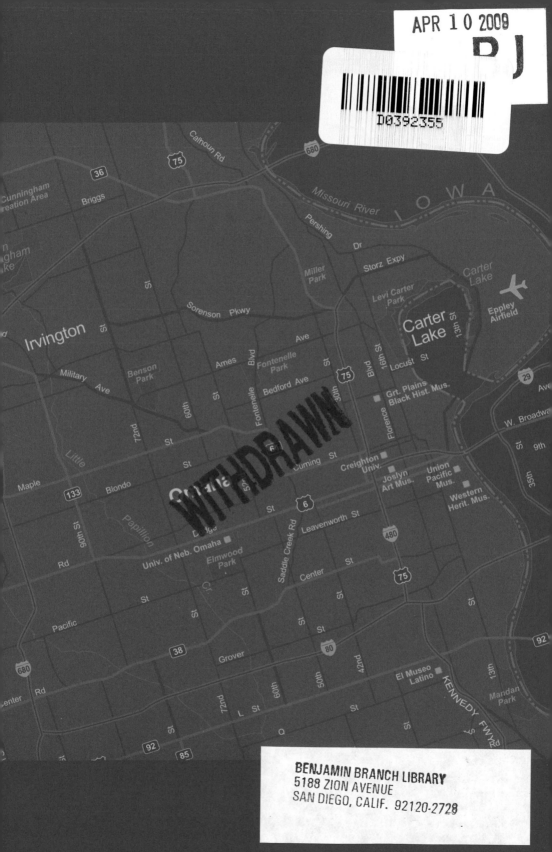

Pilgrimage to
WARREN BUFFETT'S OMAHA

A Hedge Fund Manager's Dispatches from
Inside the Berkshire Hathaway Annual Meeting

JEFF MATTHEWS

McGraw-Hill

New York • Chicago • San Francisco • Lisbon • London
Madrid • Mexico City • Milan • New Delhi • San Juan
Seoul • Singapore • Sydney • Toronto

The *McGraw·Hill* Companies

1 2 3 4 5 6 7 8 9 0   DOC/DOC   0 1 0 9 8

ISBN: 978-0-07-160197-9
MHID: 0-07-160197-X

This publication is designed to provide accurate and
authoritative information in regard to the subject matter
covered. It is sold with the understanding that neither
the author nor the publisher is engaged in rendering
legal, accounting, or other professional service. If legal
advice or other expert assistance is required, the services of a competent professional person should be
sought.

> —*From a Declaration of Principles*
> *jointly adopted by a Committee of the*
> *American Bar Association and a*
> *Committee of Publishers*

McGraw-Hill books are available at special quantity
discounts to use as premiums and sales promotions, or
for use in corporate training programs. To contact a
representative please visit the Contact Us pages at
www.mhprofessional.com.

Map images © maps.com/Index Stock
Imagery/Photolibrary

This book is printed on acid-free paper.

This is for NJB
Love, JLM

CONTENTS

PART II: *Return to Omaha: 2008*

Pilgrimage to Omaha

ach year, during the first weekend in May, Berkshire Hathaway shareholders, their friends, and their family members descend on Omaha, Nebraska for the largest financial gathering of its kind.

Seasoned professionals, amateur investors, young learners, and just plain Warren Buffett junkies, they spend the weekend renewing old friendships at Berkshire shareholder receptions and shopping for jewelry, carpeting, and high-definition televisions at Berkshire-owned stores.

But mainly they come to hear Berkshire Hathaway chairman and chief executive officer Warren Buffett, the "Oracle of Omaha," answer their questions and impart his wisdom for the better part of an entire Saturday, at the company's annual meeting.

From early morning to mid-afternoon, shareholders ask—and Buffett answers—any question at all. They ask more than 50 questions, on almost any topic, from how to be a great investor to what a good first job for an ambitious 10-year-old girl would be.

Seated at a table on a small stage on the floor inside Omaha's Qwest Center arena, the chairman of one of the largest public companies in the world, along with his close friend, partner, and vice chairman, Charlie Munger, opens a dozen microphones to investors of all stripes.

No PR flack screens the questions in advance. No lawyer shields the two men from controversial questions. And no question goes unanswered, even the most deeply personal, irrelevant, or controversial. The session lasts for more than five hours, and the questioners include everyone from antiabortion protestors to Native American activists.

It is the most remarkable, yet unadorned, exhibition of good governance in corporate America.

In May 2007, 27,000 people came from around the world to attend, and for the first time in my career, I joined them.

I manage a hedge fund. Think of it as a mutual fund without borders. We can invest in anything our investors want, from stocks to bonds to currencies to oil to real estate. We can also bet *against* companies by selling short.

One other thing that distinguishes hedge funds from, say, mutual funds is the way we earn our pay. In addition to a small fee for managing the money—1 or 2 percent—we get paid a piece of the profits we generate for our investors—usually 20 percent. No profits, no pay. So we have an incentive to make money for our investors come hell or high water, bull market or bear. That's why hedge fund managers tend to be more skeptical than the average buy-and-hold investor.

Hedge funds come in all different flavors, from trading-oriented to old-fashioned investment funds, reflecting the personality of the hedge fund manager. My hedge fund is rather old-fashioned and is invested only in stocks—no fancy stuff. Like most value-oriented money managers in the business, I've studied Buffett's writings, speeches, and investments for more than two decades.

Yet it wasn't until Chris Wagner, a friend in the business and a Berkshire shareholder invited me to go that I finally went to Omaha for the Berkshire annual meeting. For years, Chris had been encouraging me to attend. "It's a little spooky," he said. "It's a cult. You have to see it to really believe it."

This year, I decided to go with him, to see it for myself. And I expected to hear the old jokes, pithy maxims, and funny anecdotes that made the Berkshire meeting so popular; see his acerbic and (at least outside the Berkshire "family") under-rated partner, Charlie Munger, in action; take in their company's rabidly loyal shareholders; and check out one of the most famous Berkshire Hathaway landmarks—the Nebraska Furniture Mart.

Then, like aging baby boomers who go to a Rolling Stones concert mainly to be able to say they'd seen Mick Jagger, I'd be able to say, "I saw Warren Buffett."

But as it turned out, the trip meant far more than that. Even before the plane landed in Omaha, I began to grasp that I was entering a very different world. Observations both large and small took on great meaning, from the farmlands surrounding Buffett's hometown of Omaha to the remarkably low-key way in which Buffett ran the meeting in a venue the size of Madison Square Garden—glancing at his wristwatch and declaring that it was about time for the audience of 27,000 to break for lunch, for example.

Over 48 hours, I scribbled 33 pages of notes covering the profoundly engrossing question-and-answer session, a brief but enlightening conversation with two Berkshire managers, and a visit to Berkshire's fabled Nebraska Furniture Mart. The experience was an eye-opener for me, and, as I would soon find out, for the readers of my financial blog.

Now, in addition to having run a hedge fund for nearly 15 years, I also write a financial blog called JeffMatthewsIsNotMakingThisUp, reporting on whatever unusual and interesting happenings in the investment world strike my fancy.

Unusual and interesting things happen in the investment world all the time, but the most unusual—and by far the most interesting—I ever encountered was the Berkshire Hathaway annual meeting.

Returning home, I began writing about my journey to the heart of Berkshire Hathaway in what I thought might become a two- or three-part series. The response from readers, however, was overwhelming. They liked the detailed, firsthand observations about Omaha, the Berkshire shareholders, and the relationship between Buffett and Munger.

So I wrote about nearly everything I'd seen. I wrote about the way Buffett answers every question, no matter what, with a respect and an earnest manner that makes every shareholder in the building proud to say "I'm a Berkshire shareholder." And I wrote about less flattering topics that are not covered in the popular mythology, such as the absence of African American shareholders at the annual gathering of one of the most vocally progressive billionaires in history. I received feedback from novice investors and longtime Buffett admirers alike, not only from the United States but from around the world. By the time it was over, "Pilgrimage to Omaha" had become an 11-part first-person essay.

In May 2008, with Bear Stearns's collapse and the financial world in turmoil, I went back to the Berkshire Hathaway annual meeting by myself. This time, 31,000 people had come to hear the "Oracle of Omaha" and his partner take more than 60 questions from investors young and old from, quite literally, around the world. There was a new urgency in the questions.

This book is an expanded version of the original essay I wrote on my blog, and describes the 2007 and 2008 Berkshire Hathaway shareholders' meetings that covered the 2006 and 2007 fiscal years. Readers will join me as I go to the midwestern city that shaped Buffett and his investment success, discover the keys to that success, and learn why not only his shareholders but the managers of the Berkshire Hathaway companies idolize the man.

I also look at questions that are not often asked: Why has Buffett owned businesses that have withered? Does Buffett's famed penny pinching cripple his companies? Did the world's most famous financial analyst miss questionable sales practices that the SEC later investigated while he sat on the board of Coke? Why won't Buffett—a bridge partner and best friend of Microsoft founder Bill Gates—buy technology stocks? How does Buffett square his well-known social progressiveness with his lily-white audience of investors?

And, most important, how will Berkshire Hathaway survive his death?

Some of the answers surprised even me.

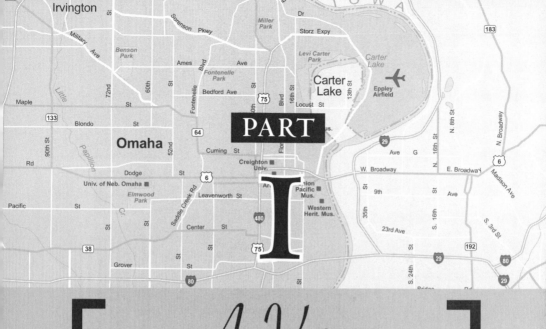

[*A Very*
Rational Place]

2007

INTRODUCTION

Wired at Birth

"I was wired at birth to allocate capital."

—WARREN BUFFETT

n May 10, 1965, a self-assured young investor who was almost unknown outside his hometown of Omaha, Nebraska, arrived in New Bedford, Massachusetts. His mission: to take control of Berkshire Hathaway, a once-proud textile company that had fallen on hard times.

The *New York Times* reported the change in a low-key article in the next day's business pages:

Textile Concern Changes Control
BERKSHIRE HATHAWAY POLICY ROW SPURS RESIGNATIONS

A policy row caused by the infusion of outside money into Berkshire Hathaway, Inc., rocked the 76-year-old textile company yesterday and resulted in the resignation of two top officers. . . .

Reached last night in New York before boarding a plane to Omaha, Warren E. Buffett, 35-year-old general partner of Buffett Partnership, said that his concern had owned an interest in Berkshire Hathaway since late in 1962 and has been the largest stockholder "for some time." . . .

Mr. Buffett said that his company was a private partnership with a few families as limited partners. As for Berkshire Hathaway, he said: "We're going to continue to sell the same goods to the same customers."

Thus began the remarkable transformation of a fading manufacturer of cotton fabrics into one of the world's biggest companies and the single best long-term stock investment in modern history, by a genial investment whiz sporting rumpled suits and thick eyeglasses, the now legendary 78-year-old chairman of Berkshire Hathaway and "Oracle of Omaha," Warren E. Buffett.

553 TIMES BETTER THAN THE DOW JONES

Far from continuing "to sell the same goods to the same customers," Buffett stopped reinvesting Berkshire's cash in textile machines and started investing it in stocks, something that he seemed uncannily good at.

In 1973, when oil prices soared and stocks crashed, Buffett bought up what is now 21.4 percent of the Washington Post Company for Berkshire at $5.63 a share. Thirty years later, those shares hit $999.50.

In 1976, he began buying up half the shares of GEICO, the direct-to-consumer auto insurer, starting at $2 a share, when Wall Street thought the company was headed for bankruptcy. Twenty years later, Berkshire acquired the other half of what was, by then, a *very* healthy company for $70 a share.

In 1988, Buffett began buying shares of Coke for Berkshire at around $5 a share, adjusted for stock splits. Wall Street thought he was crazy to pay so much for a sleepy old soft-drink company. Riding a wave of international growth, however, the company grew spectacularly over the next decade, and the stock soared to nearly $90 a share.

So it was that throughout 43 years of economic upturns and downturns, oil shocks, terrorist attacks, inflation, the Cold War, and the collapse of Communism, Warren E. Buffett—with the advice and counsel of his close partner and fellow Omaha native,

Berkshire Vice Chairman Charles T. Munger—turned an old textile company into a darling of investors around the world.

But Buffett didn't just make money buying stocks; he also bought *whole companies* for Berkshire when the price and the property seemed right. In time, Berkshire no longer looked anything like the aging textile maker of 1965. By the summer of 1983 the Berkshire "family" included a local Omaha insurance company, a small California boxed-chocolate maker, a Buffalo newspaper publisher, and a furniture retailer. Later, Buffett and Munger added more insurance companies, more manufacturers, and more furniture retailers.

In fact, they bought anything that fit their idea of being a good business with good management that they could buy at a reasonable price. They acquired what is now called NetJets, the fractional jet ownership service whose customers included Tiger Woods, and they bought a brick company whose customers were plain old home buyers.

They even bought the company that makes Ginsu knives.

And while Buffett broke his promise to the *Times* that Berkshire would "continue to sell the same goods to the same customers," when, years later, he closed down Berkshire's textile operations altogether, Berkshire shareholders didn't mind a bit.

So effectively and completely did Warren Buffett and Charlie Munger transform the old Berkshire Hathaway that the price of its stock rose 842,400 percent, from $18 on the day Buffett took control to a peak of $151,650 a share in late 2007.

The Dow Jones Industrial Average, however, rose only about 1,425 percent.

What does that mean in dollars and cents? An investor who bought $10,000 worth of Berkshire Hathaway the day Warren E. Buffett took control would have owned shares worth $84 million at their peak. An investor who bought $10,000 worth of stocks in the Dow Jones Industrial Average, on the other hand, would have owned a portfolio worth about $152,500 at its peak.

The Berkshire investor did 553 times better than the Dow Jones investor.

"WE HAVE NO MASTER STRATEGY . . ."

Remarkable as that track record is, the way Warren Buffett achieved it is equally remarkable. He used no complex investment strategies; never borrowed wads of money to make big, all-or-nothing bets; and does not employ teams of financial analysts to help him find ideas.

He never even used a computer.

Instead, Buffett sat alone in an office in Omaha, Nebraska, drinking Cherry Cokes while engaged in his favorite use of time: "reading and thinking" for hours each day and talking on the phone with an ever-widening circle of business acquaintances, searching for investments.

And when he found one he liked, he acted swiftly.

His partner all along in this venture has been Charles T. Munger, a self-assured lawyer who lives and works in Los Angeles, but who was, like Buffett, born and raised in Omaha. As Buffett's sounding board on most major investment decisions, Munger is so skeptical of most proposals that Buffett affectionately calls him the "Abominable No Man."

In addition to being a reliable sounding board, however, Munger was also a key influence on Buffett's investment style. In his early years, Buffett favored investing in cheap stocks like Berkshire Hathaway, even if they were poor businesses. Munger, however, had lived, worked, and invested in the fertile postwar boom of Los Angeles, and he preferred buying only good businesses run by good managers.

Buffett, who struggled to turn Berkshire's textile business around and then simply diversified out of it, learned the hard way that, as he says, "Good jockeys will do well on good horses, but not on broken-down nags."

Together, the two men sought "good horses"—companies in a good business, with good management, but at the kind of cheap prices that Buffett loved.

Buffett explained their investment philosophy in plain language a decade ago:

Your goal as an investor should simply be to purchase, at a rational price, a part interest in an easily-understandable business whose earnings are virtually certain to be materially higher five, ten and twenty years from now. Over time, you will find only a few companies that meet these standards—so when you see one that qualifies, you should buy a meaningful amount of stock.

Simple as that may sound, it requires a lot of work. Not physical work—there is no heavy lifting in the investment business, as Buffett likes to say—but lots of reading and thinking.

"We have no master strategy," Buffett has written. "Instead, we simply hope that something comes along—and, when it does, we act."

THE HAPPY SHOPKEEPER

Almost as remarkable as Buffett's track record and the simplicity of his investment philosophy is the fact that he does none of his work in secret, but rather opens himself up to Berkshire's investors and the public at large to such an extent that he has become the most familiar investor in the world.

Yes, Buffett accumulated shares of Washington Post and GEICO and Coke quietly, so as not to tip off copycat investors. But every time he purchased a new stock or a new business, he later wrote about it in the "Chairman's Letter" at the beginning of the company's annual report to Berkshire shareholders.

In these letters, written in clear sentences and plain language, and lightened with jokes from Woody Allen, Mark Twain, and Mae West, Buffett explained his reasoning and laid out expectations for all to see. Over time, the fame of Buffett's annual letter grew beyond Berkshire's shareholders. Soon it was being passed around among investors, analysts, and portfolio managers across Wall Street. With each annual letter, Buffett added a new chapter to what would, over time, become a lifelong course on successful investing from the world's greatest investor—himself.

Indeed, so compelling was Buffett's ability to explain himself in his letters that Berkshire shareholders began traveling to

Omaha each spring to meet the man in person at the company's annual shareholders' meeting.

For the first few years, they made their own way to the offices of the National Indemnity Company, Buffett's first insurance acquisition for Berkshire, where the meeting was held in the company cafeteria. A dozen or more investors would show up to ask "Warren and Charlie" their questions after the brief business portion of the meeting had concluded.

Attendance grew steadily thanks to word of mouth until 1985, when Buffett, who enjoyed the give and take, invited shareholders to the annual meeting in his Chairman's Letter. Two hundred fifty people showed up at Omaha's Witherspoon Hall in the Joslyn Art Museum. Informal conversation gave way to a formal question-and-answer session. Buffett and Munger would hold forth for hours with professional investors from New York and California as well as Berkshire's many loyal longtime shareholders from Omaha, including those "few families" that had been investors in Buffett Partnership, Ltd., when Buffett arrived in New Bedford to take control of Berkshire Hathaway in 1965.

The two men, equally intelligent, self-assured, and quick-witted, developed a kind of comedy routine, with Buffett's long-winded and more exuberant replies setting up dry, acerbic responses from Munger.

Buffett began concluding his annual Chairman's Letter with highlights from the previous year's shareholders' meeting and providing information about hotels, along with plugs for the Nebraska Furniture Mart, the largest home furnishings store in North America and at the time a recent addition to the Berkshire "family." He would note with pride the number of states represented by shareholders at the meeting.

Later, as Buffett's own fame grew, he began to mention the number of *countries* they represented, too.

Attendance soared along with Berkshire's stock price, soon reaching 1,000 and forcing the meeting into ever-larger venues. Berkshire began arranging buses to take shareholders to the Furniture Mart before and after the meeting. Borsheim's

Jewelers, another Berkshire acquisition, opened its doors on Sundays, against its previous policy, for shareholders who attended the meeting.

The shareholders began making an entire weekend out of it.

In 1996, 5,000 of them crowded the Holiday Convention Center for what Buffett was now calling "our capitalist version of Woodstock." Berkshire companies displayed their products and shareholders watched a low-budget movie—put together by Berkshire's chief financial officer, Mark Hamburg—that became a popular feature.

In 1998, 10,000 people filled the Aksarben Coliseum (*Nebraska* spelled backward). Buffett began offering employee discounts to shareholders shopping at the Nebraska Furniture Mart, as well as tours of NetJets' fleet at Omaha's Eppley Airfield. GEICO specialists flew to Omaha to be on hand to help shareholders get a special discount on their car insurance.

The Berkshire annual meeting was becoming big business, for Berkshire and for Omaha. When attendance outgrew every venue in the city, Omaha opened the Qwest Center, a Madison Square Garden-sized facility with an 18,300-seat arena and an exhibition hall bigger than a Costco. Buffett and Munger could hold forth for five hours answering questions, and afterward the shareholders could buy a pair of Justin western boots, a Dairy Queen ice cream "Dilly Bar," a set of Ginsu knives, and even a Clayton *manufactured home*, all under one roof.

It was a kind of gigantic flea market for the Berkshire family of companies, with Buffett acting as genial host, ringmaster, and happy shopkeeper.

And as the Berkshire annual meeting attracted attention from around the world, so too did Warren Buffett himself. Buffett had once bought and sold stocks in the isolation of a small room in his house on Farnam Street, but now the press began to converge on Omaha to report on what Warren and Charlie had to say. On Sunday afternoon, Buffett accommodated them with a press conference, where he would answer any and all questions.

The result of this steady, inexorable progression over the years is that Buffett's profile has grown far beyond his annual Chairman's Letter and the long question-and-answer sessions that he and Munger host at the Berkshire annual meeting the first Saturday in May.

Today, Warren Buffett is a worldwide phenomenon. Companies—mainly family-owned businesses whose owners need to raise money but don't want to lose control of their business by selling to an aggressive, hands-on corporate owner— seek out Buffett, hoping that he'll buy them.

And Buffett travels the world, spreading his message that Berkshire is the perfect buyer for those companies: "We have no corporate meetings, no corporate budgets, and no performance reviews."

His travels are covered by a CNBC anchorwoman who files glowing reports from cities across the globe; he holds press conferences upon arriving in countries, as the Beatles used to do. And for one weekend in May, shareholders travel all the way to Omaha from India, China, and South Africa to hear him speak.

"MY FAVORITE BILLIONAIRE"

But why does Warren Buffett bother?

Why does a man who once took a Dale Carnegie course in public speaking to overcome his boyhood shyness, who organized his time—somewhat at the expense of his family, it would appear—around *reading financial statements*, and who has been obsessed with his own mortality since boyhood spend his spare time talking to friends and strangers about how he invests?

First and foremost, Buffett wants what he calls "high-quality shareholders" for Berkshire, people who won't sell their stock when Buffett chooses to do something that goes against the grain of conventional wisdom. He put it this way in his 1983 Chairman's Letter:

> We feel that high quality ownership can be attracted and maintained if we consistently communicate our business and ownership

philosophy—*along with no other conflicting messages*—and then let self selection follow its course.

And in this he has been wildly successful. As we will see, most Berkshire shareholders don't sell their stock even when Buffett himself says that things can't get better, and they might even get much worse in the short run.

Second, Buffett views his own achievements as a force largely beyond his own control. "I had nothing to do with my own success," he insists. What made him rich, Buffett will tell anybody who asks, was not daredevil risk taking or blinding foresight, it was the luck of the draw:

> I was wired at birth to allocate capital [he told Carol Loomis of *Fortune* magazine in 2006] and was lucky enough to have people around me early on—my parents and teachers and Susie [his first wife]—who helped me to make the most of that.

Because the tools for success came to him essentially for free, Buffett is merely giving back to the community at large as much as he can of those tools that made him rich.

Third, Buffett seems to genuinely enjoy the bully pulpit his fame now provides for his views, not merely on investing, but on fiscal policy and whatever strikes this self-described "political junkie" and longtime liberal Democrat as just plain wrong.

Buffett's ties to the Democratic Party go back as far as 1968, when he raised money for "Clean Gene" McCarthy's anti–Vietnam War presidential campaign. More recently, he raised funds for both Hillary Clinton and Barack Obama, and advised them on fiscal policy matters in their Democratic presidential campaigns. Hillary Clinton calls Warren Buffett "my favorite billionaire."

Many years ago, Buffett put money into a liberal-minded magazine called the *Washington Monthly* partly as a way to promote his own views on social policy, but these days he needs no printing press of his own to air his ideas. Being the world's most famous investor gives him a far bigger platform than any magazine. And he uses it, giving chatty interviews on how "the taxation system has tilted towards the rich" with Tom Brokaw and railing against "dynastic wealth" while testifying for a stiff inheritance tax before Congress.

About the only controversial area of public policy that Buffett shies away from on camera is abortion, which he actively supports.

GLOBE TROTTING AGAINST TIME

Over the years, Warren Buffett's high public profile has taken on a serious business motive far beyond that of educating his shareholders, giving something back to society, or even making his views on taxation known.

Buffett hopes to attract new acquisition candidates to Berkshire Hathaway, and as many as possible while he is still running the company. Nearing 80 years old and keenly aware of his age, Buffett knows that he must build Berkshire while he can. "We've long wanted . . . to extend Berkshire's appeal beyond U.S. borders," he wrote to shareholders in early 2007. "And last year, our globe-trotting finally got underway."

But it won't be easy.

For years, investors have been asking Buffett what will happen to Berkshire if he "gets hit by a truck." "I'd feel sorry for the truck," Buffett used to joke.

But it is no joke. To most investors and most companies around the world, Warren Buffett *is* Berkshire Hathaway.

For Warren Buffett has not just one job at Berkshire, but *two*. First, he is its chief investment officer, in charge of investing Berkshire's money, for which he is famous.

Second, he is also chief executive officer of Berkshire, in charge of managing its "family" of companies. Those companies have been purchased by Buffett personally, and most of their CEOs report directly to Warren Buffett. After all, Buffett runs a tight ship: there are only 19 people working in Berkshire's head office.

When Buffett goes, not only will Berkshire lose the most famous investor in the world, but its companies will also lose their leader.

And even though Buffett and the Berkshire board of directors have selected a successor to replace him as chief executive officer and are evaluating four candidates to replace him as chief investment officer, it is not at all clear that the Berkshire name will be enough to attract new managers and new companies without Warren Buffett behind it.

So Warren Buffett travels the globe, from Germany to India to Israel to Italy to China, so that in future years, when companies choose to sell, they will think not of "Warren Buffett," but of "Berkshire Hathaway."

It is nothing less than a race against time.

CHAPTER I

This Is Big

"What we have created . . . is, to some extent, a cult."

—CHARLIE MUNGER

I t is Friday, May 4, 2007, the day before the Berkshire Hathaway Annual Shareholders Meeting, and I am about to find out just how big this is before I even get to Omaha.

I'm in Chicago at Gate G-19 in O'Hare International Airport, trying to switch my ticket on the late-morning Chicago-to-Omaha Flight 4128 for an earlier flight on American Airlines. It's 9 a.m. local time.

"It's sold out," the lady behind the counter tells me. "All the flights to Omaha are all sold out. But you can try standby if you want . . ."

I tell her I want to try. After a minute or two of working the keyboard, she hands me the standby ticket the way the guy at the 7-11 near my house in Connecticut hands me the Powerball ticket—a look that says, *"You might as well rip it up right now, my friend."*

Yes, I've been investing money for more than 30 years and always with Warren Buffett's famous rule in mind: "The first rule is not to lose. The second rule is not to forget the first rule."

But I do buy Powerball tickets when the pot hits $100 million. After all, where else are you going to get a shot at winning a hundred million bucks for a one-dollar bet?

Now, that is not a question I'm planning to ask Warren Buffett at the Berkshire Hathaway meeting. Buffett himself would toss me out of the Qwest Center if I suggested that Berkshire start buying Powerball tickets, no matter how high the payoff.

Knowing the lousy odds for the lottery ticket buyers, Buffett might be more inclined to try to make money *selling* lottery tickets, except that Berkshire Hathaway is not in the gaming business. Buffett and his partner, Charlie Munger, consider gambling "a dirty business."

Berkshire Hathaway is, however, very big in the insurance business. And so Buffett and his ace insurance executive, Ajit Jain, do, on occasion, insure games-of-chance sponsored by companies such as Pepsi. Buffett delighted in describing one such transaction in his 2003 Chairman's Letter:

> Ajit writes some very unusual policies. Last year, for example, PepsiCo promoted a drawing that offered participants a chance to win a $1 billion prize. . . . So we wrote a $1 billion policy, retaining the risk entirely for our own account. Because the prize, if won, was payable over time, our exposure in present-value terms was $250 million. (I helpfully suggested that any winner be paid $1 a year for a billion years, but that proposal didn't fly.) The drawing was held on September 14. Ajit and I held our breath, as did the finalist in the contest, and we left happier than he. PepsiCo has renewed for a repeat contest in 2004.

The Pepsi contest ended well for Berkshire, as most things do: the contestant lost, so Berkshire kept whatever premium Pepsi paid without having to make the billion-dollar payout. It is just one example of how Buffett's appetite for risk—well-defined, statistically calculated risk—can be enormous when the odds are in his favor.

Not only has Berkshire insured the kind of impossible-to-win games of chance on which I toss away 10 or 20 bucks a year, but it has sold insurance policies covering the 2002 Winter Olympics in Salt Lake City after the 9/11 terrorist attacks, boxer Mike Tyson's life, and baseball player Alex Rodriguez's ability to play ball after the Texas Rangers signed him to a $252 million contract, all for hefty profits to Berkshire.

With Buffett's certain disapproval of my occasional Powerball indulgence ringing in my ears, and vain hopes for the standby ticket in my hand, I wait in the terminal, computer plugged in to an outlet, and check in on my business.

Sitting here at O'Hare, with e-mails to read, instant messages from traders popping up on the computer screen, and stock tickers flickering green and red, it takes some time before I become aware of what is going on around me.

What is going on around me is this: grown men and women are filling the seats, and they are talking about Omaha and Berkshire Hathaway and "Warren," like kids going to Orlando to visit Disney World and see Mickey Mouse. It soon dawns on me that *everybody else on this flight* is also going to the Berkshire Hathaway meeting.

And they are very different from the intense, young high-tech technology warriors whom I usually see on cross-country flights; nor are they the sleep-deprived mothers and edgy fathers juggling babies and toddlers that were waiting for a JetBlue flight to Orlando this morning as I left New York.

Rather, they are mostly older men and women, nearly all of them couples, of the baby boom generation, with graying hair and wearing neat, casual clothing. Groups of younger men have also gathered, wearing jeans, open-necked Oxford shirts, and loafers. All are eager to get to Omaha.

So eager, in fact, that some of them will be left behind despite having confirmed seats on the next flight.

This is because American Airlines' computers, which routinely oversell seats based on statistical calculations regarding the incidence of no-shows among confirmed passengers, have failed to take into account the fact that this particular flight is bound for Omaha, Nebraska, on the eve of the Berkshire Hathaway annual meeting, which 27,000 people are planning to attend.

And every one of the confirmed passengers has shown up for this flight.

Soon the ticket agent is offering to pay people to stay behind, but not a single person is taking her up on it. And why would they? These people have *plans*, and they're not going to screw up those plans—and miss hearing "Warren"—by giving up their seat for a voucher on another lousy flight.

Eventually, somehow, the passengers are all on board and the door to Gate G-19 has been closed. My own standby long shot is now as worthless as an expired Powerball ticket. The gate area is almost empty, and I begin stretching out a little. I have a lot to get done before my flight leaves.

And then I hear voices from the ticket counter.

Two angry men and one desperate couple with confirmed seats on the flight are watching helplessly as the plane backs slowly away from the terminal to take its place in line for take-off. They sputter at one another, at American Airlines in general, and at the two ticket agents on the other side of the ticket counter.

The ticket agents take turns typing on one of those ancient clackety airline keyboards, shaking their heads and carefully deploying the standard non-eye-contact mode by which airline employees inadvertently goad already angry customers to the point where they want to smash something.

The wife of the stranded couple is so anxious to get to Omaha that she suggests renting a car and *driving* there, all 468 miles. Her husband, red-faced and exasperated, dismisses the notion with a snort and turns his back on her, while making calls on his cell phone as if somebody besides the American ticket agents can do something to help.

I return to my work, secure in the knowledge that I have a ticket on the next flight. After all, I checked in three hours early. The next time I look up, the ticket counter is deserted: the ticket ladies have somehow rebooked the couple and the other two men on a different flight. Either that or they're all driving to Omaha.

Now, the American Airlines Chicago-to-Omaha flight that just left the gate is an airline's dream: it left on time and *fully loaded*. Every one of its seats was occupied by a passenger who booked well in advance and likely paid full fare. By comparison, the entire airline industry is running planes that are only 81 percent full, on average, this time of year. So that Omaha flight—and all the other Omaha flights leaving here today—should be among the most profitable in American Airlines's *entire system*.

And yet the company managed to make four of its passengers irate, swearing that they will never take American Airlines again in this life *or* the next.

"MY NAME IS WARREN AND I'M AN AIROHOLIC"

No wonder Warren Buffett hates the commercial airline business, investment-wise, I muse: even when it's doing well, the airline business does poorly. To this day, two decades after his famously horrible investment in USAir, Buffett ruefully tells people that he has a 1-800 number to call should he get the urge to buy an airline stock:

> "I call at two in the morning and say 'My name is Warren and I'm an airoholic.' And they talk me down."

The stock market keeps me busy while the area around me begins to fill up ahead of the next flight—my flight. The people setting down their bags and stretching their legs, reading books, or just talking are the same kind of passengers that boarded the earlier flight: middle-aged couples interspersed with a few groups of eager young men talking and sharing stories.

I turn off the computer, make a few phone calls, and watch the crowd build, secure in the knowledge that I have my ticket on the next flight.

Or so I think.

Half an hour later I'm standing patiently in a long line of expectant ticket holders shuffling toward the door marked Gate 19. Excitement is rising. People are talking, laughing, and calling friends on their cell phones ("Guess where *I'm* going!"). I approach the ticket agent and start getting excited, too. It looks as if we'll get into Omaha on time, so I'll have a chance to get settled, check out the logistics, and meet up with a reporter for dinner.

My reverie is broken, however, when the bar-code scanner kicks out my boarding pass. The ticket agent looks at it carefully, then hands it back and says, "There's something wrong with your seat. Wait over there."

She points to the same ticket counter where two hours ago four passengers were waving their boarding passes and sputtering, while I had chuckled inwardly. Now, I am suddenly no longer part of the friendly fraternity of Berkshire shareholders. I have been rejected from the line. I walk slowly to the desk to await my fate—my mind going through alternatives for the final leg to Omaha, like renting a car.

As it turns out, there are five of us who've been rejected by the bar code scanner, and we bond by comparing when we had bought our tickets. At a minimum, three months ago. The talk turns to alternatives. One younger man has none: "My wife is on that plane," he says. "If I don't meet her, I'm screwed."

We watch the others board the plane. Now the gate area is empty. The ticket agent who banished us returns. She is remarkably helpful, and somehow we all finally get new seats. My new seat, it turns out, is exactly the same seat I'd been assigned when I got the ticket three months ago—the one that the bar-code scanner rejected. The five of us board the plane in full view of 45 smug, seated passengers. They watch impatiently while we find room for our gear in the overhead bins and take our seats. American Flight 4128 to Omaha is another completely full flight, and American has managed not only to unsettle five of its passengers but to annoy the hell out of the rest.

"If a capitalist had been present at Kitty Hawk, he would have done his successors a huge favor by shooting Orville down."

Buffett has been saying that for years, and he is right; it really is a terrible business.

But I don't care. I'm on a plane bound for Omaha.

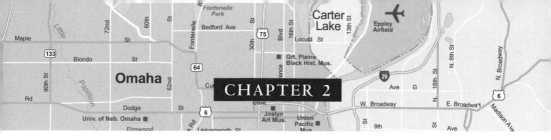

Why Omaha?

"It's much easier to think here."

—WARREN BUFFETT

Our plane descends through a dense gray cloud cover over western Iowa, and things get a little bumpy. The seat-belt sign comes on, the pilot's voice comes over the intercom telling the flight attendants to prepare for landing, and the wheels are lowered with a noisy jolt.

As we emerge beneath the clouds, the ride smoothes out, and the cabin begins to stir with palpable energy.

We are over farmland. The fields are giant rectangles that are alternately impossibly green or brown and fallow, muddy from rain. Roads run between the fields, which have been plowed in contoured patterns that reveal the subtle geography of the midwestern heartland. Occasionally, a driveway leads to a house, barns, and silos.

This geography looms large in Warren Buffett's life. In 1945, he bought 40 acres of farmland for $1,200 earned from a newspaper route—he was only 14—and to this day he frequently compares investing in stocks to buying farmland, to underscore the importance of long-term thinking.

If you were to look at a farm out here in Omaha, you wouldn't look at the price every day . . . you'd look at the value of what the farm produced relative to your purchase price. That's exactly what we do with stocks.

Buffett also once bought a farm for his son Howard's use.

Howard—now 52 years old and a Berkshire director—had sold his shares of Berkshire stock early in its meteoric rise to finance a business that didn't pan out. Later, when Howard wanted to try his hand at his first love, farming, his father offered to help. But Warren Buffett didn't offer to buy a farm for his son, or even to lend him the money. Instead, Buffett purchased the farm for himself and rented it to his son.

At market rates that varied with Howard's *weight*.

This gesture—cold as it seems—did not appear to surprise anybody, least of all Howard's two siblings. His younger brother, Peter, once bought a book for their father called *The Father's Handbook*, to try to get through to his old man, who seemed more absorbed in the stock market than his children. When their sister, Susie, was pregnant with her first child, and living in a new city, she asked her father for a loan to fix up her small kitchen to prepare for the baby. As she told the story to Roger Lowenstein, a Buffett biographer, Buffett turned her down, suggesting that she go to the bank and get a loan "like everyone else."

Warren Buffett is no soft touch, even with his children.

"I'LL PAY YOU $2.5 MILLION *NOT* TO READ IT"

The plane drops and the ground moves closer, filling the window. The fields change from lush green to muddy brown more quickly. The plane banks sharply and evens out. We pass over a highway, then more brown fields and green pastures. We are descending more quickly now, and the fields end at a bank of trees marking the edge of a fat, muddy river, the Missouri. The great, slow river passes beneath us, and we are now over grass again. Suddenly concrete appears beneath the wing, the concrete becomes a runway, the plane bangs down, and we've landed at Eppley Airfield.

We're in Omaha.

The reverse thrusters slam open and the plane slows sharply. I turn on my BlackBerry, preparing to check messages while the plane turns back toward the terminal. At JFK airport, during a busy time of day, it can take 20 or 30 minutes just to get to the gate—but a strange thing happens here. The plane rolls for a minute or two, and then stops at the gate with a slight lurch.

The lights come on, and Flight 4128 is over. The seat-belt sign is turned off, a voice welcomes us to Omaha, and the door at the front of the cabin is pushed open, letting in fresh, warm, humid air. We're all standing up, stretching, and getting our gear, and we're walking out of the plane and onto the gangway before I can finish reading the first e-mail on my BlackBerry.

Not that I'm missing out on a lot of great Wall Street research. I once got an e-mail that contained the following headlines, all in one paragraph:

> Crude Oil Little Changed Amid Weaker Outlook for U.S. Energy Demand;

> Crude Oil May Surge to $130 This Year, BlueGold's Andurand Says;

> Kornafel of Hudson Capital Energy Says Oil May Fall to $90 in Near Term;

> Lippow Says Oil to "Keep Going Higher," May Reach $110.

It is no wonder Warren Buffett doesn't read Wall Street research.

In fact, Warren Buffett and his partner, Charlie Munger, have such low regard for Wall Street research that Buffett delights in retelling the story of how Munger once turned down the opportunity to read an investment banking analysis on a company called Scott Fetzer, which Berkshire had agreed to buy, even though Scott Fetzer had already paid the investment banking firm $2.5 million for its services:

> I guess the lead banker felt he should do something for his payment, so he graciously offered us a copy of the book on Scott Fetzer that his firm had prepared. With his customary tact, Charlie responded: "I'll pay $2.5 million *not* to read it."

Despite the fact that he runs a $100 billion enterprise with dozens of different companies and close to 250,000 employees, Warren Buffett still gets much of his news the old-fashioned way: he reads newspapers. Every morning, Buffett reads the *Wall Street Journal,* the *Financial Times,* the *New York Times,* even *USA Today* and the *Omaha World-Herald.* Also, *American Banker.*

In fact, most of what Buffett reads is on paper, even the brief monthly reports he asks the managers of each of the Berkshire's companies to provide. The Eppley Airfield terminal building is about as simple and old-fashioned as Warren Buffett's news-gathering techniques. I walk through a brick-and-glass building that might have been built 30 years ago. Aside from the Omaha Beef kiosk, nothing particularly distinguishes it from any other airport terminal—not the Krispy Kreme donut counter or the shoeshine stand, and certainly not the Hudson Booksellers shop.

Or so I think.

Then I notice that the Hudson's display tables and shelves hold an unusual number of books about one particular person: Warren E. Buffett. Not only that, there are several books about Charles T. Munger prominently on display.

While some of the books are quite familiar even to the casual Buffett fan, particularly Roger Lowenstein's excellent 1995 biography, a few of them are not familiar at all. I make a mental note to check them out on Amazon later, not knowing that the Berkshire meeting will have its own bookstore set up right inside the Qwest Center's exhibition hall, devoted entirely to Warren Buffett, Charlie Munger, and Berkshire Hathaway.

I head past the baggage claim and out into the bright sunshine, pondering the fact that the world's greatest investor *and his partner* were both born and raised 1,200 miles from Wall Street, right here in Omaha.

"IT'S CHEAP HERE, YOU KNOW"

There is nobody else in line at the taxi stand. I toss my overnight bag into the first cab to pull up, slide onto the seat, and shut the door while the driver sets the meter and asks where to. I tell him, he nods "all right," and we pull away from the curb and onto a quiet, wide road. There is almost no traffic.

The windows of the cab are open, and the interior is uncomfortably warm from sitting in the midday sun. The seats are the shiny, worn, plastic New York City cab type. The suspension sags, and the cab feels springy and mildly unsafe. I ask the driver about the soccer ball on the front seat. He tells me he's from East Africa by way of Minneapolis, and he plays a lot of soccer with friends in the area.

He likes Omaha: "It's cheap here, you know."

As he drives and we talk, a Nextel phone in a holster next to the meter keeps going off. It isn't business, however. The callers are friends of his who are trying to get a soccer game together. Can't do it today, he tells each caller. He turns to me. "This is a busy day, just like they told us it would be. Busy, busy day."

Busy he may be, but not New York City busy. We're not exactly tearing down the road, jumping out at traffic lights, and doing bootlegger turns to beat the traffic. This is Omaha. Things are slower. The drive from Eppley Airfield to downtown Omaha is only five miles.

It takes about 10 minutes, and we don't even get on a highway.

We do, however, leave Nebraskan soil briefly for about a half a minute, thanks to a geographic quirk of the Missouri River that left a half-mile-wide peninsula of Iowa soil—once a loop of the Missouri River—jutting into Nebraska.

Nebraska or Iowa, the landscape is entirely what is known in real estate circles as "light industrial" and exactly what you'd expect to find near an airport on the banks of the Missouri River: fuel tanks, warehouses, grain silos, railroad tracks, and railroad yards.

There is, however, a spanking new development—the headquarters of the Gallup polling organization, the driver tells me—that sits alongside the river, and soon we're passing the modern, glass-and-metal Qwest Center, where the Berkshire Hathaway annual meeting will take place tomorrow morning, doors opening at 7 a.m.

But there's nothing here—not the farmlands or the city land-scape—that suggests why one of the greatest investors who ever lived, and his partner, were born in Omaha.

A great farmer, perhaps. Or a food mogul, certainly. Omaha Beef is famous around the world, and the Swanson TV Dinner was invented right here in the 1950s, as was Duncan Hines cake mix, dreamed up by folks at the nearby Nebraska Consolidated Mills—now ConAgra—who needed to find a way to get rid of the flour that was filling up their silos. They licensed the name "Duncan Hines" from a real person—a traveling salesman who'd been rat-ing roadside restaurants since the 1930s as sort of the *Zagat's* of his day—and turned a low-margin commodity into a highly profitable brand that ConAgra later sold to Procter & Gamble.

The lesson—that brand names carry economic power but com-modities do not— is one that Warren Buffett learned early in his life, to his shareholders' benefit over many decades. Most of Berkshire Hathaway's biggest and best stock purchases have been in companies with powerful brand names: Coke, Gillette, and American Express.

In that light, it shouldn't shock anybody that Warren Buffett wanted no part of his son Howard's farm, except to collect rent. Or, conversely, that Berkshire Hathaway would one day become a large shareholder of Procter & Gamble.

A STREET CALLED QUERULOUS

We pass beneath Route 480, an elevated highway separating North Omaha from the city center, and head west on a street so wide and yet so devoid of cars that it feels like Sunday morning—not the middle of a Friday afternoon.

There are no cabs jockeying for position at the traffic lights, no illegally parked trucks or limos, no gridlock alerts or cruising cop cars or FedEx trucks making deliveries. Just big, wide, calm streets. There are almost no pedestrians, although the sidewalks look almost as wide as the streets.

Despite the lack of traffic, we seem to hit nearly every red light—the lights aren't coordinated like those in New York City—

so I manage to get a good look at the buildings. They are a bland, midwestern mix of old-fashioned brick, granite, glass, and steel—dominated by the plain, dour Woodmen Tower. Some look straight out of the city's meatpacking heyday; others are modern and more ambitious.

Downtown is clean and windswept, with an airy, big-sky feel to it, and navigation is straightforward, with the streets laid out in a grid. Those running north to south are numbered, starting at 2nd Street along the Missouri River.

The streets running east to west are named, with many of them evoking the Old West city that Omaha used to be—Clay, Calhoun, Leavenworth—and at least one with a sense of humor about it—Querulous Street, near the Amtrak station.

My hotel is on Dodge Street.

The Western theme goes only so far, however. There are no streets or parks or hospitals or highways named for the Otoe or Ioway tribes that were already here in 1804, when Lewis and Clark stopped on their way along the Missouri River toward the Pacific, and that were slowly pushed aside as this bend in the Missouri River became an important stop for Utah-bound Mormons and California-bound gold prospectors.

Yet the old-town feel is relaxing. Being here gives one a sense of the vastness of the country, so that whatever is happening right now on Wall Street—whatever news flash is causing traders to panic and prices to gyrate and CNBC commentators to react and politicians to hold press conferences—the world continues.

And I realize I forgot to check the closing prices on my stocks today.

"HE ACTUALLY USES A CELL PHONE NOW"

The cab driver switches between talking to his friends on his Nextel and telling me about Omaha. It is a striking thing to see an East African immigrant, transplanted thousands of miles from home to the middle of America, no less, who is entirely comfortable with and very much dependent on the kind of technology that Warren Buffett, as an investor, will have almost nothing to do with.

As great as his track record is, and as wise as his pearls of wisdom are, Warren Buffett's investment philosophy does seem narrow-minded and old-fashioned. He focuses on a handful of industries he knows well—insurance, home furnishings, business services, and anything else that fits within his famed "circle of competence." And the rest he leaves alone.

Companies he has left alone include several of the most phenomenal investments of the last two decades: Apple, Google, and BlackBerry creator Research-In-Motion. Buffett even missed Microsoft, a virtual monopoly in its heyday, despite the fact that the company's founder, Bill Gates, is one of his best friends.

Times have changed since the post–World War era, when a diligent investor named Warren Buffett could buy shares of the Union Street Railway of New Bedford for $45 a share when it had $120 a share in cash on its books. Investing has become big business, and bargains are harder to come by. A new world of technology has rendered old work habits, and old investments, obsolete.

To investment managers who've made careers out of companies like Apple, or Google, or Research-In-Motion, the companies Buffett has been buying for Berkshire Hathaway—Shaw Industries, Acme Building Products, GEICO—don't exactly set the pulse racing, as Buffett himself is the first to admit.

Like pay phones in a wireless world, Buffett seems increasingly antiquated—even irrelevant—to more flexible, wide-ranging investors who have grown up in a highly connected, technologically dependent world.

Of course, neither Buffett nor his "quality shareholders" express any remorse over missing Google or Apple or even Microsoft, outside his circle of competence as those investments are. After all, while many investors have had better years than Warren Buffett, and some may have had better decades, Buffett's track record over the long haul is, quite literally, unsurpassed.

Still, if a cab driver's circle of competence can include modern technology, why not Warren Buffett's?

Partly it is age. As Richard Santulli, who founded and runs NetJets—the wildly successfully private jet timesharing business that Buffett enjoyed so much as a customer that he acquired the entire company for Berkshire—said in a 2007 interview:

> He doesn't do e-mails. He answers the phone. Ninety percent of the time—I have his direct number, he picks up the phone and says hello. If not, I get one of his assistants and he'll call me back quickly. He actually uses a cell phone now, which is very amazing.

Partly it seems that Buffett's view of technology investing dates back to the "Go-Go Years" of the late 1960s, when high-technology investing first took hold and Buffett was finding it so hard to find the kind of attractive investment ideas that he closed down his Partnership and began to focus on his single largest investment, textile maker Berkshire Hathaway.

Back then, "high technology" meant "semiconductors"—a fickle business, and one that Buffett wanted no part of.

Charlie Munger continued to reinforce Buffett's aversion to technology, having had a bad experience investing in a Los Angeles area high-technology company called Transformer Engineers that sold equipment to the U.S. military during the Korean War. "I never went back to the high-tech mode. I tried it once and found it to have many problems. I was like Mark Twain's cat that, after a bad experience, never again sat on a hot stove, or a cold stove either."

Fifty years later, of course, high technology is hardly the esoteric, fickle, unreliable business it once was. The world runs on computer systems. In a global economy, technology spending is not optional. For many companies, in fact, technology creates a "moat"—the type of competitive barrier that Warren Buffett looks for when he buys a business.

> A truly great business must have an enduring "moat" that protects excellent returns on invested capital.

In fact, heavy investment in technology created just such a moat for one of Buffett's favorite companies, Wal-Mart. Sam Walton's folksy demeanor aside, Wal-Mart adopted new technology quickly; it became the first major retailer to put satellite dishes on the roof of every store, beaming real-time sales information and new orders to suppliers.

Yet Warren Buffett makes no bones about the fact that technology investments are outside his circle of competence, and anything outside that circle represents a risk that he won't take. As he said a decade ago at the Berkshire annual meeting:

> I could spend all my time thinking about technology for the next year and still not be the 100th, 1,000th or even the 10,000th smartest guy in the country analyzing those businesses.

If Warren Buffett can't be one of the smartest guys in the country analyzing a business, he isn't interested. Period, end of story.

We pull up to the Doubletree Omaha Downtown, and I pay the driver; he is talking to one of his friends, shaking his head and saying, "No, I can't play." The dispatcher calls. They want him back at the airport. He smiles. "They told us it would be like this," he says. He leaves, pulling away onto Dodge Street.

Dodge Street is two blocks from Farnam Street. It is on Farnam—named for a Connecticut railroad speculator—that Warren Buffett lives, just a few miles west of downtown.

As most Berkshire shareholders already know, Buffett lives in the first house he ever bought, which cost $31,500 in 1957. Despite the modest price, he dubbed the house "Buffett's Folly."

Buffett simply hates to spend money, even for something as necessary and practical as a house. He *apologized* to shareholders the year Berkshire bought a corporate jet—and christened the plane the "*Indefensible.*"

"THE REAL ACTION"

Despite the fact that this is the biggest weekend in Omaha all year, the Doubletree Omaha Downtown is not exactly hopping. I expected a lot more activity than two couples ahead of me waiting to check in. It is 3:30 p.m. and the gift shop is closed for no apparent reason. The lady at the front desk tells me it reopens at 4:30 p.m., as if this is perfectly normal. The only hint of something special happening in town is a stack of *Omaha World-*

Herald newspapers on the front desk wrapped with a large photograph of a smiling Warren Buffett on the cover and with details of the weekend's events inside.

My room is as nondescript as they come. The window faces north, across the Gerald R. Ford Freeway. The buildings are run-down and industrial. The most remarkable feature on the horizon is a large sign for Sol's Pawn Shop. Not everyone in Omaha is a Berkshire Hathaway shareholder.

Later, in the lobby, near the now-reopened gift shop, I rendezvous with a reporter—an old hand at covering the Berkshire Hathaway meeting. We leave the hotel and walk several blocks in a hot, bright sun with a few fat white clouds on the horizon to the Old Market area—a quaint, busy few blocks full of bars and restaurants—for some food.

The reporter is surprisingly jaded. After several years of covering this "Woodstock for Capitalists," she sees it mainly as a weekend for shareholders to spend money at one Berkshire-owned company or another. Tonight's "cocktail reception" at Borsheim's immense jewelry store, she tells me, will be more like a giant free-for-all, with thousands of shareholders crowding the shopping mall and spilling out into a tent-covered parking lot.

"There are lines everywhere." Lines to buy Christmas ornaments, lines for food, lines for drinks, and hordes of gawking shareholders hoping to get an autograph from Warren Buffett himself. Tomorrow's "Backyard Barbecue" at the Nebraska Furniture Mart and Sunday night's dinner at Gorat's will be the same. "Avoid them at all costs," she says.

Worst of all—at least for her—is that she has to cover all these gatherings and miss "the real action."

The real action happens at events that no casual, day-tripping shareholder is going to see: a Friday luncheon with the dozens of chief executives of the Berkshire companies, hosted by Buffett himself; a Saturday night insurance dinner hosted by Ajit Jain, Buffett's ace insurance man; an invitation-only dinner, also on Saturday night, for longtime investors, analysts, and portfolio managers, hosted by a former Wall Street insurance analyst; a

Sunday brunch hosted by Buffett at his country club for old friends and longtime shareholders.

And there are cocktail parties and dinners hosted by Berkshire executives, longtime shareholders, friends and families throughout the weekend. As for Buffett, the reporter says, "Warren"—as the reporter and everybody else around here seems to call the man—"is pretty much as advertised. He's available to the press, quick to call back, amiable on the phone, and, usually, quite easy-going . . . provided he likes your work."

Buffett often picks visitors up at the airport himself; he has no chauffeur, goes into the office seven days a week, and is "unbelievably plugged in." He also has a photographic memory and "remembers everything."

Plus, he's a speed reader. The reporter knows an author who sent Buffett a book to read for accuracy, and got a call back within an hour of Buffett's receiving the book. He'd read every word, and offered a few corrections.

Still, the reporter warns me, Buffett can be prickly.

Shortly after the 9/11 terrorist attacks on New York City, she remembers, Berkshire released a snide press release calling a New York Times reporter "confused" about a point the reporter had made in an article published that morning.

Two years later, Buffett wrote an op-ed piece for the Washington Post criticizing Bush administration tax proposals that drew a sarcastic one-liner from a minor Treasury official about "a certain midwestern oracle, who, it must be noted, has played the tax code like a fiddle." The official and her wisecrack would have been forgotten by everyone, except that Buffett spent nine paragraphs of his year-end letter to investors rebutting the woman and mentioning her name three times. He finished it off with a huffy suggestion that the woman get to work making the corporate tax code fair.

Above all, the reporter says, Warren Buffett is extremely protective of his image—and of Berkshire's. Buffett has been particularly put off, she tells me, by some press coverage of a fraud investigation involving Berkshire's biggest insurance operation, General Re, and American International Group, known as AIG. Buffett once lauded one of the four former General Re executives under investigation in the probe as having "the very same qualities that I would want to see in a man who was going to marry my daughter."

That man, Ron Ferguson, would later be convicted of, among other things, conspiracy, securities fraud, and making false statements.

It's no wonder Buffett is prickly.

"A SANER EXISTENCE"

Afternoon is merging into dusk, and the reporter gloomily heads off to cover Buffett's Ping-Pong game amidst the hordes now descending on Borsheim's. I walk back to the Doubletree on my own. Outside of Old Market, the sidewalks are empty, and the streets are quiet. The wind is picking up, and the air is clean and smells like rain.

Time does feel slower here. The buildings are not so big that they block out the horizon. The sun is setting, shadows are long, and the sky is getting dark. Back at the Doubletree, the lobby is not much busier than it was before.

"I think it's a saner existence here," Buffett told L. J. Davis, writing for the *New York Times*, almost two decades ago:

> I used to feel, when I worked back in New York, that there were more stimuli just hitting me all the time, and if you've got the normal amount of adrenaline, you start responding to them. It may lead to crazy behavior after a while. It's much easier to think here.

I think Buffett was right.

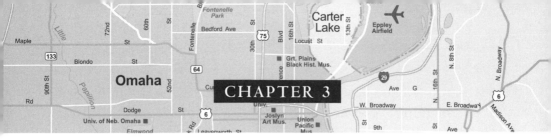

CHAPTER 3

The Newspaper Generation

"Charlie and I read five newspapers a day."

—Warren Buffett

Saturday morning dawns gray, raining, and windy. There are thunderclouds off to the north, with an occasional flash of lightning, and I realize that the rumble and booms outside my window as I came out of a deep sleep were not, as I'd imagined, roadwork being done in the street below. They were thunderstorms.

I get down to the lobby just after 6:30 a.m., and it's *busy*. Men and women—all wearing red plastic badges—are gathering, talking, sipping coffee, waiting, or heading out the door in groups of twos and fours to catch the shuttle bus to the Qwest Center.

Chris Wagner—a 25-year Wall Street veteran, friend in the business, and longtime Berkshire shareholder from California—is waiting for me, glancing through a copy of the special edition of the *Omaha World-Herald* devoted to the Berkshire annual meeting.

"See this?" he says, holding up the paper. "I told you, it's a cult."

Chris has been worried about Berkshire since attending last year's meeting. "Too much about Buffett, not enough about the business," he had said afterward, while still encouraging me to come. He's here to decide whether to keep his stock or sell it. Chris hands me a rectangular red plastic badge like the one others around us are wearing. It is a Berkshire Hathaway "Shareholder" badge, and it is my ticket to the annual meeting and the other shareholder events of the weekend. Every Berkshire shareholder is entitled to four passes to the meeting so they can bring friends and family, and since I'm not a shareholder, I'm using one of Chris's. We start to head outside, briefly debating whether to try to get to the Qwest Center before the doors open at 7 a.m. in order to get a good seat, or to head to the nearby Starbucks, which doesn't open until then.

It's going to be a long day, so we decide to get the good coffee first.

IN SEARCH OF PICKUP TRUCKS

Although the sky has cleared and the Qwest Center—Omaha's newer, cleaner, and brighter version of Madison Square Garden—is less than a mile from the hotel, Chris and I are taking his rental car. We have places to go *after* the meeting.

After stopping for coffee, we move into the line of traffic snaking its way toward the Qwest Center, which rises out of an old industrial area, all big, angular, and white. It's now 7:45 a.m., and the main parking lots are full, so we're directed to one of the satellite parking lots that handle the overflow. The reporter told me that the Buffett draw from the surrounding farms is so strong that there would be pickup trucks among the Lincoln Navigators in the parking lots.

I look for the pickup trucks, but don't see any. We join the crowds converging on the main entrance. They look much like the people who were on the plane from Chicago yesterday, making plans in the restaurant in Old Market late yesterday afternoon, and waiting for friends in the lobby of the Doubletree this morning: mostly white, aging baby boomers. Nearly all of them are couples, dressed in nice, casual clothing.

There are also those clusters of young men, dressed in their own business-casual uniform: Dockers, loafers, and long-sleeved button-down shirts with the collars open. They talk excitedly over one another, laugh and give high-fives. They egg one another on to cross at the intersections as soon as the police give the okay, and they race one another to the Qwest Center's entrance.

A fairly modern-looking hotel—"Nebraska's only four diamond property," as the Hilton Omaha proudly bills itself—sits directly across 10th Street from the main entrance of the Qwest. The Hilton is where the Berkshire elite stay, the reporter had told me, and from its doors a different kind of crowd is emerging.

They are prosperous-looking and genteel—a jacket-and-tie-wearing crowd, walking easily and without urgency to the arena. These are the directors, CEOs, and longtime shareholders with reserved seats who have been coming to the meeting for decades.

I look for familiar business faces among them—Rich Santulli, perhaps, the genius who created what is now NetJets; or Al Ueltschi, the founder of pilot instruction business FlightSafety International; or maybe carpet king Bob Shaw—each of them a highly driven entrepreneur who built a business and chose to sell it to no one but Warren Buffett.

I recognize nobody, but I do get a glimpse of the subtle pecking order that exists here in Omaha, which will be reinforced throughout the day, whereby an individual's status is determined by the length of time that person has been attending Berkshire meetings.

> "It's wonderful that we all come here each year," Charlie [Munger] told a group of friends at his own dinner party the weekend of the Berkshire annual meeting. "But why do we really do it? Yes, it's fun. But it's also a way of subtly saying, I'm very rich. It's also a way of subtly saying, I'm very smart."

That pecking order is obvious the minute we go into the giant, glass-walled complex, passing long lines at the concessions, and enter the arena on the first tier of seating, at half-court.

We see that we have no chance of getting a seat on the floor, or even close to it.

GOOD FOOD AND LOTS OF IT . . . FOR THE PRESS

The Qwest Center arena is roughly the size of Madison Square Garden and will seat about 17,000 shareholders today. Overflow rooms will accommodate the other 10,000 shareholders. At one end of the oval floor of the arena is a rectangular stage with a blue curtain behind it. On the stage in front of the curtain is a table with two microphones, water pitchers, and other paraphernalia. At that table, Warren Buffett and Charlie Munger will sit and answer questions for more than five hours—a little less than three hours before lunch, and a bit more than two hours after lunch.

On the floor in front of the stage is a VIP area for directors and their immediate families, with 60 folding chairs set up in three rows of 20. It is separated from the rest of the floor seating by a barrier of temporary gates. Many of the regular floor seats, I learn, have been reserved for families and employees of Berkshire companies. The remaining floor seats have long since been taken by early risers and Buffett regulars, who mingle comfortably by their seats like the old friends and family they probably are. There are also more than a few wide-eyed young men walking around, looking vainly for seats or talking with others who got in line as early as 3 a.m. to be first inside when the doors opened at 7 a.m.

The seats around us are all taken, but Chris and I spot a microphone several rows up—one of a dozen set up around the arena, for shareholders—and this microphone, quite miraculously, appears to have several open seats next to it.

On an impulse, Chris and I hustle up the steps to the microphone station, and then we notice an attendant standing nearby.

She is pointing to the half-dozen seemingly empty seats and say-ing, "All taken," as if she is saying it for the hundredth time. It is only then that we notice notepads, jackets, newspapers, and tote bags on the seats, holding each chair for a shareholder who plans to ask Buffett a question today.

Looking around, our eyes adjusting to the uneven lighting inside the arena, we see that every chair in the general vicinity and on this level has been taken.

We head back out to the escalators, past long, long lines of shareholders at the food courts along the perimeter of the arena, and go up to the mezzanine level, which had looked half-empty from the microphone stand. But it turns out that these seats are all spoken for, too, with jackets and newspapers and tote bags. Now we know where all those people in line at the concession stands had come from.

Back out of a tunnel and up another set of escalators, we reemerge on the highest level of the arena, where there are still plenty of open seats. The angle is steep and the legroom is a bit cramped, but we have a good view of the floor, the stage, and the small table where Buffett and Charlie Munger will sit.

Directly across the arena from us, just above eye level, is the press box. It is long and brightly lighted. Reporters are sitting at their computers, peering down on the proceedings. I was told that there is "good food and lots of it" in the press box.

Buffett likes good press, and he mostly gets it. He has been a close friend of Carol Loomis, the longtime *Fortune* magazine reporter and now editor-at-large, for decades. She plays online bridge with Buffett and edits his annual shareholder letter. "Believe me, the fact that I have known Warren Buffett all these years has been very, very good for the *Fortune* readers," Loomis has said.

Their long-standing relationship has also been very, very good for Berkshire Hathaway shareholders and Warren Buffett. Over the years, Buffett has used *Fortune* as a kind of unofficial mouthpiece for himself and Berkshire. In fact, in July 2006, he gave Loomis the first interview on his plan to give away his considerable fortune to the Bill & Melinda Gates Foundation and four other charities.

A brightly lighted electronic ticker tape rings the arena, spelling out different Berkshire brand logos as well as warnings that videos and photography are not allowed during the meeting. Two giant video monitors hang down from the high ceiling on either side of the stage.

We settle back and await the start, taking it all in and observing the crowd entering our area in search of seats.

A pattern quickly emerges. As each couple enters the arena, the husband looks around for seats, shakes his head, and then cranes his neck until he sees an open spot. He motions to his wife and they begin making their way carefully up the cement steps. I see one only man who looks like a genuine farmer—his face is craggy, he wears a large Stetson and cowboy boots, and he is carrying his things in a plastic Wal-Mart bag.

The seats around us are almost all taken now, and I notice something that I have not seen in years.

WHAT THEY'RE READING

What I notice is that almost every person sitting around us waiting for the Berkshire Hathaway annual meeting to begin is reading a newspaper.

Many of them are reading the *Omaha World-Herald*—the issue that's available free in the lobbies of the hotels, with a "Welcome Berkshire Shareholders" wrapper. Others are reading the distinctively orange-colored *Financial Times* of London, which was being given away when we came into the Qwest Center. Still others are reading *USA Today* or the weekend *Wall Street Journal*.

One or two are leafing through the Acme Brick day planner handed out as we entered. I took one, too, but strictly for sentimental reasons: it reminded me of the old-fashioned day planner that my grandfather used to keep on his kitchen table, which I found, and kept, after he died.

What these shareholders are *not* reading is a BlackBerry. Nor are they are gazing at handheld organizers, scrolling through songs on an iPod, typing on notebook computers, or sending text messages on their cell phones. And I see only one person actually talking on a cell phone.

I haven't seen this many people just sitting quietly, reading newspapers, in so long that it's almost weird. I nudge Chris. He's noticed it, too.

Maybe we've both been on Wall Street too long. Maybe this is what any gathering of middle-aged individuals anywhere in America other than Wall Street would look like right now. But still, to see a group of middle-aged men and women sitting around in public reading a newspaper, instead of staring at a tiny screen in apparent hypnosis, is really striking.

Newspaper readers sit up more or less straight with the page in front of them, and they sit still, because it takes a few minutes to actually read each page. It is an open, relaxed, inviting, approachable kind of posture.

BlackBerry readers, on the other hand, tend to be hunched over, head bowed, reading the text. They're constantly clicking or scrolling to keep the sentences coming, so they don't see much other than the little screen. It is a closed, tense, uninviting, not-very-approachable posture.

It just *looks* different.

But it's not just the looks of it that matter. That constant stream of unprompted information nurtures a kind of jumpiness, a shorter attention span that comes from knowing that whatever is on the screen right now will be followed very shortly by new, newer, newest information.

It's no wonder that Warren Buffett reportedly makes it a point never to trade stocks when he's in New York City.

CHAPTER 4

The Oracle of Omaha

"We have a reverence for logic around here."

—WARREN BUFFETT

If there is one word that describes Warren Buffett, the "Oracle of Omaha," it is *not oracular*. Nor is it *prophetic*, *divinatory*, *clairvoyant*, *extrasensory*, or *telepathic*. While he may be known as "the Oracle of Omaha," there is in truth absolutely nothing oracular about him.

Yes, it is true that in May 1969, near the peak of that era's bull market, he wrote to the investors in his partnership that "opportunities for investment . . . have virtually disappeared," closed his partnership, and kept only two stocks: a retailer that he later sold, and an old-line textile company named Berkshire Hathaway, which he decided to keep.

And it is true that in October 1974, after the Dow Jones Industrial Average had collapsed and with the America economy mired in gasoline shortages and price controls, Buffett made perhaps the most unequivocally bullish—and correct—utterance on the subject of investing ever recorded by any business publication when he told *Forbes* magazine: "Now is the time to invest and get rich."

It is also true that a week before the 1987 stock market crash, Buffett sold stocks out of a Berkshire profit-sharing plan. And that he bought nearly half a billion dollars worth of RJR Nabisco junk bonds near the bottom of the junk bond market early in 1990. And that when "old economy" brick-and-mortar companies were out of fashion during the dot-com bubble, Buffett literally bought a brick company, a carpet company, and a furniture retailer, while everybody else in America was buying Internet stocks—and would soon regret it.

And, yes, in his 2002 letter Buffett wrote to shareholders about his bearish view on the U.S. dollar, which would soon begin a long decline. And a year after that, he wrote a stern warning against "derivatives," a type of financial instrument newly popular with Wall Street banks and brokers. Their value, as the name implies, is *derived* from other financial instruments. A derivative is like a bet on a race horse instead of ownership of the horse itself. Like horse racing bets, they can get rather complicated. Buffett called them "financial weapons of mass destruction"—four years before the subprime meltdown that would spark a financial panic and lead to the demise of one of America's premier investment banks, Bear Stearns.

These stories are all true. But in every case, Warren Buffett was not attempting to predict the future, nor, except for his selling before the 1987 crash, was he anticipating a short-term move in the markets in his favor.

He was, rather, being entirely *rational*.

Closing down Buffett Partnership Ltd. near the peak of the Go-Go market in 1969, buying heavily at the bottom in 1974, snapping up discredited junk bonds from fear-stricken investors in 1990, selling the U.S. dollar near its peak, and buying a brick company near its bottom were all rational decisions based on the intrinsic values offered in a particular market at a particular moment in time. What's more, those investment decisions were based on information that was freely available to anybody with the time and the desire to look for it.

They were not predictions, prophecies, or forecasts. "We've long felt that the only value of stock forecasters is to make fortune tellers look good," Buffett wrote in his 1992 Chairman's Letter, and he meant it.

If there is one word to say about Warren Buffett—and it is a word that more than any other defines the basis of his great investment success—the word is *rational*.

And while most staggeringly rich, successful investors might try to cloak their investing methods in an aura of mystery and intrigue, Warren Buffett has never attempted to hide his methods or keep them a secret.

Instead, he shares them all with anyone who wants to listen, and 27,000 people are now assembled here inside the Qwest Center in Omaha, Nebraska, on a muggy spring morning to do just that.

Then a voice booms over the speakers, announcing, "The movie will start in 10 minutes." An excited buzz begins to fill the arena. As the lights dim, people fold their newspapers and put away their reading glasses, take a last sip of their coffee, and check their watches. It is 8:20 a.m.

THE ORACLE OF OMAHA

Chris and I soon notice a kind of bustle far down below on the floor of the arena. Its locus appears to be near the stage, where there is sudden movement. Others notice, and all around us a collective arm grabbing, finger pointing, and whispering begins. The fingers are pointing toward a man in a rumpled dark suit with unruly white hair who, we now can see, is walking casually up the main aisle toward the center of the arena. He is being led by an efficient-looking woman, and his progress is slowed by shareholders reaching out, shaking his hand, and patting him on the shoulder.

It is the Great One. The King. The Boss.

It is John, Paul, George, and Ringo all rolled into one.

It's the chairman of the board himself—and quite literally, too, for it is Warren Buffett, chairman of the board of Berkshire Hathaway, and every inch the "Oracle of Omaha."

He sits down amiably in a reserved row right at half-court, in a seat that will give him a good view of the movie on the giant screens hanging alongside the small stage where he and Charlie will sit and conduct the meeting. The crowd swells around him, and that's when the camera flashes start going off.

Polite, nicely dressed men and well-dressed women approach him, timidly, to snap a picture and then retreat into the crowd, which is building and disrupting the movement of others who are attempting to get to their seats.

The camera flashes go off rapidly now, and the crowd closes in on the man, who is still sitting casually, one leg crossed over his knee, and chatting with the middle-aged woman who led him to his seat. She is his daughter, Susie, who has put together the movie that is about to be shown.

"The movie will start in two minutes."

Several nice-looking young men in suits now appear—they are bodyguards—and make friendly gestures to disperse the picture takers, but the flashes keep going off, so the men in suits do their job a bit more forcefully, pointing people to their seats. The crowd breaks up as the lights go down and the place gets dark, and the movie begins.

WOODSTOCK FOR CAPITALISTS

The movie that starts the 2007 Berkshire Hathaway shareholders' meeting begins with a cartoon. While nobody will mistake it for a Disney classic, it's meant to be fun, and that's how the audience takes it. Warren and Charlie are two rather square hippies conducting business at the original Woodstock festival, playing on the theme that Berkshire's annual meeting is a "Woodstock for Capitalists," as Buffett first began calling it in his 1996 Chairman's Letter.

Warren and Charlie drive their VW wagon to the music festival and swap their Fruit of the Loom T-shirt collection for a truckload worth of a "groovy" soft drink called Coke. The Coke sells out immediately, and the partners use that windfall to buy a van full of See's Candies. The inside joke, which everybody in the room gets without being reminded, is that all these brands— except Volkswagen—are part of the Berkshire "family." Buffett bought See's Candies for Berkshire in 1972 and purchased Fruit-of-the-Loom out of bankruptcy in 2002. He began buying shares of Coke in 1988, and Berkshire today owns 9 percent of the company. Buffett considers the investment in Coke, which he says "is like Mom and apple pie," to be one of Berkshire's "permanent" holdings.

As the cartoon continues, the two hippies meet a young Bill Gates, who is talking gibberish about some new fad called computers. The joke, of course, is on Buffett, whose famous distaste for technology investments left Berkshire out of many of the greatest acts of wealth creation in history—Apple, Cisco, Google, and Microsoft have a combined value of more than half a trillion dollars, yet Berkshire has never owned a share.

Ironically, Buffett himself owns 100 shares of Microsoft, which he bought after first meeting Bill Gates in 1991 and bonding with the young technology genius over a discussion about IBM. Microsoft was still early in its growth, and the shares traded for about $1.50 a share, adjusting for stock splits. But Buffett did not buy 100 shares of Microsoft as an investment: he bought them to get on the company's mailing list for financial information, something he has done his entire career with companies he wants to study.

Nevertheless, it was very likely the best $150 that Warren Buffett ever spent; the current price of Microsoft stock is over $25 a share.

Also, Gates has since become one of Buffett's closest friends and a Berkshire board member. The two play online bridge every week; Gates uses the name "Challenger X," while Buffett is "T-Bone." Gates even bought his wife's engagement ring at Borsheim's, with Buffett's help.

How did the "Oracle of Omaha" miss seeing the value of Microsoft's monopoly on computer operating systems—a "moat" if ever there was one—when he was playing bridge, attending board meetings, and taking vacations with the man who founded Microsoft?

It's a great question, and one day somebody might ask it. But Buffett knows that the best way to deflect criticism is to offer it yourself before somebody else does. Buffett's cartoon encounter with Gates makes the point so that not only do his own shareholders not mind, but they can laugh about it.

PURPLE HAZE FOR AN ELVIS AUDIENCE

The rest of the "Woodstock" cartoon is a jumble of 1960s-era references, mystifying to most of the straight-laced, Elvis-era audience and downright unintelligible to the high-fiving young men in the crowd. A singer named Janis asks Warren and Charlie if they have seen "Bobby McGee," and a guitarist named Jimi comes by looking for a guitar riff for a song about "Purple Haze." It can't end too quickly, but fortunately it does.

A video of Warren strumming the ukulele, which Buffett has played all his life, and singing "Ain't She Sweet" with his supposed distant relative, Jimmy Buffett, picks things up. This is followed by a strange mix of riveting moments and odd film clips, including plenty of television ads for Berkshire companies. There is, for no apparent reason, a "Mean Joe Greene" Coke commercial—a hit when it aired almost 30 years ago, but meaningless today—and seemingly random highlights from old University of Nebraska football games.

These images have great meaning, however, to Buffett, Munger, and their families and old friends in the audience. Coke looms large in Berkshire lore—after all, one of Buffett's first commercial ventures involved buying six-packs of Coke at his grandfather's store and reselling the individual bottles for a profit. He was six years old.

Fifty-eight years later, Buffett began accumulating 9 percent of the entire company.

As for the football clips, Buffett, like many Nebraskans, is a rabid Cornhuskers fan, going so far as to produce the Berkshire

Annual Report in team colors to mark a special occasion in Nebraska football lore: the 1997 retirement of revered coach Tom Osborne.

In these parts, the football plays we've been watching are famous.

What look to the casual observer to be random, unrelated moments are in fact reminders that this movie, and the entire weekend, are not marketing ploys designed to showcase a company. They are, rather, the outgrowth of what began as a few shareholders driving to Omaha to ask questions of a man whom they regarded as an extraordinary steward of their money.

Over the years, this meeting, which first took place in the cafeteria of a local insurance company, has become a worldwide phenomenon. The movie has become a visual and audio shrine to Warren Buffett and the values—both investment and otherwise—that he has consistently espoused to Berkshire's directors, managers, employees, shareholders, friends, and family over a consistently successful investment career.

When the movie finally ends, we get to see Buffett himself, on stage, ready to perform.

CHAPTER 5

This Motley Group

—✦—

> "Berkshire has the best managers—and shareholders—anywhere."
>
> —WARREN BUFFETT

uffett strides out from behind the blue curtain. He is wearing a bright Hawaiian shirt, and his gray hair is pulled back in a ponytail. He is smiling broadly and carrying an acoustic guitar.

It is *Jimmy* Buffett, the singer.

Outside Omaha, this aging troubadour is famous for relentless touring and a mildly catchy drinking song—"Margaritaville"—that made him spokesman for a laid-back lifestyle, on which he has built a chain of restaurants, and a fortune.

Here in Omaha, however, Jimmy Buffett is famous for his early and canny purchase of Berkshire shares in the early 1980s, as well as persistent speculation—which he seems to encourage—that he is related to another, far wealthier Buffett, whom he calls "Uncle Warren."

Jimmy approaches a microphone stand, a pair of bifocals balanced awkwardly on the end of his nose, and jokes about the lack of a teleprompter. Then, to the tune of "Margaritaville," he begins to play a version called "Berkshire Hathaway-ville."

Cue cards spread out at his feet contain the revised lyrics ("Some people say that Charlie Munger's to blame"), but unfortunately Jimmy Buffett can't seem to read his own lyrics. He muffs some words, stumbles to a halt, and tells us that he'll have to start over. By this time, however, the audience is more interested in seeing him finish. When he finally does, he introduces the Buffett that everybody has come to see and hear—Warren Buffett—and his partner, Charlie Munger.

The two men emerge from a curtain behind the stage to great applause. Warren Buffett still looks rumpled, despite the Italian-made Zegna suits he wears. "I wear expensive suits," he likes to say. "They only look cheap on me."

Charlie Munger, taller and stiffer, looks very much the six years Buffett's senior that he is. He wears a dark suit and tie, and he walks stiffly.

Munger sits down and Buffett starts the meeting.

He first introduces the directors and other notables seated in the roped-off section down front, making a special mention of Susan Decker, the Yahoo! executive who is joining the board this year.

Decker stands and acknowledges the applause. What distinguishes her from the existing board members is not just her job running one of the original dot-com companies (Yahoo!) or the fact that she is a woman and will be one of only two women on the Berkshire board of directors.

It is her age: 44.

The Berkshire board of directors is *old*. Four of its members are 80 or older. Decker single-handedly reduces the average age on the board from almost 70 to a little over 65.

The reason the Berkshire board is so old is that a majority of its members are early business partners, classmates, or childhood friends of Warren and Charlie.

And most of them are legends in their own right.

Tom Murphy is the media executive who built Capital Cities Communications into a giant by taking over the ABC television network, and later merging with Disney. Berkshire was the largest shareholder in "Cap Cities/ABC," as Murphy's company was known, and made a $2 billion profit on the sale to Disney in 2001.

David ("Sandy") Gottesman built First Manhattan into an investment giant and was one of the first Wall Street professionals to recognize Buffett's talent. The respect was mutual; when Buffett closed his partnership in 1969, he recommended that his investors consider investing with Gottesman.

Walter Scott is a local Omaha businessman and childhood friend who built Peter Kiewit Sons Inc. into a major construction firm and helped form MidAmerican Energy, which Berkshire later acquired. Donald Keough is another Omaha native, and another childhood friend of Buffett's, who was president of Coke when Buffett began buying the stock in 1988. Keough deduced that the stranger who was buying up large blocks of Coke shares through a midwestern stockbroker might in fact be his old neighbor. When he called Buffett to ask if this was the case, Buffett said it was.

Ronald Olson is senior partner at Charlie Munger's old law firm—Munger, Tolles & Olson.

"Are any of these guys going to tell Warren Buffett he's doing something wrong?" Chris wonders out loud.

It's a great point. Even the younger directors owe something to Buffett. Bill Gates (51), of course, is one of Buffett's best friends. Charlotte Guyman (50) is a former Microsoft executive, and Howard Buffett (52) is Warren's oldest son and the only one of his three children who is on the board.

While Berkshire's board of directors might not be the toothy watchdogs you'd expect of a public company, being a Berkshire board member is not a shady path to prosperity. GE, for example, pays its directors $250,000 in compensation a year, and also lets them buy appliances at a discount through one of those ridiculous big-company perks called, in this case, "The Executive Products and Lighting Program."

Berkshire, on the other hand, pays its directors a measly $900—plus expenses—for each meeting they attend. And if they don't make it to a meeting but listen in on a teleconference instead, they get $350.

More important, unlike most public companies, Buffett does not provide his directors with the standard "Directors and Officers" insurance that companies provide in the event somebody sues the company's directors and officers for doing something stupid.

The irony that one of the world's largest insurance companies doesn't even provide its own officers and directors with standard insurance coverage can't be lost on the directors he has just introduced, but Warren Buffett wants Berkshire's directors to think, and act, like true owners. And given the company's track record, who'd argue that the board hasn't done its duty?

Certainly nobody in this room.

HOW QUALITY SHAREHOLDERS REACT TO BAD NEWS

Introductions over, Buffett reviews in a sentence or two the first-quarter 2007 earnings, just released. It soon becomes clear that we are in for something quite different from the standard corporate shareholders' meeting.

The Berkshire Hathaway income statement displayed on the giant screens hanging down from the ceiling shows strong quarterly net income of $2.6 billion. Thanks to a mild hurricane season, Buffett says, the insurance businesses that contribute most of Berkshire's earnings were terrific.

But Buffett doesn't take the time to enjoy them.

"It couldn't get any better than it was last year, from our point of view," he says, not mincing words. "The insurance earnings are going to go down, there's no question about that."

Now, if we were attending any other annual meeting—IBM's, say, or Microsoft's, or GE's—and the CEO stood up in front of 27,000 shareholders, Wall Street analysts, mutual fund managers, and hedge fund guys and said, "It couldn't get any better than it was last year," and "profits are going down," the rush for the exits would have swamped whatever contingency planning the Qwest Center has in place for emergency evacuations when something bad happens at Strategic Air Command headquarters 10 miles south of Omaha.

Yet not a single person stirs in his seat, gasps, coughs, or makes a sound of displeasure or disappointment to mar the convivial and expectant atmosphere.

Buffett's search for "quality shareholders" has been a success.

These shareholders understand that Berkshire's results can—and will—be volatile. After all, nearly two-thirds of Berkshire Hathaway's earnings are related to insurance, from GEICO automobile insurance to Ajit Jain's huge reinsurance business, specializing, in Buffett's words, "in mammoth and unusual risks."

That is a huge change from two decades ago, when most of Berkshire's profits came from Buffett's stock-picking skills and a hodgepodge of seven noninsurance companies that he and Munger acquired for Berkshire after Buffett took control in 1965.

Those seven companies included See's Candies, Scott Fetzer, Kirby vacuum cleaners, a work uniform company, the Nebraska Furniture Mart, the *Buffalo News*, and World Book Encyclopedia. For years they performed so well that Buffett anointed them "the Sainted Seven" in his 1987 shareholder letter.

Today, however, not one of the original "Sainted Seven" is big enough to receive its own line on the income statement. In fact, only See's Candies still generates enough income to be mentioned in the quarterly financials filed with the SEC. The rest have faded with the changing global economy. And one of them, World Book Encyclopedia, has disappeared almost entirely.

Still, the seven served their purpose by providing Berkshire Hathaway with a steady stream of cash that, Warren Buffett, in his role as the company's self-described "capital allocator," could use to buy other companies. And this is what allowed him to acquire most of the 76 or so companies that make up Berkshire Hathaway today.

THE POWER OF FLOAT

Berkshire is essentially a giant insurance conglomerate (including GEICO and General Re) with some other large businesses on the side. This may seem odd since Buffett didn't even buy *himself* a life insurance policy as a young father, figuring that he could grow his own money faster than any insurance policy.

What attracted Buffett to the insurance business in the first place was the fact that, unlike the products or services sold by almost any other business in the world, insurance is paid for by the consumer *before it is actually used.*

People pay for their health insurance, their life insurance, their car insurance, and their property insurance—often for years before ever needing the insurance. That money —called "float" in the industry—accumulates at the insurance company, a sort of ready-made investment fund for an investor who can make it grow before it has to be paid out. Buffett figured out that as long as he could at least break even on the insurance itself, he knew that he could make a lot of money by investing the float in stocks and bonds.

That insight—perhaps the biggest of Buffett's career—has been copied by many other investors, and it has worked even better than Buffett might have dreamed, because the insurance operations have, on average, been profitable in their own right. So the float, which is today close to $60 *billion,* has cost Berkshire nothing at all.

In effect, Berkshire's insurance operations have provided Warren Buffett with an interest-free loan of $60 billion to invest for his shareholders' benefit.

Beyond insurance and the profits that Buffett has earned by investing Berkshire's float, energy is now Berkshire's single most important business. Through MidAmerican Energy Holdings, Berkshire controls hydroelectric power dams in Washington State, natural gas pipelines that carry 8 percent of the natural gas consumed in the United States, and the third largest electricity distributor in the United Kingdom.

After energy, there is a "motley group" of companies—as Buffett himself describes them in his Chairman's Letter—manufacturing everything from bricks to paints to insulation, recreational vehicles, carpet, and manufactured housing. While most of these businesses have suffered from the decline in housing, others—particularly NetJets and FlightSafety International, along with the newer ISCAR metal tools business—are flourishing.

In fact, Buffett today dismisses the housing-related declines as a short-term problem, not a long-term concern, and finishes up his brief comments on the numbers with a well-received flourish: "Berkshire has the best managers—and shareholders—*anywhere.*"

Now, this kind of cheerleading is not mere puffery for the reporters watching in the press gallery across the arena, or for the newcomers among us. Buffett has always given full credit to the managers—"All Stars" he calls them—who run Berkshire's businesses.

> I've taken the easy route, just sitting back and working through great managers who run their own shows. My only tasks are to cheer them on, sculpt and harden our corporate culture, and make major capital-allocation decisions.

With the management team recognized and near-term earnings expectations reduced, Buffett checks his watch and moves on. It is nearly 9:30 a.m., time for the real reason that 27,000 people are here.

The question-and-answer session.

CHAPTER 6

The Math Has to Make Sense

> *"It can continue to go on for a long time after you're in a state of total revulsion."*
>
> —CHARLIE MUNGER

It starts simply enough. Buffett repeats the "ground rules" for the questions, which are also spelled out in the meeting guide that all shareholders receive with their badges. Here are the rules:

- State your name and hometown.

- Ask your question promptly—speak loud and clear.

- Do not ask more than one question or attempt to "bundle" several questions together.

The only thing that is off-limits, Buffett tells us, "is what we're buying now." He asks that shareholders speak up—"Charlie can hear and I can see," he says, "so we work well together."

This gets a laugh, but Buffett isn't kidding; he will frequently cup his hand to his ear as the questions are asked, and Munger will occasionally prompt him with the gist of the question that's been asked. Munger, being blind in his left eye, wears extremely thick glasses and frequently gazes off, seemingly in a different world, but, as we will learn, very much in the present.

Fifty-four questions will be asked over the next five-plus hours, by my count, from individuals of all ages—10-year-old girls to grown men. The shareholders generally will stick to the rules, and Buffett will answer their questions thoughtfully and in full—rarely discoursing for less than five minutes on a topic before asking his partner, who is seated silently at the table, "Charlie, you have anything to add?"

Munger will occasionally decline. "Nothing to add," he'll say, or "Nothing on that one, either"—frequently drawing appreciative laughter for his tight-lipped manner.

But when "Charlie," as Buffett invariably calls him, does have something to say, it nearly always will be a well-thought-out and tightly constructed set piece, both dour and judgmental. Munger brings a sense of moral outrage to the session that Buffett shares but rarely voices, and takes delight in crafting the kind of harsh and condemning phrases that thrill and, sometimes, shock the audience.

Munger also frequently concludes his remarks with a joke from his well-worn repertoire. These invariably get titters, laughter, and sometimes applause even though they often sound dated and for the most part politically incorrect. The audience, it is clear, expects to hear them. Buffett settles in behind his microphone, checks a legal pad that he keeps at hand, and calls on the microphone in "Area 1."

"THE INVESTORS CAN'T LEAVE"

The first person to ask a question is a shareholder from Chicago. He thanks Buffett profusely for hosting this gathering and taking his question and then asks about the "private equity" boom that is currently raging across America and most of Europe.

"Is it a bubble?" he wants to know. "And what could cause it to burst?"

In a gruff, folksy, matter-of-fact voice, Buffett starts to speak.

The mark of an original thinker may be that you never know how he's going to answer a question you've never heard him asked before. And this question about private equity should be a layup, particularly for Warren Buffett.

"Private equity" firms buy entire companies using a lot of borrowed money, the same way people buy houses. Thanks to low interest rates and easy credit, private equity is at the moment one of the hottest things going right now. It is Wall Street's version of the housing bubble.

Private equity firms have been buying everything from semiconductor companies like Freescale Semiconductor to fashion-dependent retailers like Neiman Marcus at what Buffett has in the past called "nosebleed prices." Like subprime borrowers buying a house that they can't afford, the private equity firms have been taking on debt loads that might make even Donald Trump nervous.

It would be simple enough for Buffett to shake his head and offer a stark warning about the silliness of running with the herd and doing deals just to do deals, and about how these kinds of fads always end badly.

Furthermore, Buffett could point out that with Berkshire's fabulously large cash reserves and his own unerring eye for a bargain, Berkshire will be one of the few companies that will be able to take advantage of the ensuing bargains.

Buffett, however, doesn't take the easy way. He answers the question that was *asked*. Buffett explains that only wealthy investors can get involved in private equity funds, and those investors are "locked up" for long periods of time and can't pull their money out of the funds on short notice. "The private equity funds lock up their money for five or ten years and buy businesses that don't price daily. It takes many years for the score to be put on the board, and the investors can't leave."

"It isn't really a bubble that will burst." It is, however, a *boom*, Buffett says, and one that he's not happy about.

The people who manage private equity funds get paid only when they buy companies, he points out. "So there's a great compulsion to invest it quickly so you can raise another fund and get more fees." And that mindless drive to make acquisitions has also driven up the price of acquisition candidates, hurting Berkshire's ability to acquire companies at the kind of reasonable prices that Buffett seeks.

"We can't compete against these buyers. We buy forever, and it's our own money." He shakes his head. "I started to cry while you were asking your question, thinking about it," he says, drawing laughter. Meantime, he adds, Berkshire is not going to change its investment standards in order to participate in the current fun and games, because, he concludes, "The math has to make sense to us."

As to the question of when the private equity boom might end, Buffett says he thinks it could be "quite some time" before investors become disillusioned and attempt to pull their money out. He then asks Charlie Munger if he has anything to add.

Munger stirs and says laconically, in a dry, thin voice, "It can continue to go on for a long time after you're in a state of total revulsion."

"The voice of total optimism has spoken," Buffett says, to laughter. He makes a check on his yellow legal pad and calls for the next question.

"Okay, Area 2."

It is unlikely that anyone in attendance is imagining that the "Oracle of Omaha" and his partner will be proven wrong about private equity before summer is over.

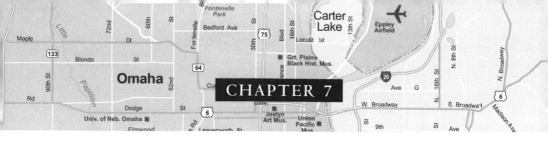
Buffett's Table

"The first rule is not to lose. The second rule is not to forget the first rule."

—WARREN BUFFETT

The questions are asked politely and with great respect. Most of the shareholders have written them out beforehand and read them into the microphone. Young and old, they tend to rush from nervousness, stammer, or get tongue-tied and repeat themselves. It's understandable: they've been waiting a long time to ask the Oracle of Omaha their question.

Oh, and 27,000 people are watching.

Only a handful of older professionals and longtime shareholders—some of whom Buffett recognizes and acknowledges by name—appear genuinely relaxed and unhurried at the microphone.

Relaxed or not, before they get to whatever they actually intend to ask, everyone offers thanks, usually to "Mr. Buffett and Mr. Munger," sometimes so profusely that Buffett has to nudge them along to ask their question. Buffett does not interrupt anyone or cut anyone off, but he is very sensitive to the mood of the crowd, and when the audience gets restive, he will ask in a gruff but friendly voice, "Is there a question in there?"

Eventually they get to it, but first they just want to thank Warren and Charlie for hosting this meeting, for sharing their collective wisdom, and most especially for the long-term benefits that have accrued to shareholders owning Berkshire Hathaway stock.

And those benefits have been immense.

Each year, the Berkshire Hathaway annual report opens with a full-page table, titled "Berkshire's Corporate Performance vs. the S&P 500."

Beginning with the year 1965, when Warren Buffett took control of Berkshire Hathaway, the table publishes in black and white the annual increase in value of Berkshire Hathaway and compares this to the stock market as a whole, using the Standard & Poor's 500 (S&P 500) index. At the bottom is the cumulative gain in Berkshire compared to the S&P 500.

And what a gain it is: Berkshire's value has grown 21.1 percent compounded over 43 years. That's double the growth rate of the S&P 500, which has managed a 10.3 percent compounded gain over the same span of time.

Now, 10.3 percent compounded over 43 years is not a bad rate of return; the cumulative gain amounts to 6,840 percent.

However, 21.1 percent compounded over 43 years is a staggering amount: precisely 400,863 percent—more than *58 times better* than the S&P 500.

To the careful observer of Buffett's track record, the most remarkable thing that jumps off the page is the impact of putting Buffett's only rule of investing—"The first rule is not to lose; the second rule is not to forget the first rule"—into action.

Even when the U.S. stock market, as measured by the S&P 500, was getting its clocked cleaned—1966, down 12 percent; 1969, down 8 percent; 1973, down 15 percent; 1974, down 26 percent; 1977, down 7 percent; 1981, down 5 percent; 1990, down 3 percent; 2000, down 9 percent—Berkshire's net worth grew *each year*.

In fact, Berkshire didn't have a down year until 2001, a *36-year span* that included, as Buffett once wrote,

> the huge expansion of the Vietnam War, wage and price controls, two oil shocks, the resignation of a president, the dissolution of the Soviet Union, a one-day drop in the Dow of 508 points, or treasury bill yields fluctuating between 2.8% and 17.4%.

And these figures don't even include the nine years prior to 1965, when Buffett took control of Berkshire Hathaway and was running a partnership with money from family, friends, and acquaintances. During those nine years, Buffett Partnership, Ltd. never had a down year, and his partners had already gained some 400 percent by the time Buffett took control of Berkshire Hathaway.

Combining the two periods of Buffett's investment career, Buffett Partnership Ltd. and Berkshire Hathaway, Warren Buffett has had *one* down year in over 50 years.

Yet Buffett's table is astounding for more than the magnitude and consistency of the returns. In fact, the reported compound growth rate actually *understates* Buffett's achievement.

First, many of Berkshire's operating businesses—such as See's Candy, MidAmerican, and NetJets—are worth more than the value recorded on Berkshire's books, which is based on cost, not current value.

Second, Berkshire's 400,863 percent gain in value from 1965 through the end of 2007 is *net of income taxes*, while the S&P 500 gain is not. If both were net of taxes, Berkshire's gain might be more than 100 times the S&P 500's, not 58 times.

Of course, the Buffett faithful have a simpler way of measuring the worth of Berkshire Hathaway—one that is purer and more reliable than calculations of economic wealth.

They look at the stock price.

When Warren Buffett became chairman of Berkshire Hathaway on May 10, 1965, the stock price was $18 a share.

And gathered here in Omaha on May 5, 2007, almost exactly 42 years later, that price is now $109,250 per share.

But $18 invested in the S&P 500 on May 10, 1965, would today be worth only about $300.

That's why we're all here.

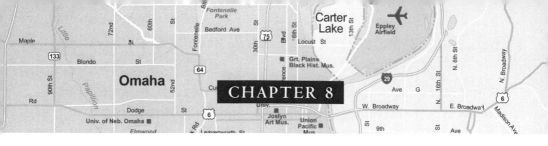

CHAPTER 8

The Time Value of Warren Buffett

"This is not the forum in which to address these comments."

—FORMER HOME DEPOT CEO ROBERT NARDELLI

T he contrast with most annual shareholder meetings couldn't be greater. Annual meetings of even the largest companies—and Berkshire Hathaway is among the 50 biggest private employers on earth—are sparsely attended by shareholders and mostly ignored by the national press, except during a company crisis.

Yet the Berkshire annual meeting draws shareholders, reporters, and news cameras from, quite literally, around the world.

The first shareholder to ask a question came from Chicago; the second from Germany. And the third shareholder, who is ready at a microphone now, has come all the way from India to be here.

By the end of the day, shareholders from Kentucky and Kuwait, Minnesota and Munich, Iowa, Nebraska, Vancouver, Australia, Michigan, Florida, Seattle, Great Britain, New York, New Jersey,

San Francisco, San Jose, Santa Monica, Los Angeles, Indiana, Kansas City, and Hong Kong will have asked questions.

So many international shareholders have traveled to Omaha for today's meeting, in fact, that before the questions got underway, Buffett announced that he and Charlie would be hosting a meet-and-greet with them after the formal session ends.

He explained that if so many shareholders had come all that way to be in Omaha, "I just feel I ought to thank them."

Hearing Buffett talk this way about his shareholders calls to mind another famous—or, if you like, infamous—CEO: Home Depot's Robert Nardelli.

THE BOARD WORE CHICKEN SUITS

Robert Louis Nardelli was a rising star from GE whose disappointing and stormy tenure as CEO of Home Depot ended not long after a shareholders' meeting during which two large digital clocks timed shareholders who were asking questions. The questions were limited to 60 seconds, but it didn't matter because Nardelli didn't respond anyway—although he did say, "Thank you."

The meeting was over in half an hour.

Nardelli's fellow members of the Home Depot board of directors—the folks who are nominally in charge of the company—did not witness that particular mockery of corporate governance, for the simple reason that not one of them attended the meeting.

"I tried a new format," Nardelli blandly said afterward. "It didn't work."

Sparked by *New York Times* columnist Joe Nocera's brilliant account of the meeting—"The Board Wore Chicken Suits," May 27, 2006—a shareholder revolt eventually led to Nardelli's ouster. The same board of directors that had failed to show up at the annual meeting awarded Nardelli a $210 million severance package. Nardelli reportedly helped to seal the deal by, among other things, dropping his right to use the six Home Depot corporate jets for his personal use. He is now CEO of Chrysler.

Appropriately enough, the shareholder from India is asking Buffett about the seemingly outrageous compensation packages today's corporate boards are offering in order to attract the next Jack Welch, even if he turns out to be Robert Nardelli. That isn't exactly what the fellow from India says, but it's the gist of the question, and it galvanizes Buffett.

Buffett says flat out that he does not care much for meticulously crafted compensation systems in the first place. "There are more problems with having the wrong manager than having the wrong compensation system," he says—a lesson that the Home Depot board of directors learned the hard way.

Buffett contrasts the friendly negotiations between a compensation committee and a CEO that always result in a nice, fat contract for the CEO, with the intense negotiations between companies and labor unions. "You read about labor negotiations going on for weeks, both sides declare an impasse, they negotiate until 3 a.m., etc. When was the last time you heard about anything like this when a board negotiates pay with a CEO?"

The difference, he says, is that to the compensation committee negotiating with a chief executive, it's "play money"—but to the chief executive, it is life and death. "One side really cares and the other doesn't."

Despite having served on 19 corporate boards himself, Buffett, who in the past has referred to compensation committees as "tail-wagging puppy dogs," says he's been nominated to only a single compensation committee.

"They're looking for cocker spaniels, not Dobermans," he tells us. "I try to pretend I'm a cocker spaniel, but nobody's fooled."

Chris is shaking his head. "So why doesn't he just ask to be on the committee?" he whispers. It's a great question. Buffett's been using this line about cocker spaniels and Dobermans for years, and it always draws a good laugh from the crowd. But surely the world's greatest investor could simply *ask* to be put on the compensation committee—and if refused, simply mention his request to one of his many friends in the press.

What board of directors of any public company is going to want to admit to shareholders that it wouldn't nominate the "Oracle of Omaha" to its compensation committee?

THE FIRST BILLION-DOLLAR CEO

Furthermore, Buffett's presence on Coke's board of directors for 17 years certainly did nothing to stop the escalation of public company CEO salaries.

In fact, it may have *helped* it.

Roberto C. Goizueta, the Cuban-born CEO who led the turn-around of Coke that caught Buffett's eye in 1988, received more than a billion dollars in salary, bonuses, and stock grants during his tenure—the first professional manager to break the $1 billion ceiling, according to press reports at the time.

Buffett, who called Coke under Goizueta "a shareholder's dream," still regards Goizueta—who died of lung cancer in 1997—as a heroic figure. He was famous on Wall Street for obsessing over the company's stock price, and a favorite saying was reported to be "Set expectations, meet expectations. Repeat."

For years Coke did just that. Earnings soared, and so did the stock.

Berkshire's 200 million shares of Coke were acquired at an average price of $6.50 per share starting in 1988. When Goizueta died, those shares were worth about $60 a share.

Goizueta, whose pay came mainly from grants of Coke stock, had become a billionaire. And while Goizueta benefited greatly, so did all Coke shareholders—Berkshire included.

After Goizueta's untimely death, however, things began to fall apart.

In 2000, Coke cut 20 percent of its global workforce and announced $1.6 billion in charges to streamline operations. It also noted that some bottlers were cutting orders because of too much inventory.

In 2003, the "shareholder's dream" under Goizueta turned into a nightmare when the SEC began investigating charges brought by a whistle-blower that Coke's immensely profitable Japanese unit had been inflating income through a practice known as "gallon pushing" from 1997, the last year of Goizueta's reign, to 1999.

Coke settled the charges in 2005 without admitting or denying the SEC's findings. The *New York Times* reported the news:

The commission found that at the end of every quarter, Coke pressured its Japanese bottlers to buy additional soda concentrate so that it could increase its earnings. The practice allowed Coke to meet analyst expectations in 8 of 12 quarters, the S.E.C. said.

One SEC official said at the time:

"Coca-Cola misled investors by failing to disclose end-of-period practices that impacted the company's likely future operating results."

Did Goizueta's ambitions for Coke and his own heavy investment in Coke stock create pressures to inflate the company's revenues and earnings to meet the enormous expectations set by his leadership?

We'll never know, but it all happened right under the nose of a board of directors that included one of the most financially astute individuals in the world: Warren Buffett.

ENVY, NOT GREED

If anybody considers Roberto Goizueta's billion-dollar pay at Coke part of the problem when it comes to outrageous executive compensation, they're not saying it here.

In fact, Buffett and Munger place the blame on public disclosure *rules* as much as on the individuals involved. These rules require the details of all such compensation to be disclosed to the SEC. The unintended consequence, according to both men, is that it fuels compensation inflation, because everybody knows what everybody else is earning.

"What really drives it is *envy*, not greed," Buffett says. "You pay someone $2 million and they might be quite happy until they hear that someone else got $2.1 million."

"Charlie said of the seven deadly sins, envy is the worst," Buffett concludes. "You feel miserable—but the other guy has no idea how you're feeling." He makes a great show of picking out a chocolate candy from the See's Candies box. "Envy—where the hell is the upside?" he asks rhetorically, and declares gluttony to be a far more worthwhile sin.

"There's upside to gluttony," he says, happily popping the piece of chocolate in his mouth—both he and Munger will pick out morsels from the box throughout the day—to great laughter.

Buffett makes another checkmark on his pad and calls for the next question.

THE *INDEFENSIBLE*

This shareholder is from the United Kingdom. He cites a study showing that companies with corporate jets underperform their peers, and he wants to know how best to measure the effectiveness of corporate managers.

Munger jumps in before Buffett speaks. "I want to report that we are solidly in favor of private jets." The arena erupts in laughter: most everyone here is familiar with the story of the *Indefensible*, a corporate jet Berkshire Hathaway acquired in 1986.

To most companies, this would have been no big thing. Most companies don't even disclose the existence of their corporate jets to their shareholders, although all the big companies have at least one, thanks to that envy thing Buffett was talking about. Home Depot had six under Robert Nardelli.

Still, to Berkshire Hathaway, acquiring one was an earth-shaking event. Indeed, Buffett announced it in his 1986 annual letter using exceedingly small type:

> We bought a corporate jet. Your Chairman, unfortunately, has in the past made a number of rather intemperate remarks about corporate jets. . . . Travel is now considerably easier—and considerably costlier—than in the past.

He even named the jet the *Indefensible*.

However, if anybody is worth the cost of owning a corporate jet, it is Warren Buffett. Since time is money, as the saying goes, and Warren Buffett's net worth is the largest in the world, his time should be more valuable than that of anyone else who ever lived.

To put some figures on the matter, start with Berkshire Hathaway's recent market value of approximately $200 billion, nearly all of which has been achieved since Buffett took over as chairman in 1965.

Assuming that Buffett worked 12-hour days over the course of 43 years—and he probably worked no less than that—the value of Warren Buffett's time works out to about a million dollars an hour.

EXEMPLARY BEHAVIOR

Nevertheless, Buffett eventually ditched the *Indefensible* and all the attendant costs that go along with having a plane—pilot, hangar, and insurance—after he discovered NetJets, the executive jet time-sharing service. In fact he liked NetJets so much that three years later Berkshire bought the company. He has no hesitation about defending Berkshire's use of the service. "Berkshire is significantly better off because we use corporate jets," he tells the U.K. shareholder. "I don't know which deals wouldn't have been made, but I do know I would not have had the enthusiasm to travel thousands of miles to see deal after deal" without NetJets. "It's a valuable business tool."

Still Buffett is wary of the abuses of privilege. He tells the story of the CEO of a company in which Berkshire once owned stock who used to fly to Idaho on corporate business. As it turned out, the guy also happened to have a vacation home there.

"It can be misused like everything else," he says.

Asked whether he'd like to add anything, Munger reaches a bit further back in time for an example. "The Roman Emperor Marcus Aurelius had no trappings of power, though he could have. The best way to combat" excesses of leadership, Munger says, "is to have examples of *exemplary* behavior."

Being an "exemplar" is a familiar theme of Munger's, and he clearly thinks that Berkshire Hathaway, under Warren Buffett's leadership, provides just such an example of exemplary behavior.

As for what kind of compensation plans work best, Buffett—being a pay-for-performance kind of guy—says that he would pay all managers for value-added performance, not just for being in the right place at the right time.

He uses the example of oil companies that have been benefiting from the recent rise in oil prices. "It's crazy to pay management more" just because oil prices went up, he says. But if an oil company's drilling and exploration costs were lower than the competition, "I'd pay 'em like crazy."

It is simple, concise, and clear, and hard to argue with.

While Buffett calls for the next question, Chris wonders out loud how different Robert Nardelli's tenure at Home Depot might have been if he and his board of directors had allowed themselves to be subjected to five hours of questions from shareholders, employees, and retirees, where *everything* was on the table.

At the very least, we decide, Nardelli probably wouldn't have had six corporate jets at his disposal.

And he certainly wouldn't have been asked the question that turns out to be the most commonly asked question of the day from the younger generation of Buffett fans.

From 10-year-old girls to twentysomething graduate students, they all want to know essentially the same thing.

CHAPTER 9

Budding Buffetts: Where to Begin

"Read everything you can."

—WARREN BUFFETT

The questions show no sign of having been arranged ahead of time. There is no invisible hand of a PR flak guiding things, no particular order by theme or subject matter.

There is nothing that makes the shareholders themselves, their questions, or even the delivery of those questions come across as insincere or planted—although one or two seem to have an agenda. Still, there is almost nothing to tip off Warren Buffett to what's coming.

It's just a lot of people asking questions, unfettered.

A dichotomy begins to emerge. Professional investors from the East Coast and from California tend to enunciate their own names clearly—you get the sense that one or two of them want to make an impression on Buffett himself—before launching into tightly scripted questions about specific financial topics.

Shareholders who aren't professional investors, on the other hand, often hurry through their identities and ask loosely constructed, but farther-ranging questions, from "What advice do you have for long-suffering shareholders of the *New York Times*?" to "How would you fix the healthcare system?"

There's even a rambling question about John and Abigail Adams—two of Munger's favorite historical figures, as almost everyone in the arena already knows. ("Did you know them, Charlie?" Buffett quips, to laughter.)

The question that is asked most frequently comes from younger members of the audience.

The question is, "What should I do to become a great investor?" and it is asked for the first time by an earnest 17-year-old from San Francisco who says he is attending his tenth consecutive meeting.

Buffett's emphatic answer is simple and straightforward: "*Read everything you can*," he says with finality.

This is advice that Buffett has been giving for years, and it is advice that he will give in different ways throughout the morning and afternoon, for he strongly believes—and Munger concurs, calling Buffett "a learning machine"—that it was the reading he did in his formative years that shaped his approach to investing and prepared the groundwork for the next 50 unprecedented successful years.

And Buffett isn't kidding when he tells the young man, "Read everything you can."

"By the age of 10," he goes on, "I'd read every book in the Omaha Public Library with the word *finance* in the title, some twice."

Buffett's reading habits did not stop when he was 10. He still reads literally thousands of financial statements and annual reports each year—as he has done for each of the last 50 or more years that he's been investing. Friends and acquaintances who are invited to share a jet with Buffett report that he'll chitchat briefly and then start reading. Andrew Kilpatrick, author of the massive Buffett hagiography—*Of Permanent Value*—reported

that Buffett once mentioned, while the two were at a book signing, that he had 50 books at home, waiting to be read.

Buffett does not advise the 17-year-old from San Francisco to
read any particular books, although he does mention the profound impact that value-investing guru Benjamin Graham's
The Intelligent Investor had on him when he read it for the first
time. "What I'm doing today, at age 76, is running things
through the same thought process I learned from the book I
read at 19."

Nor does he steer the budding Buffett toward any particular
investment style. Instead, he advises reading everything possible
to find the style that suits the individual. "If it turns you on, it
probably will work for you," he says.

Buffett also recommends doing something else besides reading: "Invest—on a small scale—don't just read."

"Charlie," he says, "you have anything to add?"

Munger stirs from the implacable position he maintains
throughout—seated stiffly in his chair, arms folded, eyes dis-
torted by Coke-bottle-thick glasses—and leans slightly forward
toward the microphone on the table before him. He suggests a
logical approach that's typical of *almost* everything he will say
during the session.

"Ask, 'What do you own and why do you own it?'" Munger
says. "And if you can't answer that," he declares with absolute
finality, "*you aren't an investor.*"

Buffett concurs, and repeats for the budding Buffetts in this
crowd what he has told shareholders and students alike over
many years (Buffett taught an investing course at the University
of Omaha in the 1950s and speaks to as many as 30 student
groups each year): "If you can't write an essay describing 'why
I'm going to buy the entire company at the current valuation,'
you have no business buying 100 shares of stock."

Of course, there is more to what has made Buffett a great
investor than this—as we will come to understand as the day
continues.

But it all began by *reading*.

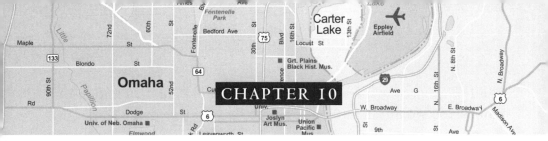

CHAPTER 10

The Most Versatile Investor in the World

"We have at least 60 derivatives . . . and believe me: we'll make money on all of them."

—WARREN BUFFETT

ith the question answered, Buffett makes another check on his yellow pad and calls for the next microphone.

The shareholder says that he's from Nebraska, although he sounds a bit too breathless, too serious, and too on edge to be one of the early Berkshire millionaires. Those longtime shareholders, who are now sitting in the seats near the stage and will be attending brunch tomorrow at Buffett's country club, are a pretty relaxed-looking bunch.

They are also, of course, much older than the baby boomers who make up most of the crowd here. Some of them have been with Buffett since he raised his first money from friends and family in 1956. As Buffett has described it, "I sat down with seven people who gave me $105,000 to manage in a little partnership, and those people made the judgment that I could do a better job amassing wealth than they could do for themselves."

As the years went by, and word of Buffett's results spread, his partnership took on more investors. Buffett takes enormous pride in these investors' loyalty, longevity, and faith in his stewardship. He even keeps track of how many Berkshire investors live in his zip code ("about 125," he wrote in the 1993 Chairman's Letter).

But this shareholder from Nebraska doesn't seem like an old friend of Buffett's or even a distant neighbor. He is far from relaxed, and he's asking his question in conspiratorial tones, as if he's about to expose the biggest scandal since Watergate and Teapot Dome combined—unless a government agent cuts off his microphone before he can spill the beans.

The scandal, it turns out, is a modestly topical issue that has been widely promoted by a public company CEO who, ironically enough, was once employed at a now-minor Berkshire Hathaway subsidiary. The issue is "naked short selling," and the man wants to know what Buffett thinks of it.

Buffett, it turns out, doesn't think much of it at all. To sell a stock short is to bet the stock will go down—hence the familiar expression "Don't sell yourself short." In order to sell a stock short, the investor first borrows shares of the stock through a stockbroker, and then sells those shares in the stock market, just as if he or she had owned them. The short seller hopes to buy those shares back, deliver them to the broker, and book a profit.

The controversy at the moment involves the claim that some short sellers don't properly borrow the shares. They just sell and sell and sell until a stock becomes worthless, then buy the shares back. This is called "naked short selling."

Now, I've known a lot of short sellers in 28 years on Wall Street, and I have never known anybody who sold stocks short naked. Chris, who works at one of the largest Wall Street firms around, doesn't know anybody either. But if there are two men who can contradict our own experience on this or any other issue, they are Warren Buffett and Charlie Munger. Their combined investment experience is approaching 120 years.

Buffett begins his response with a sort of amused recap of the question for Munger, who for the first and only time of the day could not make out the question: "It's about this so-called failure to deliver and naked shorting." Buffett is clearly not impressed by any supposed naked shorting crisis. He doesn't even have a problem with legitimate short selling.

"I do not see the problem with shorting stocks," Buffett says, "but it's a tough way to make a living." He's right, too: the stock market tends to rise over time, so betting on stocks to fall is a low-probability bet—the kind Buffett avoids.

Instead, he sometimes takes the other side.

Recalling that Berkshire Hathaway made good money lending out its shares of U.S. Gypsum to short sellers when that company was under siege from asbestos lawsuits, before the stock went up tenfold, Buffett says: "If anyone wants to naked short Berkshire, they can do it until the cows come home. In fact, we'll hold a special meeting for them," he says, to laughter.

If the world's most successful investor, who doesn't see a problem shorting stocks, has never encountered a massive naked shorting conspiracy, it probably doesn't exist. Buffett's experience, after all, encompasses pretty much everything that has happened on Wall Street since World War II, and, thanks to his voracious reading, most of what happened before he even started.

"SOME DAY YOU WILL GET A VERY CHAOTIC SITUATION"

The breadth of Buffett's knowledge is staggering. This is, after all, a man who counted the discarded bottle caps at vending machines to measure the popularity of soft drinks, who reportedly counted railroad cars to track shipments of oil additives, and who once arbitraged cocoa beans against the shares of a Brooklyn, New York, chocolate maker.

He purchased shares in a trolley line in New Bedford, Massachusetts, that were trading for less than the cash the company had in the bank, bought 25 percent of the only privately owned bridge between the United States and Canada (and later sold out to the current owner), and accumulated enough stock to control a Los Angeles, California, trading-stamp company.

During a family vacation with the Munger clan in the 1960s, the two men evaluated the rides at California's Disneyland, leading to Buffett's buying 5 percent of the company's shares for his partnership. In 1961, Buffett took over a Nebraska windmill manufacturer—more than 40 years before a Berkshire subsidiary began developing wind farms in the midwestern United States. He even bought into a map company, then engaged in a very early form of "greenmail" by getting a seat on the board and then agitating for the company to buy him out.

Decades later in the months following the 9/11 attacks on the World Trade Center, Buffett helped to price intricate insurance policies covering North Sea oil platforms, the World Cup Soccer Tournament, and the Sears Tower in Chicago.

He has purchased bonds with no risk of default issued by the U.S. government and bonds with a very real risk of default from the Washington Public Power Supply System; and he has purchased bonds issued by companies, including Texaco, Inc., that had already filed for bankruptcy.

He has acquired entire companies, in businesses as diverse as direct-to-consumer auto insurance, chocolate candy, tufted carpet, Western boots, and door-to-door vacuum cleaner sales.

Warren Buffett may be known for never buying technology companies, but he is in fact one of the most versatile investors in the world, and he demonstrates that versatility here today.

"We're not limited," he says, in response to a question about the merits of certain alternative investment vehicles. "We buy businesses, bonds, currencies, futures . . . " And he isn't kidding.

Take what are called derivatives—financial instruments with fancy names like "collateralized debt obligation" that lie at the heart of the subprime mortgage debacle.

Warren Buffett first warned his shareholders about the risks posed by derivatives in 21 scathing paragraphs on the subject in his 2002 Chairman's Letter—calling them "time bombs, both for the parties that deal in them and the economic system" and "financial weapons of mass financial destruction, carrying dangers that, while now latent, are potentially lethal."

And he repeats those warnings about the risks posed by the explosion of derivatives in today's financial markets. "Some day," he tells us, "you will get a very chaotic situation."

Yet he then goes on to say quite matter-of-factly, "We have at least 60 derivatives" in the Berkshire portfolio. "And believe me," he says, "we'll make money on all of them."

We believe him.

"CHARLIE HAD NOTHING TO DO WITH IT— IT WAS ALL ME"

Not only does Buffett know derivatives, but he also knows currencies. Berkshire began making currency bets in 2002 and increased those bets in 2003, when Buffett told shareholders that he had become "increasingly bearish on the dollar."

Today, he says he still thinks the dollar is going lower, and after discussing why, he leaves us hanging with a terrific teaser: "We have one currency position that will surprise you," he says. "We'll tell you about it next year."

Now, think about that statement for a minute.

Consider it from the perspective of a nervous, caffeine-addled Wall Street currency trader whose position book changes by the hour, if not the minute or the second. I know of one currency trader who moved from Greenwich, Connecticut, to Germany in order to save the *milliseconds* it took to send electronic orders across the Atlantic Ocean.

Yet Buffett is talking about a currency position he quite seriously expects to hold until sometime later this year. That's conviction, backed by a fundamental understanding of his investment position.

Buffett not only knows—and does—derivatives and currencies, he also knows commodities.

Asked for his opinion on commodities late in the day, Buffett says that he has "no opinion." But he then notes in an offhand way, "If we thought oil was going up, we could buy oil futures, which we did once."

In fact, Buffett made a large bet on oil in the mid-1990s, buying contracts on nearly 50 million barrels of crude oil when the price was close to $12 per barrel.

He also made a large bet on silver bullion in 1997, when Berkshire bought control of 111 million ounces of silver at a little less than half the current price. Unfortunately, Buffett sold before silver prices took off. Asked about the infamous silver trade of 1997 today, Buffett ruefully acknowledges having left money on the table. "I bought too early; I sold too early. Other than that it was a perfect trade," he says, getting a laugh.

He also takes the entire blame for Berkshire's silver trade. "Charlie had nothing to do with it—it was all me," he says.

This is typical of Buffett. He takes full responsibility for an even bigger mistake while reminiscing about his disastrous investment in USAir. "I bought into a high-cost airline thinking it was protected . . . but that was before Southwest Airlines showed up."

But what is remarkable about Buffett's brief rehashing of the USAir investment is not that he again takes the entire blame. It is the way he tosses off two obscure numbers that summarize the heart of the problem facing USAir: the cost per seat-mile of fanatically efficient Southwest Airlines ("8 cents"), and the cost per seat-mile of the aging, inefficient USAir ("12 cents").

Cost per seat-mile happens to be the single most important financial variable in the airline industry. By measuring how much money an airline spends on labor, fuel, and all the other costs of moving one passenger one mile, cost per seat-mile allows investors to easily compare any airline with any other, anywhere around the world.

Buffett knows this—and not by happenstance. During the course of the day, whatever industry is brought up by a shareholder, he almost invariably zeroes in on its most vital statistic.

Discussing the poor prospects for the newspaper industry—an important part of Berkshire's early success, through both its large stake in the *Washington Post* and full ownership of the *Buffalo*

News—Buffett mentions the recent problems encountered by a new chief executive of the *Los Angeles Times*. "This smart fellow came along and said he was going to take its circulation up to 1.5 million. Well, it's now at 800,000."

And the actual circulation figure for that newspaper, it turns out, was precisely 815,723 as Buffett spoke.

Bemoaning the state of annual reports, Buffett—who believes that CEOs should write their own letters to investors—mentions an oil company report "Charlie and I read recently" that didn't give the information Buffett was looking for. "There was no discussion of finding costs in the letter," he says, speaking about the money an oil company spends to discover and develop its oil reserves. "Because, of course, it was a terrible figure."

TOO TOUGH TO ANSWER

Throughout the day, questions about the arcane—derivatives, currencies, managed futures funds, and commodities—compete with questions about everyday issues, from how to protect against inflation to favorite role models, all of which Buffett discourses on with ease and absolute knowledge.

Only one question all day completely stumps Buffett—and it was not the question from the nervous man about naked short selling.

The question that stumps Warren Buffett is asked by a doctor from Salinas, California, who points out that Berkshire, being a large insurance company, has a stake in the country's healthcare system, and asks "What can Berkshire do to help solve the healthcare problem in the United States?"

Both Buffett *and* Munger appear nonplussed.

Buffett fidgets and gropes for words, but it is Munger who finally breaks the silence. "It's too tough," he says simply, and Buffett concurs.

"We look for the easy problems," he says. "We don't try the tough ones."

That's a little scary, coming from an investor known for his supreme intelligence, grasp of facts, and never shying away from seemingly dangerous investments. It was Buffett who put together a complex rescue package during the Long-Term Capital crisis of 1998, when a brainy bunch of bond traders borrowed billions of dollars and made huge bets on bonds that went wrong, and nearly brought down the financial system. (Buffett made a lowball bid for Long-Term Capital's portfolio, in partnership with Goldman Sachs and other investors, while on vacation with Bill Gates; the bid was rejected.)

Berkshire entered even murkier waters with a $13 billion commitment to pay future claims and expenses on insurance written by the Lloyds of London syndicate prior to 1993, including "long-tail" asbestos claims that may not appear for decades. It is one of the most arcane reinsurance deals ever made.

Furthermore, Buffett once used his own considerable personal charm and hardheaded brand of moral rectitude to help rescue securities giant Salomon Brothers—in which Berkshire had a $700 million investment—from a near-death experience in the early 1990s after the company's aggressive bond traders cheated the federal government and nearly lost their business.

Buffett's self-deprecating, apologetic, and highly effective testimony before Congress during the Salomon scandal—"Lose money for the firm, and I will be understanding. Lose a shred of reputation for the firm, and I will be ruthless"—received broad coverage at the time; a clip of that testimony was a centerpiece of the movie this morning.

In his long career, Warren Buffett has not only rescued a major banking firm from near bankruptcy, he has also publicly offered his own notions for balancing the federal budget deficit (it would involve huge consumption taxes) and the national trade deficit.

Yet he offers no thoughts on the healthcare system. "Maybe we'll hear about it in the presidential campaign," he says rather blandly, reaching for a piece of fudge from the bowl of See's on the table.

With the question checked off, Buffett crooks his arm and looks at his watch. Despite the let-down after hearing him pass on the healthcare question, it is a charming moment: a billionaire, presiding over the annual meeting of one of the largest companies in the world, is seated alongside his longtime partner at a small table on a small stage on the floor of an arena the size of Madison Square Garden. He is running this meeting of 27,000 people as if there were a dozen of us sitting around a table in the company cafeteria—which is how the whole thing got started back in the early days of Berkshire Hathaway.

And still today there is no master of ceremonies and no corporate counsel keeping tabs on what comes out of Buffett's mouth. There's just a guy in a suit keeping track of the questions on a yellow legal pad and checking his watch from time to time.

"Charlie and I'll take one more question, and then we'll break for lunch."

The next question is the twenty-fourth of the day. And for the most versatile investor in the world, it should be the easiest one so far. It involves nothing as intractable as the U.S. healthcare system, as outré as naked short selling, or as complex as derivatives.

Instead, it comes straight off the front pages of the same newspapers that nearly every person in this giant room seemed to be reading before things got underway.

It is about the subprime mortgage crisis that has begun to engulf the landscape of American housing.

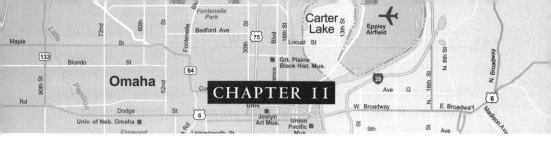

CHAPTER 11

An Insider's Information

"Dumb lending and dumb borrowing."

—WARREN BUFFETT ON THE SUBPRIME CRISIS

This last question before we break for lunch should be easy enough to handle. It involves the most basic of human needs—shelter—and it has been front-page news for months: What does Warren Buffett think about the subprime issue?

Now, Omaha, Nebraska, is hardly Ground Zero of the subprime problem. With a median price of only around $130,000 for a single-family house, this is hardly the province of overpriced "McMansions" and condos built on spec. Warren Buffett's own house, which he bought nearly 50 years ago for $31,500 and fixed up over the years, sits in a nice, quiet neighborhood not far from Berkshire's offices, on the same street. It is appraised at all of $710,000 by the local tax assessor's office, and that includes an indoor racquetball court.

While Buffett does not have any subprime horror stories of his own to share, he does, of course, have some stories he has learned by *reading*.

"I've read a lot of 10-Qs and 10-Ks," he says, employing the shorthand for quarterly and annual financial filings that public companies must make with the Securities and Exchange Commission. "And a number of financial institutions gave a large number of people the chance to make below-market payments first . . . and of course they'll need to make *above*-market payments later."

"It was," he says, reducing the issue to its core, "a bet on housing prices." He then provides what could go down as the epitaph of the subprime mania: "That's dumb lending and dumb borrowing."

If Buffett always presents the rational, objective view of a situation, Munger delights in offering a moral judgment on the underlying issue. And on the subprime issue, Munger takes a strident stance. "There's been a lot of sin and folly," he says, "a lot of it due to accountants who let lenders book profits when no one in their right mind would have allowed them to book profits. If accountants lie down on the job, you see huge folly."

He peers sternly through his glasses. "It's in the national interest to give loans to the deserving poor—but the moment you give loans to the undeserving poor or the stretched rich, you run into trouble." This draws an appreciative murmur of approval from the audience.

And then Munger really lets loose:

"I don't know how these people shaved in the morning," he says of the lenders who pushed subprime loans, "because what was looking back at them was a face that was evil and stupid."

The crowd erupts in laughter, then applause. "Did he really say that?" somebody behind us exclaims.

He did, and his crack about the "undeserving poor"—a line from George Bernard Shaw's play, *Pygmalion*—lingers in my mind. He appears to be making a moral judgment that distinguishes between poor people who deserve a home and those who do not. Buffett jumps in and brings the conversation back, as he often does, to specific numbers.

"We saw this in the manufactured-home business," he says. Berkshire owns Clayton Homes, a large manufactured-home company purchased in 2003 and Buffett has witnessed the subprime issues through Berkshire's experience in that industry. "When someone only has to make a $3,000 down payment to someone who gets a $6,000 commission," he says, referring to mortgage brokers who were getting large commissions, "then believe me, you'll see a lot of bad behavior."

Compounding the problem, he says, was "securitization," the bundling and reselling of all these loans to investors far away from the local markets. "A local banker wouldn't allow this because he'd see what's going on, but when the loans are bundled and sold by Wall Street, that discipline disappears."

Such firsthand knowledge—which Buffett employs to help explain the subprime mortgage crisis—also explains another reason for Buffett's investment success.

By owning entire companies, not just shares of stock in publicly traded companies, Warren Buffett has placed himself on the inside of American industry. Berkshire Hathaway owns companies in so many different businesses, in fact, that Buffett has insight into nearly every aspect of any business that you could name—Apple and Google aside, of course.

Berkshire's in-house companies not only help Buffett assess different industries and the companies within those industries, but also help him find other companies to acquire. As he wrote in a letter to shareholders a decade ago:

> Whenever we buy into an industry whose leading participants aren't known to me, I always ask our new partners, "Are there any more at home like you?"

Virtually every retailer that Berkshire owns, for example— including Borsheim's, R.C. Willey, Star Furniture, and Jordan's— came to Buffett, directly or indirectly, through the management of Nebraska Furniture Mart.

As CEO of a $100 billion enterprise with more than a quarter of a million employees, Warren Buffett possesses, quite possibly, the widest information network available to any investor trading on any stock exchange in the world.

Still, Buffett's unique position on the inside of the subprime crisis doesn't give him a unique insight into how the problem will end. "I don't think it'll be a huge anchor dragging down the rest of the economy," he says.

No oracle he. Before the year is out—in fact, even before the summer ends—the subprime crisis will start to spread, and eventually drag the country into precisely the recession he doesn't seem to expect. But for now, we are comforted.

Buffett checks off his yellow pad, looks at his watch, and announces a break for lunch. "We'll be back in about a half hour."

CHAPTER 12

"You Don't Want to Let Him Down"

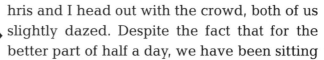

"He just wanted to see us tell him in person that we thought it was a good deal."

—BERKSHIRE MANAGER

Chris and I head out with the crowd, both of us slightly dazed. Despite the fact that for the better part of half a day, we have been sitting quietly in the upper mezzanine of a large arena that has been temporarily given over to nothing more intense than watching two men listening to, and answering, questions, we find ourselves very hungry.

It is as if we have been burning calories just *listening*.

And we're not the only ones feeling this way: there are long lines of blank, hungry-looking people forming at the Qwest Center concession stands. Unfortunately, the concessions offer nothing but burgers—no surprise, this being Omaha, but not what we're looking for at noon on a Saturday. We head down an escalator to an "Express Lunch" stand where 10-dollar tickets get you a choice of a few different wraps, a bag of chips, a cookie, and something to drink—but the line is long and getting longer as more people pour out of the arena.

We finally get Greek salads at a food stand run by Katie's, a popular local restaurant, and eat standing up at a railing overlooking the main lobby, squeezed together. Other shareholders carrying their food hover nearby, waiting for openings at the railing.

Crowds continue to emerge from the arena in a steady flood. Chris and I eat, talk a little, and people-watch. I count four African American faces among the thousands streaming past us. That makes seven I have seen so far today.

When we entered the Qwest Center early this morning, the only types of people I was interested in counting were cowboys and farmers, to see if it was true what the reporter said about seeing pickup trucks in the parking lot. The number of African Americans crossed my mind only as I was looking at all the newspaper readers seated around us, before the movie began. Among the all white faces, I could not help but notice an African American woman sitting a few rows away with a friend.

I saw one more as we were getting food, and I decide now— hey, we just spent half a day listening to a numbers-obsessed guy talk about cost per seat-miles and oil-finding costs—to keep track of the number of African Americans instead. It will not be difficult. For a man who thinks the tax code should be used to promote the redistribution of wealth, the immense prosperity he has created for Berkshire's shareholders has not been distributed very far at all.

BOOKWORMS, CAMPERS, AND DILLY BARS

Greek salads finished, Chris and I head down to the lower lobby, moving with a part of the crowd that is now flowing into the giant exhibition hall next to the arena. "Wait'll you see this," he says, as we go through the doors into the hall.

"This" is a vast space, bigger than a Costco, filled with shareholders and crammed from one end to the other with nearly every product and service Berkshire Hathaway's companies offer.

We go with the counterclockwise flow.

A Fruit of the Loom store occupies one corner, and it is packed with shareholders combing racks of T-shirts and shelves of boxer shorts, or standing at temporary cash registers with armloads of the stuff. I can't fathom why anybody would come to Omaha, Nebraska, to buy Fruit of the Loom boxer shorts until Chris points out the Berkshire Hathaway–themed slogans emblazoned on everything.

A small stage has been set up where men dressed as Fruit of the Loom advertising characters are singing "Help Me Rhonda" to enthralled children while their parents wait in line at the cash registers. Absolutely nothing is being given away here, but the shareholders don't mind. The shelves and racks have been stripped bare of most of the normal-sized merchandise, and what remains is disappointingly cheap stuff.

Across from the Fruit of the Loom store is an entirely different sort of product. It is a NetJets display, where shareholders can buy a fractional ownership of a jet. While not as busy as the underwear store, there are a few very comfortable-looking couples talking to NetJets representatives. (Shareholders with a serious interest can go to the Omaha airport and tour the actual product.)

The flow of the crowd carries us past the NetJets display to an actual house, assembled right here inside the Qwest Center. It is a Clayton manufactured home, with a neatly landscaped "yard" in front, and it is open for inspection—and offered for sale at $139,900. "An excellent value," Buffett called it in his Chairman's Letter, and sure enough, a long line of shareholders are waiting patiently to go inside.

A GEICO counter staffed by friendly looking young men and women is busy with shareholders, several deep, talking insurance, and a Dairy Queen stand is doing a land-office business selling (there are *no* giveaways here, even snacks) chocolate-covered ice cream sticks called Dilly Bars, which nearly every shareholder in the place seems to be in the process of devouring. Nearby, we see the opposite end of the popularity spectrum: the World Book Encyclopedia display, one of the few square feet of the giant hall that is almost devoid of people.

We pass a Forest River camper that has been parked inside the hall, the entrance landscaped with an atmospheric fence and a small water-filled pool; another long line of shareholders is waiting to go through.

In the far corner of the hall, a satellite branch of the Bookworm—Buffett's favorite local bookstore—has been constructed and filled entirely with books about Warren Buffett, Charlie Munger, and Berkshire Hathaway.

And the bookstore is *packed*.

"Read everything you can," Buffett has been telling his younger acolytes all morning, and it seems as if every shareholder is taking him at his word. The line to the register is like Disney World's Splash Mountain on a hot Florida day during spring break. I abandon the idea of picking up one of the books I'd noticed at the airport bookstore. Squeezing and pushing our way out of there, Chris and I decide the exhibition is starting to wear a bit thin.

PICKING STOCKS OUT OF TRASH CANS

We head past a Justin Boots shop with salesmen wearing cowboy hats. Intricately patterned Western boots are on display, and a lot of paunchy middle-aged men are trying them on. Nearby is a stage where Buffett entertained reporters and early-rising shareholders with his ukulele before the meeting and a small, dirt-floored rodeo ring that is now empty.

We end up at a Shaw Flooring Center, where Shaw carpets and tiles are laid out and salesmen are on hand to take your order.

I knew Shaw Industries when it was a public company run by Bob Shaw—about as plainspoken a guy as ever ran a public company. And I recall vividly a day in the fall of 1990, when he came to New York City for a meeting with Wall Street's money managers and investment analysts.

Now, nobody at that time, at least on Wall Street, cared much about Shaw Industries, because the American consumer was not in the mood to buy much of anything, let alone new carpeting. Saddam Hussein had occupied Kuwait, sending the price of oil to all-time highs and everything else, including consumer confidence, to all-time lows. Shaw Industries, being a carpet manufacturer, was losing two ways: sales were going down, and at the same time costs were going up, since most carpets are made of petroleum-based nylon and polyester fibers.

Shaw's stock was dropping as fast as the sales of its carpets.

And yet, to the Wall Street analysts who followed Shaw, the company's reaction was a head-scratcher: Shaw was *buying* its own stock back, in size. Wall Street didn't think the share buyback was a good use of cash for an up-and-down business whose future looked as dark as Kuwait's. Why, the analysts wanted to know, didn't Shaw hang onto its cash and wait for things to pick up?

Bob Shaw, self-assured and headstrong, answered the same basic question, asked in only slightly different ways, many times in a row, until he finally lost his temper and dropped all pretense of explaining the share buyback in rational economic terms.

"Look," he said, "if Wall Street is gonna throw my stock in the trash can, I'm gonna pick it up."

I thought it was as good an explanation for a company's buying its stock as I'd ever heard. And Bob Shaw was soon proven smarter than every Wall Street analyst in the room. First, low-flying B-52s bombed Saddam's "Elite Republican Guard" back to the proverbial Stone Age while troops on the ground chased the remnants back to Baghdad. Then, legendary Texas oil well firefighter Red Adair put out the oil fires Saddam left behind so quickly that oil prices collapsed. Housing sales went up, Americans started buying carpets again, and Shaw's business— and the company's stock—boomed.

By buying back the company's stock aggressively when nobody else wanted it, Bob Shaw was ahead of his time, and he came out looking pretty smart. Ten years after that meeting, almost to the day, Bob Shaw did something else that was slightly ahead of his time.

He chucked the public company rat race and sold his company to Berkshire Hathaway. Buffett told the story of how he acquired Shaw in his annual letter that year and concluded with a pun:

Leaving aside our insurance operation, Shaw is by far our largest business. Now, if people walk all over us, we won't mind.

The Shaw story illustrates another simple reason for Buffett's success: the self-selection process of those who want to sell to him.

If you're a mediocre but successful-in-a-ladder-climbing-way type of CEO, it's not going to occur to you to try to sell out to Berkshire Hathaway, for the simple reason that running a public company is far too lucrative—not to mention comfortable—what with corporate jets and golden handshakes and stock options granted by your friends on the board of directors.

The man or woman who wants to work for Warren Buffett is, by definition, highly ethical, hardworking, and not in it strictly for the money, because the management team always stays on after selling to Berkshire Hathaway.

So if you're "able and a straight shooter"—to use Buffett's own description of his favorite kind of business partner—you may well end up with the name of your company flashing in lights inside the Qwest Center and a booth selling whatever you specialize in selling, here in the exhibition hall.

Not to mention a story about you in Buffett's annual Chairman's Letter.

"HE JUST WANTED TO SEE US"

Chris elbows me and nods toward a pair of men in front of another display. They stand out for one reason: instead of the large plastic "Shareholder" badges worn by everyone else in the crowd, they are wearing "Manager" badges.

We maneuver through the crowd, introduce ourselves, and ask what company they manage. And then we begin to talk.

The company these men are with, like each of the dozens represented in the exhibition hall, had been in business a long time before selling out to Berkshire. The company has a familiar brand name that was once highly regarded but is now somewhat tired and old-fashioned.

Also, its business is no longer a good one. While the company hasn't been driven almost out of existence, like World Book

Encyclopedia, or hurt by the recent housing slowdown, it is vulnerable to lower-cost competitors, and no longer has the kind of "moat" that Buffett seeks.

The two men we meet are soft-spoken and friendly—in a wary sort of way. We chat a bit and learn that they've both worked at their company for many years, and stayed on after their company was purchased by Berkshire a number of years ago.

"How's business?" we finally ask.

They shrug, a little leery of giving too much away, and don't say much more than "It's tough," which we already know.

Finally, Chris asks what we *really* want to know: "So what it's like to work for Warren Buffett?"

They both smile and the mood lightens. This is a topic that they can discuss without worrying about who might overhear us. "No quarterly nonsense, for one thing," says one.

The other agrees. "We don't have to do any stupid stuff to hit numbers," he says. Public companies hate to disappoint Wall Street analysts when they report their quarterly earnings. Most companies push for business at the end of each quarter to hit their targets. Some companies resort to fraud. Berkshire Hathaway, of course, never bothers trying. Buffett wants companies to focus on the long run.

"What kind of stupid stuff?" Chris and I ask at once.

"Oh, we used to do dumb things—really dumb, expensive things."

"Like what? Price cuts? Giveaways?"

They both smile and shake their heads. "All kinds of stuff."

We don't pry for specifics. "What else changed?" Chris asks. They shrug, look at each other, and say, "Nothing."

"Nothing?"

"No, nothing. Same systems, same everything."

This is hard to believe. Most companies send financial SWAT teams into newly acquired subsidiaries, looking for people to fire and buildings to empty. "What about your external reporting?" I ask.

"No change."

"But how do you report your numbers to Berkshire?"

They look at me as if I've asked them how they get out of bed each morning. "We send them the numbers," one of them says slowly, "once a month."

"Well, who talks to Buffett?"

"Our CEO talks to his CFO."

When Buffett says he doesn't want to manage the companies he buys, he's not kidding.

We ask about an acquisition that their company made fairly recently—how it came about, who suggested it, and why Berkshire went ahead with it.

"We thought it would be a good fit. We sent the idea to Warren."

"Did you meet with him to discuss it?"

"Once."

"What did he ask?" I'm thinking now's the chance to hear the juicy details about the kind of number crunching Buffett does to convince himself to buy a billion-dollar company.

"*He just wanted to see us tell him in person that we thought it was a good deal.*"

"Wow. He didn't look at numbers?"

"A lot of numbers had already gone back and forth," they say.

"So what did he say to you?"

"He said, 'Okay, well, Charlie and I want to noodle on this over the weekend.'" The man smiles at the memory. "He said that, he wanted to 'noodle on it.'"

The other man says, "They took it from there."

I ponder the notion that Buffett merely wanted to *see* the men tell him that they thought the deal made sense. It makes a huge impression on me, yet I will not fully comprehend its significance until the afternoon session, when Buffett and Munger respond at length to what, in retrospect, is the best question of the day.

Chris, meanwhile, asks the two men, "What's it like not having that quarterly earnings pressure? It must be great."

"It's great," they both agree. "But, in a way, the pressure is worse," one says quietly.

"Why?"

"Because," the man says with a kind of awe in his voice, "you don't want to let him down."

CANDY, SHOES, AND GINSU KNIVES

We thank them, shake hands, and continue walking in a glassy-eyed state of mind, trying to take in the crowds, the noise, and, especially, what we've just heard.

Chris says what I'm thinking. "So they did a multi-hundred-million-dollar deal, and Warren Buffett *just wanted to see these two guys tell him it was a good idea.*"

We walk past booths selling Dexter shoes, See's Candies, and novelties like the deck of Berkshire Hathaway playing cards. Warren is the King and Charlie, of course, is the Joker. Before we leave the hall, we pass by the most surprising display of all: Ginsu knives.

Yes. Warren Buffett owns Ginsu knives.

Actually, Warren Buffett controls about one-third of Berkshire Hathaway, which owns a conglomerate called Scott Fetzer, which owns Douglas Quikut, whose Quikut division manufactures Ginsu knives.

Ginsu knives were made famous—and profitable—by a late-night TV commercial. The voice-over started, "In Japan, a hand can be used like a knife. But this method doesn't work with a tomato," and showed a hand smashing a tomato.

The kitschy commercials were a hit, and Ginsu knives became a hot item even though they have nothing to do with Japan. Like a good many Berkshire products we have seen here today, they were conceived in the United States and are still manufactured here. Berkshire may be a great company with a wonderful collection of brand-name products, but as businesses go, it is not exactly on the front lines of globalization. We head back into the arena and find that our section has been largely deserted. Almost everybody else that was here in the upper mezzanine has moved down to get closer to the action, leaving behind empty popcorn boxes, soda cups, and plenty of folded-up newspapers.

The arena floor still looks crowded, except for the fenced-off VIP area for directors and friends. Out of the 60 chairs in that section, only 20 or so are now occupied—and Bill Gates is not among those present.

It's a shame for those who haven't returned: Buffett will soon get what I think is the best question of the day.

In the meantime, the extra legroom is fine with Chris and me. We can stretch out a bit and ponder what we've been witnessing.

Buffett and Munger soon return to the stage, this time without applause or ceremony. They take their seats, and Buffett checks his watch in an old-fashioned sort of way, crooking his arm enough for the watch to appear from beneath his jacket sleeve and tilting his head back to read it.

It is 12:50 p.m., and the afternoon session begins—with no pomp and circumstance: just a man checking his watch and, next to him, an older man who moves almost not at all.

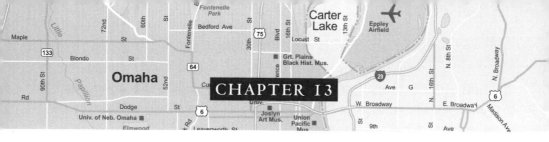
Intrusion

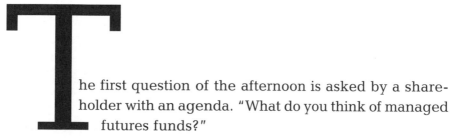

"Many annual meetings are a waste of time, both for shareholders and for management."

—Warren Buffett

The first question of the afternoon is asked by a share-holder with an agenda. "What do you think of managed futures funds?"

The man, it turns out, runs a family of so-called managed futures funds—mutual funds that trade futures contracts. The guy is plugging himself in front of nearly 27,000 people.

Buffett does not appear to be exactly sure what the question is getting at. He answers it as he does all questions—straight ahead, without fishing for background or trying to guess the intent—and it is not exactly the answer the man is looking for.

"We think the most logical fund is like the one we manage at Berkshire, where we can do anything, but aren't *compelled* to do anything."

Charlie Munger, for all his sphinxlike appearance most of the time Buffett speaks—he sits nearly motionless, except when he reaches for a See's chocolate candy or drinks from a water glass—seems to know exactly what the speaker is getting at. As soon as Buffett finishes, Munger dismisses the idea of such "managed futures," or any other type of fund. "Averaged out," he says, "the returns will be somewhere between lousy and negative over time."

"I'd agree," Buffett says, finishing off with the kind of aphorism that seems to pop out of his mouth as spontaneously as most people sneeze. "*Areas* don't make opportunity. *Brains* make opportunity."

Still, the managed futures funds guy did what he wanted to do: he planted in the minds of 27,000 Berkshire Hathaway shareholders—somewhat fewer, actually, considering those who didn't return from lunch—that there is such a thing as a managed futures fund.

It's surprising that more people don't try something like this: all it takes is a shareholder badge—most shareholders use only one or two of the four badges they can request—and the willingness to get in line at the Qwest Center early enough for a spot at the microphone.

"YOU CAN'T HAVE A DEFINED ROAD MAP, BUT YOU *CAN* HAVE A RESERVOIR OF THINKING"

Buffett makes a checkmark on his legal pad and calls for "Area 12." The twenty-sixth question of the day is a variation on what has become, by now, a familiar theme.

"I'm a 23-year-old with limited capital and high ambitions," the young man at the microphone says. "What are the best investment opportunities for the next fifty or one hundred years?"

"Read everything in sight," Buffett again advises, "and when you get the opportunity to meet someone like Lorimar Davidson, as I did, jump at it."

Lorimar Davidson was an executive with an obscure insurance company who happened to be the only person in the company's headquarters one Saturday morning in January 1951 when a 20-year-old investment analyst knocked on the front door and asked the custodian if there was anybody he could talk to.

The young analyst was Warren Buffett, the insurance company was GEICO, and the meeting started a lifelong relationship between the two men as well as the companies: Berkshire eventually acquired GEICO nearly 45 years later. A videotaped reminiscence of the encounter—recorded by Davidson the year before he died—was shown earlier. In it, a frail-looking Davidson says that the 20-year-old Buffett asked questions like a veteran insurance analyst. Buffett, watching with the rest of us, got choked up watching the tape.

Buffett could probably stop here and move on to the next microphone—after all, there are only so many times anybody wants to hear an ambitious young investor ask for advice from Warren Buffett. Yet he continues his habit of answering the entire question by addressing the young man's "fifty or one hundred years" time horizon.

"Charlie and I have made money in a lot of different ways," he notes, "some of which we didn't anticipate 30 or 40 years ago." So he advises keeping an open mind. "You can't have a defined road map, but you *can* have a reservoir of thinking."

This open-mindedness is another key to Berkshire's great success. In fact, it led to one of the most important events in Berkshire's history.

"I DON'T THINK WE WANT TO BE IN THE CANDY BUSINESS"

When the family behind See's Candy Shops put its small, Los Angeles, California-based premium confectionary business up for sale in 1971, it was a lousy time to own a company that made expensive confectionary treats.

The Vietnam War was still raging, consumer confidence was low, inflation was high, and President Nixon had just enacted a freeze on wages and prices at about the time an investor in Omaha, Nebraska, got a call asking whether he had any interest in buying a privately held company called See's Candy Shops.

Buffett's initial reaction to the idea was negative. He had not yet acquired companies outside Berkshire's textiles, insurance, and publishing areas. "I don't think we want to be in the candy business," he told the intermediary.

After looking at the numbers, however, Buffett changed his mind. Founded in 1921 by Charles See, using his mother Mary's recipes, the company had a devoted following in its home state, selling boxed chocolates from old-fashioned stores in a black-and-white motif, modeled, as the company proudly notes, after "Mary See's home kitchen."

But Buffett didn't care about the kitchen thing so much as the numbers; war, inflation and price controls notwithstanding, See's generated strong sales and fat profit margins. So Buffett and Munger bought the company for $25 million in January 1972, a bargain at just six times the chocolate maker's pretax earnings and less than its $30 million in total sales.

It was one of the greatest acquisitions any company would ever make. In 25 years, See's has contributed $1.3 *billion* in pretax income to Berkshire. In the year 2007 alone, See's generated $82 million in profits on $383 million in sales.

And if the recent sale of Godiva Chocolatier for nearly 15 times pretax earnings is any indication, Berkshire could probably sell See's for more than $1 billion today—all because Buffett and Munger proceeded without a "defined road map."

"IF YOU HAVEN'T HAD A DATE IN A MONTH . . . "

There is certainly no road map for today's meeting.

The 23-year-old with "high ambitions" is followed by an older shareholder from Florida asking whether his state's insurance regulators might penalize the insurance companies, after severe hurricanes in 2004 left insurers and homeowners squabbling over the damage.

Buffett handles the question quickly, and Munger—as he frequently does on questions involving insurance issues—says, "I have nothing to add."

The Florida shareholder is followed by a New Yorker who wants to know why Berkshire invested over $5 billion in common stocks during the quarter, despite the fact that Buffett doesn't seem to think that stocks offer good value.

Buffett rephrases the question for the audience, asking rhetorically: "Have we changed our standards?" He shrugs. "I don't think so, but if you haven't had a date in a month . . . " He smiles, and the crowd laughs.

"It doesn't reflect our giving up on finding an elephant of a business," he says. "We're well prepared to acquire a very large business."

Checking off his legal pad, Buffett then calls for "Area 1."

"I HOPE YOU'LL RESPECT MY OPINION, AS I DO YOURS"

The spotlight moves to Area 1, the microphone nearest the stage on our side of the arena. The speaker identifies himself and, without needing to—his accent is straight out of one of the New York City boroughs—says that he's from New York. He has brought his daughters with him, he says, and they are all fans of Warren Buffett. "You're my hero," he says. "You're our hero."

Buffett, who can smell a setup coming a mile away, leans back in his chair and nods warily, his right hand cupped behind his ear. The crowd, too, begins to get restless as the man continues talking. "I've always looked up to you," he says. "You're my hero."

Buffett isn't biting. He nods appreciatively. "You're doing pretty well so far," he says warily. This draws relieved laughter from the crowd, and Buffett adds, "What's your question?"

The question, when the man finally gets around to it, is about abortion. He wants to know why Warren Buffett funds Planned Parenthood.

Now, Warren Buffett does more than fund Planned Parenthood. He and Munger helped overturn a key California abortion law in a landmark case decided in 1969, and his Buffett Foundation has funded research on the RU-486 "morning-after" pill.

While Buffett has never sought to hide his views on the subject or his activities in its support, he prefers not to talk much about either publicly. As he told *Barron's* in 1997, "I'd end up getting 50 letters a day. It would change my life too much."

It has certainly changed the mood inside the Qwest Center.

Shareholders in the crowd who might have taken the New Yorker's side probably wish he'd never brought up the issue, while those who share Buffett's point of view begin to make their displeasure at the man's views known, loudly and aggressively.

The noise level rises as the man keeps going. "Cut him *off!*" a voice near us yells, dispelling the good vibrations of the day's events.

Buffett quickly seizes control of the mood, stifling the crowd's more hostile elements.

He does it simply by answering the question.

In no uncertain terms, Buffett says that he thinks Planned Parenthood is a "terrific organization"—this generates raucous applause—and that he thinks it's "too bad" that women have been forced to bear children, "generally by governments of men." This brings more applause.

"If we'd had a Supreme Court with nine women on it from the beginning," Buffett says, "I don't think a question like yours would even be asked." Applause again interrupts him, and while Buffett could certainly let that be his final word, he adds, "I hope you'll respect my opinion, as I do yours."

It is an interesting moment. Buffett, with the more vocal part of 27,000 people on his side, still wants those who might disagree with him—on one of the most divisive issues of our age—to understand why he believes what he believes. Still, the atmosphere is a little sourer now. Irrationality has reared its ugly head, both in the man's erratic, rambling question and in the shockingly hostile reaction—"Cut him *off!*"—from what had been such a relaxed, friendly crowd.

It's as if an aunt and uncle had gotten into a screaming match midway through Thanksgiving dinner. The outside world has suddenly intruded, and it is a downer.

Buffett quickly calls for the next question.

"FIFTY PERCENT TWADDLE"

A Los Angeles shareholder asks about "beta," a mathematical calculation of volatility that is widely used by professional money managers to measure the risk in an investment portfolio. The theory goes that the higher a stock's beta, the greater the risk in owning it. (Google, for example, would be a high-beta stock because it bounces around so much; Berkshire, on the other hand, would certainly be a low-beta stock because it does not bounce around much at all.)

High beta or low, Buffett is having none of it. "Beta is nice and mathematical," he says. "But it's wrong. It is *not* a measure of risk." Buffett then compares beta—as he frequently compares other investment concepts—to the price of farmland.

"Take farmland here in Nebraska: the price of land went from $2,000 to $600 per acre. The beta of farms went way up, so according to standard economic theory, I was taking more risk buying at $600." He lets this sink in. "That's nonsense," he says flatly.

"The whole concept of volatility is useful for people whose career is teaching"—both Buffett and Munger make frequent digs at academics throughout the day—"but useless to us."

"Risk comes from the nature of certain kinds of businesses—the simple economics of the business—and from *not knowing what you're doing,*" he emphasizes. "If you understand the economics and you know the people, then you're not taking much risk."

Buffett turns the question over to Munger, who sums up their dissection of beta far more economically: "We'd argue that what's taught is at least 50 percent twaddle," he says before settling back in his chair, while laughter erupts throughout the arena.

We're a family again.

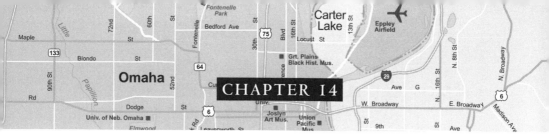

CHAPTER 14

Whom Do You Trust?

"Over time, markets will do extraordinary, even bizarre
things. A single, big mistake could wipe out a long string
of successes. We therefore need someone genetically
programmed to recognize and avoid serious risks,
including those never before encountered."

—WARREN BUFFETT

n investor from New York asks how Buffett
evaluates management simply by reading
annual reports.

Buffett's answer, by now, is somewhat predictable: "We read a
lot," he says.

"We've spent many years buying many things without meeting managements at all." In fact, he says, of the $5 billion worth
of stocks Berkshire bought in the first quarter, most were in companies that "we've never talked to."

"We read the annual reports," he says, especially the CEO's
letter to shareholders. "It tells us a lot about the individual running the company."

"MOTHER NATURE, BLESS HER HEART, WENT ON A VACATION"

It is no coincidence that the individual speaking these words writes the longest and most self-critical letters to shareholders of any CEO in America, if not the world. Buffett writes them in longhand on a yellow legal pad, and *Fortune* magazine editor-at-large Carol Loomis edits them.

Buffett's Chairman's Letter in the Berkshire Hathaway 2006 annual report we have with us at today's meeting is *24 pages long*. By comparison, the 2006 letter to shareholders from Jeffrey Immelt, chairman and CEO of GE, runs seven pages—six excluding the fancy tables with meaningless graphics depicting "Growth as a Process" and "Winning in the Future."

Buffett's letter starts, as always, with the table showing "Berkshire's Corporate Performance," and then defines the two yardsticks by which Buffett and Munger measure their own performance. The first yardstick is the amount of cash, stock, and bonds owned by Berkshire, which exceeded $80,000 per share; the second yardstick is the pretax earnings of Berkshire's noninsurance companies, which exceeded $3,600 per share.

Buffett moves on to his favorite topic: new acquisitions. He starts with "the highlight of the year," the $4 billion investment in ISCAR, a dynamic, fast-growing Israeli metal cutting tool company, and concludes with what is, to outsiders, the positively mystifying purchase of Russell Corporation, an apparel company whose best days are long behind it.

Buffett then goes straight into the strong results from the insurance business—"Mother Nature, bless her heart, went on a vacation"—and the rest of the Berkshire businesses.

And that's just the first 15 pages.

The next four pages review Berkshire's common stock investments, a wide range of currency bets starting with the Australian dollar and ending with the Taiwan dollar, and one of the frankest descriptions of a company's CEO search ever written

Now, Warren Buffett wears two hats at Berkshire. First, as chief executive officer, he oversees the Berkshire companies, which he leaves pretty much alone. Second, as chief investment officer, Buffett decides how to invest Berkshire's enormous insurance "float" as well as the cash earnings from its noninsurance companies.

It is his role as chief investment officer that made Buffett famous, and it is the role that most outsiders pay attention to, for as chief investment officer, Warren Buffett *is* Berkshire Hathaway.

It is also the role Buffett seems to think the company hasn't got a replacement for just yet. He writes:

> I have told you that Berkshire has three outstanding candidates to replace me as CEO and that the Board knows exactly who should take over if I should die tonight. . . . Frankly, we are not as well-prepared on the investment side of our business.

Buffett then discloses a plan to hire a person or persons to succeed him in that role, and he spells out the main criteria, with this extraordinary caution:

> Over time, markets will do extraordinary, even bizarre things. A single, big mistake could wipe out a long string of successes. We therefore need someone genetically programmed to recognize and avoid serious risks, including those never before encountered.

How many other companies think that way? Continuing his letter under the heading "This and That," Buffett riffs on Berkshire's $4.4 billion worth of federal tax payments and puts it in a rather striking perspective:

> In its last fiscal year the U.S. Government spent $2.6 trillion, or about $7 billion per day. Thus, for more than one half of one day, Berkshire picked up the tab for all federal expenditures.

Buffett also discloses a modest increase in the famously small corporate staff at Berkshire's "World Headquarters," from 17 to 19 at year-end; ridicules free-spending "corporate bigwigs"; rails at executive compensation abuses; outlines his plan to give away his Berkshire holdings (the largest charitable donation in history); and mocks "Wall Street's Pied Pipers of Performance"—hedge funds.

Buffett concludes the letter with two pages on the annual meeting:

> But nothing is more fun for us that getting together with our share-holder-partners at Berkshire's annual meeting.

And he means it.

Already this weekend, Buffett has lunched with Berkshire's CEOs, played bridge with Bill Gates and Ping-Pong with an 11-year-old champion, attended a dinner hosted by a former Wall Street analyst with some of those same "Pied Pipers of Performance" he likes to tweak, played the ukulele on stage . . . , and he is still going strong after fielding 34 questions since 9:30 this morning.

"WE GET SUSPICIOUS VERY QUICKLY"

The thirty-fifth question of the day is a follow-up of sorts to the question about evaluating managements.

A young shareholder from Seattle wants to know how, precisely, to evaluate something that Buffett values even more highly than numbers—management integrity.

"I can read annual reports and financial statements, but I don't have access to meet with managements," the young man from Seattle says. "How can I learn whom to trust and whom not to trust?"

Aside from the healthcare question that he declined to even attempt to answer, this is the first and only question of the day that Buffett has a hard time with.

"I get letters all the time from people who've been taken advantage of," he starts off. "Charlie and I have had very good luck buying businesses and putting our trust in people," he says, working toward a concrete answer. "It's been overwhelmingly good," he says, "but we filter out a lot of people."

"We haven't batted 100 percent, but it's above 90 percent."

Munger speaks up. "We're deeply suspicious if the proposition sounds too good to be true," he says, and gets a laugh describing one supposed deal, "a company that wrote fire insurance on underwater concrete bridges." As he frequently does after the punch line, Munger looks around with a straight face and settles back in his chair.

But Buffett is not finished. He hasn't put his finger on the answer.

"It goes beyond ridiculous propositions," he says. "People give themselves away," he says, "and maybe it's an advantage being around awhile and seeing how people give themselves away."

"They make certain kinds of comments," he says, again fumbling for the key. "What they laugh about . . . if they say 'it's so easy.'" He snorts. "It's never easy. We get suspicious very quickly. We rule them out 90 percent of the time."

What he's talking about, of course, is body language. And while Buffett makes many of his investments just by reading "a lot," when it comes to buying companies or investing in deals, he wants to see the body language.

"It's the very things they talk about," he says. "There are a lot of clues in the things they think are important."

I recall what the two Berkshire managers had told us during the lunch break: "He just wanted to see us tell him in person that we thought it was a good deal."

Warren Buffett may be known for his ability with numbers—even before computers came along, Buffett had never owned a calculator in his life—but what he cares most about when he buys a company is character. And he makes sure everyone in the Berkshire "family" knows it, writing to his managers:

> We can afford to lose money—even a lot of money. We cannot afford to lose reputation—even a shred of reputation. Let's be sure that everything we do in business can be reported on the front page of a national newspaper in an article written by an unfriendly but intelligent reporter.

Buffett is not content to have his managers hide behind the letter of the law when his reputation is at stake.

Yet he soon appears to do just that.

CHAPTER 15

Grumpy Old Man?

"I don't think [global warming] is likely to be an utter calamity for mankind. You'd have to be a pot-smoking journalism student to think so."

—CHARLIE MUNGER

Warren Buffett seems eager to please. "I like applause," he has said. And throughout the day, he goes to great lengths to make everyone feel welcome, comfortable, and happy.

Charlie Munger, on the other hand, seems eager to appear not to care what anybody thinks of him.

On stage, Munger projects an aloof, somewhat haughty sensibility that comes across as righteous, hardheaded, and unwavering. Unlike Buffett, who leans forward and leans back, cups one ear and then the other, shuffles papers, and moves his hands to make points as he speaks, Munger barely moves at all, except to lean slightly toward the microphone to speak when Warren asks, "Anything to add, Charlie?"

And yet, while the crowd often stirs in anticipation of whatever politically incorrect zinger Munger might be about to get off, he is far more than a wisecracking sidekick to Warren Buffett. He is also largely responsible for Buffett's transformation from a strict value-oriented investor in the style of Benjamin Graham—

Buffett's first mentor—to an investor who seeks to buy very good businesses at reasonable prices.

"HE'S A PERFECT PARTNER"

Born in Omaha on January 1, 1924, six years before Buffett, Munger worked in the Buffett family grocery store as a youth, although the two men did not meet until 1959, when Munger returned to Omaha on business from Los Angeles, where he settled after law school.

A stern moralist, he has said, "The safest way to get what you want is to try to *deserve* what you want." Munger is intensely rational, a voracious reader and self-styled "biography nut" who averages a book a day. He considers the acquisition of wisdom a "moral duty."

Munger pursued a legal career, like his father, who was an attorney, and graduated magna cum laude from Harvard Law, Class of 1948 (two years before Warren Buffett was rejected by Harvard Business School). Munger returned to Los Angeles, where he had been stationed during World War II, and started a law firm, Munger, Tolles & Olson LLP, which still performs legal work for Buffett, Berkshire, and its subsidiaries. He also began to involve himself in business deals, particularly real estate, which in postwar southern California was as close to a sure thing as ever existed.

A card player like Buffett who learned to wait for the odds to be in his favor before betting—and then betting heavily—Munger was likewise extremely focused on making money. But whereas Buffett liked money as a means of keeping score, Munger valued wealth for the *freedom* it brought him. He and Buffett became fast friends almost immediately upon their meeting in 1959, and they eventually formed one of the most famous partnerships in American business history.

"I would have to say," Munger told Carol Loomis, "that I recognized almost instantly what a remarkable person Warren is."

Buffett thinks just as highly of Munger. "Charlie can analyze and evaluate any kind of deal faster and more accurately than any man alive," Buffett told Janet Lowe. "He sees any valid weakness in 60 seconds. He's a perfect partner."

And while Munger did not take his current position as vice chairman of Berkshire Hathaway until 1978, more than a decade after Buffett took over as chairman, it is no stretch to say that Berkshire would not be what it has become without Charlie Munger.

"IF WE HADN'T BOUGHT SEE'S, WE WOULDN'T HAVE BOUGHT COKE"

When Warren Buffett ran his partnership, Buffett Partnership Ltd, he followed the strict "value investing" methodology pioneered by Benjamin Graham, an investor, author, and Buffett's professor and mentor at Columbia Business School. Graham had survived the Great Depression, and he prospered in its wake. Lingering fears of another 1929-style market crash meant that shares of companies traded far below their intrinsic value—sometimes even for less than the cash on their books. "Cigar butts," Graham called these investments: stocks that could be picked up for almost nothing yet still had some value. He bought them based strictly on the mathematical value of their assets, without regard to the business they operated.

Buffett absorbed and refined Graham's teachings and steered Buffett Partnership Ltd. to huge gains over its 13-year life.

Munger, meanwhile, started his own law firm and made his first million in Los Angeles real estate. He also did legal work for different companies, and in this way Munger witnessed firsthand both the ease of making money in a booming economy and the difficulties of turning around bad businesses. And he thought a lot of Graham's theories "just madness."

"Ben Graham had blind spots," Munger once said. "He had too low an appreciation for the fact that some businesses were worth paying big premiums for."

Buffett learned Munger's lesson after the pair acquired See's Candy Shops at what appeared at the time to be a high price—three times the company's book value—but was, in retrospect, a steal. Buffett admits the experience with See's opened his eyes to the value of buying great businesses at reasonable prices, rather than bad businesses at great prices. He told shareholders at the 1997 meeting that owning See's led him to buy what is now 200 million shares of Coke; at the time, Berkshire's Coke holdings had gained $12 billion in value. "If we hadn't bought See's, we wouldn't have bought Coke," he said at the meeting. "So thank See's for the $12 billion."

In reality, Berkshire shareholders should thank Charlie Munger for that $12 billion, for without Munger, there might not have been See's *or* Coke among Berkshire's holdings.

LOLLAPALOOZA IDEAS

Close as their relationship is, the two men are distinctly different.

While Munger calls himself "a Nebraskan to my soul" at today's meeting, he left Omaha for the University of Michigan and never returned. Buffett returned to Omaha at age 26 after leaving for the University of Pennsylvania and a stint working in New York City—and stayed.

Buffett famously hoarded his wealth until recently. Munger has given away Berkshire stock over the years, to Good Samaritan Hospital—whose board he has chaired—and other charities, with a particular focus on education.

Munger is a staunch Republican; Buffett a staunch Democrat.

Munger is also more relaxed about his work. While Buffett prefers work over vacation—"I tap-dance to work," he likes to say—Munger spends time each summer with his extended family on the northern Minnesota lake where he spent his childhood summers. Like Buffett, however, he is a patient investor, and believes that the key to investment success is to patiently search for a few "lollapalooza" ideas . . . and when you do find them, make a major commitment.

"You really want one that you don't have to sell," he's said. "Then you can sit on your ass for 30 years."

Munger's role at Berkshire has declined as Buffett's visibility has expanded. "We don't talk as often," Buffett told *Forbes* magazine in 1993. "Charlie doesn't have his ego wrapped up in Berkshire the way I do, but he understands it perfectly."

Although nowhere near as wealthy as his partner, Munger is Buffett's equal intellectually. As chairman of Wesco Financial Corporation (a publicly traded Berkshire subsidiary), Munger even hosts his own version of this "Woodstock for Capitalists" for Wesco shareholders the weekend following Berkshire's, in Los Angeles. There Munger fields questions solo, and so many "Mungerisms" have come out of that meeting—and Berkshire's—that they have been assembled into *Poor Charlie's Almanack: The Wit and Wisdom of Charles T. Munger.* The book runs 512 pages long and, of course, is available for sale in the exhibition hall bookstore.

Many of the 27,000 shareholders here today expect Charlie to deliver not only investment wisdom but also a full complement of "Mungerisms" in his role as the erudite Joker in the Berkshire deck of cards that is also on sale in the exhibition hall.

He does not let them down.

"A FACE THAT WAS EVIL AND STUPID"

When Munger speaks, discussions of hurdle rates and Gaussian distributions mingle easily with references to Marcus Aurelius, Benjamin Franklin, and Mozart.

After Buffett spends several minutes explaining in some depth Berkshire's refusal to invest in the gaming industry, despite its attractive returns, Munger says simply, "It is a dirty business."

After Buffett laments that Berkshire learned about the perils of low-cost foreign labor the hard way—by owning a shoe company—Munger quotes Will Rogers: "You should be able to learn not to pee on an electrified fence without actually trying it."

The audience loves it, and over the course of the day, a pattern seems to emerge: while Buffett tends to try to wrap up his answers on an amusing or upbeat note, Munger's voice is sardonic and downbeat, its delivery dry and deadpan.

Asked about global warming and his thoughts on the science behind it, Buffett says, "I believe the odds are good that global warming is serious. There's enough evidence that it would be foolish to say there *isn't* a problem."

"If you have to make a mistake," Buffett continues, with his usual brand of plainspoken logic, "err on the side of the planet. Build a margin of safety to take care of the only planet we have."

Buffett's concerns about global warming might be dismissed as a reflection of his political philosophy. That would be a mistake. Buffett is, above all things, rational. Furthermore, he probably *reads* more than almost any other individual on the planet. By way of example, Bill Gates credits Buffett with sparking his interest in world health issues by recommending an obscure document on poverty published by the World Bank in the early 1990s.

Also, and most important for the people in this arena, global warming is a serious issue for Berkshire Hathaway's insurance operations, which could be exposed to huge losses in the event of a catastrophic hurricane where Berkshire has reinsured other insurance companies against loss. "We think much more about whether global warming will produce atmospheric changes that will change the frequency and intensity of major storms," Buffett says. "We think the exposure goes up every year, even though we don't know exactly what goes on in the atmosphere."

Munger, who has been stirring in his seat, dismisses the entire notion. "Carbon dioxide is what plants eat," he says dryly. "The Midwest would be more comfortable if the world were a little warmer."

This draws titters of approval, prompting Buffett—who likes to engage Munger when the two are at opposite ends of a spectrum—to ask, "You don't think it would be a problem if the sea level rose 15 or 20 feet?"

"With enough time, these things can be adjusted to," Munger says, without specifying how much time for adjustment is needed. He finishes with the kind of crack that says more about his age than about the science behind the issue:

"I don't think this is likely to be an utter calamity for mankind. You'd have to be a pot-smoking journalism student to think so."

It draws laughter, and a certain amount of silence, too. There is a fine line between a brilliant, acerbic 83-year-old investor and a grumpy old man.

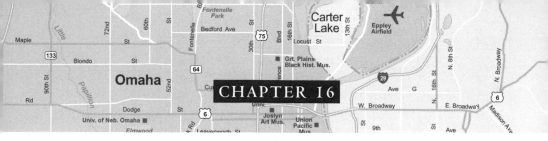

CHAPTER 16

Artful Dodging

"I'm in a peculiar position on this, because when we bought PacifiCorp, Walter Scott and I signed affidavits."

—WARREN BUFFETT

T he questions come at Buffett out of left, right, and center field. Except for the rambling question about Planned Parenthood in the morning session, Buffett does not get much forewarning of what might be coming at him. And because the questions aren't prescreened by a moderator—it's first come, first served at the microphones—he has no time to prepare an answer in advance.

Except once.

The exception comes midway through the afternoon session. Buffett is answering a question about how frequently he reviews Berkshire's portfolio ("I have more money than ideas, so we aren't really thinking of selling," he says) when an odd sound, like a bamboo curtain rattling in a soft breeze, begins to fill the arena.

We see five quiet, respectful women in full Native American tribal dress making their way down a side aisle toward a microphone on the floor of the arena. As they walk—slowly, in single file, their heads slightly bowed—their native dresses make the sound we're hearing.

Chris and I had seen the women waiting in the corridor outside the arena as we came back from the exhibition hall and our chance meeting with the Berkshire managers. They were lined up along the wall just outside one of the entrances, looking about as out of place in that sea of middle-aged baby boomers as you can get.

At the time we had no idea what they were doing there—but they were clearly on the agenda, and now one of them is stepping up to a microphone.

Buffett finishes his answer, makes a checkmark on his legal pad and calls for the next question. It is the first, and as far as we can tell, the only question for which Buffett has had advance notice.

The spotlight shines on the American Indian woman at the microphone. The others stand together several paces back. It has become so quiet that we can hear their clothing as they shuffle together, even in this giant arena.

"I am Wendy George," the woman says in a soft, respectful voice, "of the Hoopa Indian reservation in northern California." She begins to speak about dams on the Klamath River that generate electricity for PacifiCorp—a Berkshire company.

The question is not new today: a woman identifying herself as the wife of a commercial salmon fisherman who had been hurt by the "Klamath River crisis" had earlier told Buffett that she had come from California with her 14-year-old daughter to "join the protest." She spoke quickly and emotionally of the economic toll, and blamed it on the PacifiCorp dams and Bush administration policy.

The issue both women raise is clear-cut: four aging hydroelectric power dams on the Klamath River need to be either replaced or removed. On one side are farmers who want the water for their crops; on the other are environmentalists, fishermen, and the Native American tribes that had fished the river for generations before the dams were built in the early 1900s.

In the middle sits PacifiCorp, the regulated utility that owns the dams and would have to spend over $100 million of its customers' money to remove them, assuming that the tab isn't picked up by a state or federal agency.

When the fisherman's wife asked for Buffett's position, he answered her with straightforward abruptness. "Our position is simple," he said. "We're a public utility . . . and in the end we'll do what exactly what the regulators say."

But Wendy George is not going to be so easy.

"My people are river people," she says quietly, slowly, and emotionally. "Our culture, our religion, our sustenance is based on the river." She stops, crying quietly. Buffett waits, along with the rest of us, for the woman to collect herself.

He does not hurry her a bit.

When she recovers her voice, she asks a straightforward question: "Would you be willing to meet with tribal leaders to learn about our issues?"

It seems reasonable enough, and we sit back, ready for Buffett to answer it reasonably.

He speaks earnestly and with conviction. "As I said earlier, we will not make the determination in the end. It will be made by FERC [the Federal Energy Regulatory Commission] the same as with coal, gas, or wind generation."

"Any time you get into public utility plants, people are unhappy or happy with the decisions because no one wants a power plant in their yard," Buffett says, "but the world wants more electricity. We will do *exactly* what FERC and the state commissions decide."

Buffett doesn't stop with that answer: he has come prepared.

He picks up a document from the table—it has been there all along—and holds it up. "I'm in a peculiar position on this, because when we bought PacifiCorp, Walter Scott (a Berkshire director) and I signed affidavits."

The document he is holding just happens to be the affidavit he signed.

Buffett adjusts his glasses and reads from it: "I agree that we will not exercise decisions except those ministerial in nature."

Now, I am not sure what "ministerial" means, and I don't know if anybody else here does, but to Buffett it means that the matter is closed.

He ends—as always—by accentuating the positive. "This was part of the order that allowed MidAmerican to buy PacifiCorp. The acquisition went through in record time, by the way, because MidAmerican has such a great track record of being responsive to regulators."

Munger, for his part, adds nothing.

Wendy George bows her head and walks slowly back to her companions, and together they begin to file out. The rustling of their tribal dresses fills the arena. The atmosphere has gone flat.

Buffett's response seemed about as corporate, legalistic, and positively unexemplary as it could be. He held up that affidavit—like a student holding up a hall pass—as if it gave him immunity not just on the substance of the issue, but on the style of it as well.

It's hard to fathom. The same man who upbraids U.S. Treasury officials in his Chairman's Letters, slams government fiscal policy in op-ed pieces, and calls for Congress to maintain stiff inheritance taxes on "the lucky sperm club" of his fellow well-to-do *without a bit of concern for whom he might offend* won't even tip his hand on whether he thinks four dams belong in a river?

Not being a lawyer, and never having invested nearly $7 billion in a regulated utility as Warren Buffett did on behalf of Berkshire Hathaway, I can only guess that this affidavit business is as serious as he makes it out to be.

But watching these women walk quietly out of the arena, I think more than a few people are shocked at the un-Buffett-like nature of his response.

I sense some in the audience expected something more along the lines of this: Buffett, after reading the affidavit and explaining why he couldn't get involved in any decision making at PacifiCorp—and certainly being unable to negotiate with "tribal leaders"—breaks into a smile and says, "But I never promised FERC I wouldn't *listen*."

He didn't. He dodged her question, artfully.

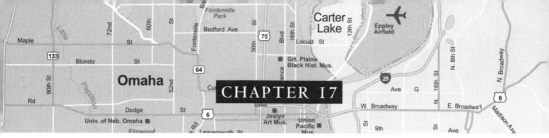
One-Half of 1 Percent

"I haven't given up anything."

—WARREN BUFFETT

The Hoopa Valley women are still walking out of the arena as Buffett calls for the next question. It is another shareholder from Florida and another question about insurance.

The dull discussion calls to mind the Woody Allen movie in which a prisoner gets sentenced to "solitary confinement with an insurance salesman," and my thoughts drift back to the colorfully dressed Native American women.

Though gone from the arena, they are a startling reminder that the Berkshire "family" of companies is large and varied, with an impact that extends well beyond the Qwest Center, the Omaha city limits, and the banks of the Missouri River. They are also an exotic contrast to this audience of, for the most part, middle-aged, nicely dressed, Berkshire Hathaway-owning, Warren Buffett-idolizing white people.

I've seen eight African Americans today, not counting Qwest Center employees: six men and two women. Assuming that's only one-quarter of those in attendance today, it would suggest that no more than 32 African American shareholders of Berkshire

Hathaway are attending today's meeting. I run this number by Chris. He says 32 sounds too low, and I agree. But even tripling it to, say, 100 amounts to less than one-half of 1 percent of the 27,000 in attendance. African Americans make up approximately 13 percent of the U.S. population.

Despite Buffett's avowed social progressiveness, the Berkshire audience is not merely "predominantly" white. It is almost exclusively white.

Of course, this is America. Nobody stops anybody from buying shares of stock in a company and attending the shareholders' meeting. Furthermore, the racial mix of Berkshire Hathaway shareholders is very likely not much different from that of any other U.S. company's shareholders.

Nor would it be any different from a gathering of snooty Wall Street hedge fund types.

The fact is, in 28 years on Wall Street, I have known and worked with exactly three African American investment professionals. Three professionals out of the hundreds that I have worked with over the course of nearly 30 years is not a much better ratio than the one prevailing here at Berkshire.

I wonder if Warren Buffett keeps track of that kind of number, the way he keeps track of everything else—including, for example, the number of Berkshire shareholders living in his zip code.

And if he does, does it bother him?

"THE PROPER WAY TO RUN OUR COUNTRY"

You'd think it might, being as socially progressive as he is fiscally conservative. The son of an isolationist, hard-right, John Birch congressman, Buffett—who lived in Washington, D.C., as a teenager and parlayed his profits from delivering the *Washington Post* into $1,200 of Nebraska farmland and that first investment in GEICO—went the opposite way on political issues.

In 1969, Buffett personally crusaded to open his downtown eating club to Jewish members, doing so in a typically low-key, rational way: Buffett simply applied for membership in the local *Jewish* club. Once he was accepted there, the rationale for having a non-Jewish club evaporated, and the Omaha Club opened to Jews.

A few years later, Buffett hosted antiwar presidential candidate George McGovern at his Omaha house even before McGovern had won the Democratic nomination. In recent years, he backed Hillary Clinton in her first U.S. Senate bid and has hosted fund-raisers for the 2008 presidential campaigns of both Hillary Clinton and Barack Obama.

He has also ratcheted up both his rhetoric and his public profile on social issues, stepping out from behind the candidates themselves to appeal directly to Congress and the American public by appearing on television and testifying before Congress in support of the inheritance tax.

"I don't believe that passing a huge fortune intact to people who just happen to be members of the lucky sperm club is the proper way to run our country," he tells the press later this weekend. By very effectively combining high-minded rhetoric with his uncanny ability to make large concepts simple, Buffett has increasingly made his case for higher taxes and wealth redistribution to the public.

Still, Buffett was not always so vocal.

In the 1970s Buffett invested in and joined the advisory board of the Community Bank of Nebraska, a minority-controlled bank that was being promoted by a friend of his first wife, Susan. Wary of the poor success rate of minority banks, Buffett refused to invest more when loan losses increased, and eventually "distanced himself" when the bank "began to flounder" in the words of Roger Lowenstein, the author of *Buffett: The Making of an American Capitalist.* Urged by the bank's promoter to "take some black students under his wing and teach them finance," Buffett—who taught a night class on investments at the University of Omaha in the early 1950s—"did not respond."

And for all the accolades Buffett received in 2006 for his mammoth gift of Berkshire stock to the Bill & Melinda Gates Foundation, Buffett did not have a reputation for generosity around his hometown. "Warren is *renowned* for not giving money away," one Omaha businessman told Roger Lowenstein.

To Buffett, that reputation was derived entirely from a rational thought process. "I always felt I'd compound money at a higher rate and it would have been foolish to give away a significant portion of my capital" early in life, he told us in the morning session, when he was asked about his plan to start giving the bulk of his Berkshire stock to the Bill & Melinda Gates Foundation so late in life.

Nevertheless, Buffett did offer his ability to "compound money at a higher rate" to others outside Berkshire during his peak years. In fact, Buffett has served on the board of trustees of Grinnell College, a small liberal arts school in Iowa, since 1968. It is no coincidence that Grinnell's endowment-per-student is among the highest in the country—ahead even of Stanford University.

Buffett also helped advise FMC Corporation in the selection of money managers during the 1970s, as a favor to the company's CEO.

There is no report of Buffett offering his investment prowess to others outside his circle of friends during those peak "compounding" years.

In any case, he is now standing near the edge of the stage, his hand shielding his eyes from the glare of the lights trained on the stage, and searching for Joe Brandon, the CEO of General Re, to help answer the Florida shareholder's question on the state's new insurance laws.

Perhaps Buffett notices the racial mix in the sea of faces before him; perhaps not. It is hard to miss, and Buffett is nothing if not observant. A friend who met with him in Omaha years ago about a potential business deal described the experience of being grilled by Warren Buffett this way: "It was like a long, low-dose x-ray."

And Buffett is also, certainly, compassionate, at least when his sense of social fairness is offended.

In response to a question about his recently announced plans to give away his fortune, for example, he dismissed the notion that his commitment to donate $37 billion worth of Berkshire

Hathaway stock to various charities is some kind of sacrifice on his part.

"I haven't given up anything," he said flatly. "A sacrifice is when someone gives up an evening out or a lot of time, or a trip to Disneyland because they donated to a church."

"I haven't changed my life."

When asked why Berkshire has no investment in the gaming industry, Buffett called gambling "a tax on ignorance," and said, "I find it kind of socially revolting when a government preys on the weaknesses of its citizens rather than acting to serve them."

And during the morning discussion of the subprime debt meltdown, both Buffett and Munger had nothing but scorn for the mortgage brokers who took high, hidden fees out of the deals thanks to the easy availability of credit and the naïveté of the borrowers. Yet while Munger concluded his remarks with scorn for those who had made the loans—calling them "evil and stupid"—Buffett expressed concern for those who had been hurt who were least able to afford it.

"You'll see plenty of misery," he had told us.

And in this observation, Buffett would, of course, be proven correct much faster than even he knew.

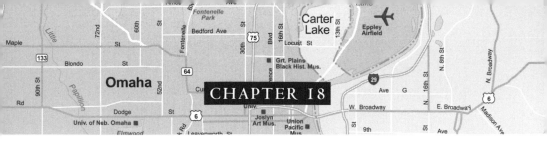

CHAPTER 18

What Now?

$\smile$

"Corporate America is living the best of all worlds—and history has shown this is not sustainable."

—WARREN BUFFETT

The afternoon is moving quickly by, and it is clear that not every shareholder who is at the microphones will get to ask a question before the session ends.

We're now on number 44 with maybe half an hour to go.

Still, Buffett and Munger will manage to answer more than 50 questions before the 3 o'clock deadline. Buffett continues to answer expansively, while Munger continues to fulfill his role as the sardonic voice of outrage and scorn at humankind's foibles.

Asked about inflation, Buffett tells us that "the best protection against inflation is your own earnings power." The second best, he says, is "owning a wonderful business—not buying metals or raw materials."

Buffett, who personally sets the price of See's Candies every December—the only time he gets involved in Berkshire's non-insurance businesses—sums the lesson he learned by owning such a "wonderful" business: "The truth is, if you own Coca-Cola or Snickers bars or anything that people are going to want to give a portion of their current income to keep getting, and it

has low capital-investment requirements, that's the best investment you can possibly have in an inflationary world."

"IT WILL NEVER BE A FABULOUS BUSINESS"

A question about Buffett's recent, large purchases of railroad
stocks starts Buffett on a brief but detailed discussion of a business that is not as wonderful as selling Coke or Snickers bars,
but which clearly is something he knows a lot about. After all,
the headquarters of the Union Pacific Railroad is a few blocks
from where we are seated and only two miles from Berkshire's
offices; also, in his younger days, Buffett owned shares in Des
Moines Railway.

"Railroads have finally gotten their act together," he tells us.
"The competitive position of the railroads has improved from 20
years ago. There's been progress on labor issues and an
improved competitive position against the trucking industry."

He doesn't sound *too* excited—although he will continue buying
them heavily in the months following the meeting. "What was a
terrible business 30 years ago, operating under heavy regulation,
has become a decent business—and could be better over time."

He adds one note of caution: "It will never be a fabulous business; it's too capital intensive."

"THERE'S BEEN A *HUGE* FLOW OF PROFITS TO BANKS AND INVESTMENT BANKS"

A shareholder from Nebraska asks a variation on one of the most
frequently asked questions of the day: *What now?*

Each time the question is asked, Buffett makes it clear he is not
sure where the world is going and what will happen now, but
things are about as good as they'll ever get. "Corporate profits as
a percent of gross domestic product have increased from 4 to 6
percent to 8 percent. I think there have only been two or three
years in the past 75 where corporate profits have been as high."

He says flatly that it won't last. "You have lots of businesses
earning 20 percent on tangible equity in a world where corporate

bonds are yielding 4 to 5 percent. That's astonishing. If you read a book, it would say it's not possible." Buffett holds his palms wide apart to illustrate the high level of profits. "It means someone else's share is going down," he says, bringing his palms together. "Namely labor."

Buffett also discusses the "extraordinary" profits now prevailing in the banks and the financial sector. "We've invested in and owned banks. If 20 years ago you'd asked me whether it was possible, in a world of 4.75 percent bonds, that countless banks would earn 20 percent–plus returns on tangible equity, I'd have said no. In part this is due to leverage."

Munger follows with his own observation, one that will prove, in retrospect, at once unremarkable yet quite profound. "A lot of profits are not in manufacturing or retailing," he says somberly, "but in *financial* sectors. There's been a *huge* flow of profits to banks and investment banks. It has no precedent."

Buffett finishes with a coda for the times: "Corporate America is living in the best of all worlds—and history has shown this is not sustainable. I would imagine that it will not be."

"I THINK YOU MIGHT SEE . . . A SHOCK TO THE SYSTEM"

As for the potential of a credit crisis, Buffett says it certainly wouldn't happen as a result of Federal Reserve policy: "The Fed doesn't want to contract credit."

Buffett thinks the crisis, if and when it comes, will be beyond the government's control.

"I think you might see an exogenous event, a shock to the system that causes a huge widening of credit spreads and a cheapening of equities." If it happens, he is ready. "This would be good for Berkshire because we have money to take advantage of it."

Asked about the potential for a catastrophic failure caused by financial derivatives, Buffett repeats what he has been saying for years:

"We may not know when it becomes a super danger or when it will end precisely, but I believe it will go on and increase until very unpleasant things happen because of it." As to what might trigger a derivative crisis, Buffett shrugs:

"It's a crowded trade. Someday, you will get a very chaotic situation. As to what could trigger this and when—who knows?"

"Who had any idea that shooting an archduke would start World War I?"

Munger winds up the derivatives discussion with an equally stark warning: "As sure as God made little green apples, this will cause a lot of trouble. This will go on and on, but eventually will cause a big dénouement."

At that moment, nobody in the arena—except possibly Warren Buffett himself—is thinking of an investment bank called Bear Stearns.

"THERE'S JUST TOO MUCH MONEY FLOATING AROUND"

In addition to wondering "what now?" for the economy, shareholders want to know what Buffett thinks of the stock market. "Today, if you give me a 20-year time horizon, I'd buy equities versus a 20-year bond," he says, but he is clearly not too excited by the market's prospects.

And Munger flatly warns shareholders not to expect great things from Berkshire's recent investments, "We won't make the kind of returns on these investments that we made on investments 10 to 15 years ago. There's just too much money floating around."

Buffett emphatically agrees: "We won't come close."

"I HAVE A GREAT IDEA: LET'S CHOP TREES DOWN . . ."

The information load is taking its toll. The crowd is slowly thinning. I take a quick, head-nodding-to-the-chest nap, and snap out of it refreshed while Buffett is discussing the problems at the *New York Times*.

Now, Warren Buffett loves media in general and newspapers in particular. Not only does he read five or more each day, but

Berkshire owns 21.4 percent of the *Washington Post* and also owns the *Buffalo News* outright. Yet he turned cautious on Berkshire's media investments as long ago as 1990, when he wrote to shareholders:

"While many media businesses will remain economic marvels... they will prove considerably less marvelous than I, the industry, or lenders thought would be the case only a few years ago."

And *that* was before the Internet came along. Today he sounds even more bearish, particularly about the newspaper business:

"Imagine that someone came along saying, 'I have a great idea: let's chop trees down, buy expensive printing presses, and buy a fleet of delivery trucks, all to get pieces of paper to people to read about what happened yesterday.'"

He makes his point and gets a chuckle, but Chris and I simultaneously recall the advice he gave earlier in the day to a 10-year-old girl from Kentucky who wanted to know what she can do to earn money.

He suggested that she deliver newspapers.

CHAPTER 19

Road Trip

"We try to look for easy problems."

—CHARLIE MUNGER

Warren Buffett crooks his arm and looks at his watch one last time. Charlie Munger sits in his familiar position, arms folded, head slightly bowed. The arena—now half-empty—rustles with people gathering their things.

It is close to three o'clock in the afternoon, more than seven hours after Chris and I walked through the main doors into a jam-packed Qwest Center. My old-fashioned steno notebook is nearly out of blank pages. Since no recording devices are allowed at the meeting, and since I hadn't thought to bring my computer, my only backup is the old-fashioned Acme Brick day planner with a picture of Warren Buffett on the inside flap and the words "Since 1891."

But we're done. The day planner goes into my knapsack as a keepsake.

Buffett uncrooks his arm and announces that the session is adjourned. The May 2007 Berkshire Hathaway annual shareholders' meeting is over.

Actually, only the Q&A portion of the meeting is over, he tells us. The true business portion of the shareholders' meeting—in which votes are counted and directors are elected—will start after a short break.

In fact, Buffett encourages the crowd to "stick around," because, among other things, the proposal that Berkshire Hathaway should divest its PetroChina holdings—which he earlier told us had been defeated 25 to 1, "even excluding my own vote"—will be debated. "It should be an interesting discussion," he says earnestly.

Interesting, maybe, but meaningless: the votes are in, and the resolution lost. Chris and I are not sticking around.

Also, the business portions of shareholders' meetings are dry, formal, and surprisingly brief affairs involving calls to order, seconds to nominations, vote tallies, and other necessarily uninteresting fluff—even for Berkshire Hathaway.

Besides, our time in Omaha is running out, and we want to use what remains of the day today to see for ourselves one of Berkshire Hathaway's most storied enterprises operating right here in Omaha.

THINGS NOBODY DARED ASK

Well, I can't say Chris didn't warn me.

The biggest surprise of the day has not been the spectacle of 27,000 people converging to hear two old men speak, or the number of questions they answered, or the sincerity and thoughtfulness behind each answer, or the repartee between Buffett and Munger, or even the absence of African Americans.

It is that with so much high-level discourse about the state of the world—from the U.S. dollar ("It's going down") to the inadequacies of a portfolio theory concept known as beta ("Beta is nice and mathematical, but it's *wrong*")—there has been almost no discussion of the Berkshire Hathaway businesses themselves.

Ironically, the names of those businesses flashed all during the meeting across a bright electronic band ringing the balcony between levels of the Qwest Center arena—starting with Acme

Building Brands and ending with XTRA Corporation, with other names, familiar and unfamiliar, in between.

Nevertheless, familiar or not, we have learned almost nothing new about any one of them, aside from Buffett's observation during his brief review of the first-quarter earnings report at the start of the meeting: "Most of the noninsurance businesses did fine."

He did not define *fine*, nor did he give any details about the impact of the homebuilding downturn on Shaw Industries (carpeting), Acme (bricks), and the other residential construction-related businesses within the Berkshire portfolio, except to say that they were "hit, and in some cases hit hard."

Without a single number to back it up, the normally numbers-conscious Buffett had boasted, "Compared to other companies in the sector, our managers continue to do a sensational job."

And that appeared to be enough for the crowd.

Not one shareholder asked about any of the businesses in the Berkshire "family," except for two insurance-related questions from a pair of sleep-deprived Floridians who managed to get up early enough to find out what Buffett thinks about their hurricane-prone peninsula.

Over the course of listening to both Buffett and Munger respond to 54 questions, we have heard plenty about the bleak prospects for the U.S. dollar, why the stock market seems more attractive to Buffett than the bond market at the moment, how it is that the private equity bubble will not burst, and why the derivatives market continues to scare Buffett, even as Berkshire benefits from many derivatives contracts—"We have at least 60 derivatives . . . and believe me: we'll make money on all of them."

We have also learned something about Klamath River dams, the cost of moving an airline passenger on Southwest versus USAir, the competitive position of railroads versus truckers, the virtues of gluttony as opposed to envy, and Charlie Munger's best advice for investment success: "The key is to avoid making mistakes."

We were also told precisely what Buffett is looking for in his replacement as Berkshire's chief investment officer, and how he plans on going about finding the right person or persons: Buffett will be giving "a chunk of about $5 billion" to several money managers and watching how they do over a period of time. Then, he said, "we'll turn over the entire portfolio to one or more of them."

No gunslingers or hotshots need apply: "We will need somebody who basically doesn't do any dumb things, and occasionally does something smart."

We have heard all this but not a word about See's Candies, Dairy Queen, NetJets, Fruit of the Loom, Justin Boots, or even GEICO.

And while Chris and I leave the Qwest Center with a far better understanding of the Berkshire culture and how deeply embedded Buffett and Munger's core beliefs about investing and behaving reside within the Berkshire "family," we've seen and heard almost nothing we didn't already know about Berkshire Hathaway as a business.

Now, Buffett did not avoid speaking on the topic of, say, how Fruit of the Loom is managing to compete against offshore competitors these days, or why Dairy Queen seems outdated compared to so many fast-food chains, or what the long-term prospects for Kirby's door-to-door vacuum cleaner sales might be in an Internet age, or why See's Candies is still mostly a West Coast business nearly 35 years after Berkshire bought it.

It's just that nobody in the building particularly cared enough—or dared—to ask.

After all, if *you* had a chance to ask Warren Buffett a question in front of 27,000 people, you probably wouldn't ask something as mundane as why See's Candies has no stores east of Chicago, while Starbucks—a coffee shop, for goodness sake—is an authentic worldwide brand. Or why the old Dairy Queen store in your hometown always looks so down and out compared to the alternatives. Or why Nebraska Furniture Mart never took its big-box model across the country, the way Best Buy did.

You're going to thank Warren Buffett and Charlie Munger for making you rich. Then you're going to ask them where to invest.

Still, it is a fact that Berkshire Hathaway owns more than a few businesses that, while profitable, are not exactly prosperous.

Fruit of the Loom, for example, is an apparel manufacturer with a once-proud name that is getting squeezed by big customers such as Wal-Mart on one side and low-cost imports on the other. "We do not want to buy a business with a high labor content that can be shipped from overseas," Munger said near the end of the afternoon session.

Yet Fruit of the Loom is just that type of business.

See's Candies, to pick another brand name from the flashing sign ringing the arena, is certainly not a candidate for low-cost competition from overseas, but it must certainly be getting hurt on the expense side of the business. Fudge, after all, is made with sugar, cocoa, butter, and corn syrup—commodities that have been soaring in price—and it uses lots of energy. You'd never know this, however, or what management is doing about it.

Nor do we know what See's management is doing to expand in the developing countries that are quickly evolving into seriously big markets. See's "international" operations consist of two stores in Hong Kong, three in Japan, and some sales in Mexico.

About the closest we came to understanding a Berkshire company was when Buffett proudly showed a brief film of Munger and him touring the completely automated, human-free factory of ISCAR, the Israeli metalworking company that Berkshire acquired in 2006 for $4 billion. "We bought it without looking at it," he told us. "But after we looked at it, we *really* liked it." There was not one word, however, about ISCAR's current business or the potential return on that investment.

If Buffett wasn't going to volunteer anything about the more mundane aspects of the Berkshire family of companies—and since no shareholder was willing to ask about them—Chris and I are going to take a look for ourselves.

We're going to pay a visit to one of the original "Sainted Seven"—Nebraska Furniture Mart, possibly the most warmly regarded of all the stars in the Berkshire firmament by Warren Buffett himself.

"A PAPER ROUTE IS A GOOD IDEA"

Chris and I head down the crowded escalators and exit from the Qwest Center into warm, humid afternoon air—the remnant of last night's storms, which are expected to get more serious later tonight and on into tomorrow morning, when we're both planning to fly out.

The rental car is hot and stuffy—and bizarrely, we can't unlock the doors using a regular old door-unlocking remote control. Chris has to use the key to unlock the driver's door, get inside, and scooch over the front seat to unlock the passenger door *from the inside*.

Not only that, but in order to put our gear in the backseat, we have to virtually climb over the seats and unlock the back doors *from the inside*. General Motors has apparently concluded that one way to solve the fact that it has been losing money on each car it sells is to try to discourage people from buying them in the first place. It is no wonder that Warren Buffett has never purchased shares of General Motors for Berkshire's portfolio— although he did buy a Cadillac DTS as a show of support for the struggling company after seeing an interview with its CEO on television.

Eventually, we're behind the wheel, and we quickly leave behind the modern, soaring metal-and-glass Qwest Center for the more familiar, plainspoken brick-and-granite buildings in the city center. After just a few more minutes driving up and over a long, rolling hill and passing through half a dozen traffic lights, we leave downtown Omaha entirely. Office buildings give way to bars, insurance brokers, and apartment complexes.

Passing the cracked sidewalks and squat brick buildings, Chris and I discuss the advice Buffett had given to the girl from Kentucky who asked in a timid but clear voice, "What would a 10-year-old do to make money?"

"That's a subject I gave a lot of thought to when I was 10," Buffett had started his answer. "I got half my capital from delivering newspapers," he said, adding, "You're probably a little too young."

He then mused on one of the keys to success: "I saw a study that correlated business success with a range of variables like grades, parents, whether one attended business school—and they found it correlated best with the age at which you first started in business."

He was telling the 10-year-old that she already had a head start on her peers. "Look for what people don't want to do for themselves," he told her. "Ask around and see what other kids are doing."

He concluded by going back to his first thought: "A paper route is a good idea."

A paper route is actually a pretty lousy idea these days, with the demise of afternoon newspapers and 1950s-era *Leave It to Beaver*-type neighborhoods. And not many parents today would want their 10-year-old daughter to go to strangers' houses. Of course, not many newspaper companies want 10-year-olds— boys *or* girls. Routes today require a car, a driver's license, and insurance—not a bicycle and a strong throwing arm.

LOOKING FOR EASY PROBLEMS

But only one bum response out of 54 questions is still a sensational ratio for anybody of any age—especially considering that Buffett had answered every question at length and in detail, with only two exceptions.

The first exception was the healthcare question; the second a more obscure one about the merits of the New York Stock Exchange's merger with Euronext. This had elicited a brief but meandering answer from Buffett, who then asked Munger for his thoughts.

Munger passed: "I don't know anything about it."

Buffett quickly followed: "I don't either; I just took longer to say it."

Apartment buildings yield to brick houses. The University of Nebraska at Omaha campus suddenly appears on both sides of the street. The road slopes down a long hill, to a very busy intersection. We turn left at the light and follow a long line of cars moving slowly past a drive-through Starbucks on one side and a Borders Bookstore on the other, toward a motley collection of huge buildings that loom up on the west side of 72nd Street.

The buildings appear so large that it is as if some old airplane hangars had been converted into a gigantic store.

We follow the cars into a parking lot—actually many parking lots, of various sizes and shapes, that connect the immense buildings. After finding a space, we go through the laborious process of manually locking every door of the car, and each of us remarks that he is never buying a GM car, no matter what Buffett thinks. We then follow shoppers streaming into the nearest entrance of the largest retail enterprise I have ever seen.

It is the Nebraska Furniture Mart, and inside its cavernous walls is a stunning assembly of merchandise and hordes of eager buyers in a setting that, in certain respects, seems nearly as out of date as Buffett's advice to the 10-year-old girl from Kentucky—"a paper route is a good idea."

And I begin to wonder just how healthy "this motley group" of businesses that we have learned almost nothing about might be.

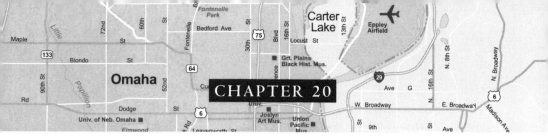

CHAPTER 20

Buffett's Last Nickel

"I'm a 'one-price' guy."

—WARREN BUFFETT

Warren Buffett is one of the richest men who ever lived. He also may be one of the cheapest.

His license plate, THRIFTY, was famous around Omaha—too famous, in fact; he gave it away along with his 2001 Lincoln Town Car in a charity auction, owing to worries about his safety.

And with reason: for a billionaire, Warren Buffett is a very casual guy. He has no chauffeur, drives himself the mile or two between his house and his office—he comes in seven days a week—and even drives to the airport to pick up visiting reporters, friends, and dignitaries making their way to Omaha to see him.

Moreover, if his visitors have time, Buffett likes nothing better than to drive them to the Nebraska Furniture Mart to see one of the crown jewels of the Berkshire "family."

The Nebraska Furniture Mart is actually a collection of buildings—including a separate furniture store, a carpet store, and an electronics store—scattered across 77 acres of what used to be prairie in such a random fashion that it feels as if each time the business outgrew one building, somebody decided to put up the next building right *here*, without much forethought as to how it all fit together.

It looks kind of like an old-fashioned lumberyard.

To complete the setting, an enormous white tent has been raised high above the cars on a far corner of the Furniture Mart property, where a gigantic Berkshire shareholders' "reception" will take place later today. We pass a husband and wife changing—in the shade of their minivan—from their shareholders-meeting clothing into more formal attire for the shareholders' reception. They have traveled a long way by car to be here: the minivan is *packed* with clothing, coolers, and just plain stuff.

We head to the electronics store, opened by Nebraska Furniture Mart in 1994—11 years after Buffett purchased the business for Berkshire. Banners on the lampposts display various electronics brand names, simultaneously enticing shoppers into the store and reminding them of where they parked.

The unintended effect of these banners, however, is to make the place seem *old*, for we see not a single brand that electronics shoppers care about these days—Garmin, for example, or LG or even Apple. Instead, the banners carry stodgy old names, like IBM and Maytag and Whirlpool. Some of the brands no longer even exist in any meaningful fashion. We're parked under a sign for "Compaq," for example. That name disappeared almost as soon as the company was taken over by Hewlett-Packard five years ago this week.

They might as well be advertising Underwood Typewriters.

Inside, the Nebraska Furniture Mart electronics "superstore" seems like any other electronics superstore, except a bit bigger and a bit older—circa 1994, not 2006. The no-frills atmosphere is a bit less inviting than the local Best Buy, although it does give shoppers the impression that they could do no better, and probably a whole lot worse, buying electronics gear elsewhere.

And there are a lot of shoppers, although we notice that a good many of them are wearing the now-familiar Berkshire "Shareholder" badge. They wear the badges not out of mere habit: shareholders get a steep discount on their shopping here this weekend. It is a big business for the Mart. Buffett likes to brag that shareholder weekend sales can be 10 percent of this location's annual total sales (there are two other Nebraska Furniture Marts, one in Kansas City and another in Des Moines).

That means the Mart will do something like $40 million this weekend alone. It also means that Berkshire Hathaway is very likely the only public company in the world that actually earns a *profit* from its annual meeting.

"THEY HAD WRUNG THE LAST NICKEL OUT OF ME"

And that fact certainly warms Warren Buffett's heart, for Buffett did not become the world's richest man by wasting money. He was, as he likes to say, "wired at birth" not only to make money but to hang onto it.

Buffett and his sisters, Doris and Roberta ("Bertie"), grew up not far from here in a hardworking family. Buffett was extremely close to his father, Howard, a stockbroker and four-term Republican congressman with high ethics, who once refused to accept a salary increase that had been approved *after* the election. Buffett's relationship with his mother, Leila, appears to have been quite different: her family had a history of mental illness and she was subject to dark mood swings.

By all accounts, Buffett was, from the start, a math whiz and intensely interested in making money. By the age of 17, he had earned more than $5,000 from his newspaper routes, owned income-producing Nebraska farmland and a pinball machine business in Washington, D.C., and was buying stocks and even selling them short.

He had also been filing his own tax returns for four years.

But Buffett did not make money in order to spend it. He preferred to invest his earnings and watch the money grow. Acutely aware of the power of compound interest, Buffett memorized the Union Carbide "Compound Interest Tables" in the days before handheld calculators made them obsolete, and in later years wrote an essay to his partnership investors on "The Joys of Compounding." He once complained to a friend after his first wife, Susan, spent $15,000 on home furnishings, "Do you know how much that is if you compound it over 20 years?"

He met and wooed his wife, Susan Thompson, by visiting her house and befriending Susan's father while she went on dates with other young men. On their honeymoon, Buffett read a book coauthored by his future mentor, Benjamin Graham, *Security Analysis*—to his bride. "It might not seem romantic," he told the *Philadelphia Inquirer* in 2007, "but I felt she ought to read it."

Buffett's single-minded focus on making money was reinforced by an iron-willed discipline; he once famously refused to bet $10 that he'd get a hole in one over three days of golf at Pebble Beach—despite the $20,000 payoff.

As legendary insurance executive Jack Byrne, who rescued GEICO from near-bankruptcy and turned Berkshire's $45.7 million investment into $2.3 billion, told the story, all the other members of the group took the bet except Buffett, who had decided that the odds weren't with him. "He said if you let yourself be undisciplined on the small things, you'd probably be undisciplined on the large things, too."

Years later, that discipline would be evident in one of those "large things," the initial acquisition of MidAmerican Energy for precisely $35.05.

Buffett wrote about the odd price to shareholders:

> Why the odd figure of $35.05? I originally decided the business was worth $35.00 to Berkshire. Now, I'm a "one-price" guy . . . and for several days the investment bankers representing MidAmerican had no luck in getting me to increase Berkshire's offer. But, finally, they caught me in a moment of weakness, and I caved, telling them I would go to $35.05. With that, I explained, they could tell their client they had wrung the last nickel out of me. At the time, it hurt.

Chris and I had been told by the Berkshire managers at lunch that the only thing that changed after they were acquired by

Berkshire was where they kept their cash: it went to Berkshire, for Warren Buffett to invest.

Seeing the Nebraska Furniture Mart firsthand, it shows.

The warehouse-sized store feels behind the times. Modern electronics retailers such as Best Buy are opening smaller stores, not larger, thanks to the digitization of music and video, which has done away with many of the products these stores used to sell. More unsettling than the cavernous size and out-of-date displays, however, is what we find at a nearby customer service desk.

The computer monitor on which one of the salespeople is checking inventory for a potential customer is an ancient, pre-Windows type of screen. I haven't seen one of these point-of-sale monitors with block white letters and a blinking white cursor in so long that I actually can't remember where I last saw one.

Of course, not having the latest and greatest software isn't necessarily a sign of back-office chaos. For all we know, the Nebraska Furniture Mart's computer systems might offer every piece of vital information a salesperson or an accounts payable staffer can need at a keystroke.

But this seems unlikely—and it seems even less likely when we move on and pass by a door opening into a small room that contains a bunch of less-than-cutting-edge servers stacked on cluttered shelving.

TOO THRIFTY?

Retailing has come a long way since 1983, when Warren Buffett bought Nebraska Furniture Mart on a handshake from Rose Blumkin, the late Russian immigrant whose motto—"Sell Cheap and Tell the Truth"—is displayed on the company's Web site alongside her photograph. And *electronics* retailing has come even further, thanks to the constant downward spiral in prices, fickle consumer tastes, the digital revolution, and the rise in online shopping.

But not so much here, it seems.

Disappointed and not having spent a dime, we head outside and cross a busy driveway to the furniture superstore of the Nebraska Furniture Mart.

And super it is: big, cavernous, and *very* long. The longest store I have ever walked through.

Fully loaded showrooms meld into one another with endless displays of sofas, recliners, tables, and chairs—almost literally as far as the eye can see. There's even an entire section devoted to *bar stools*, with different styles of bar stools displayed at different types of bar countertops. And that's before we reach the lighting area, which appears to offer every fixture ever created since Thomas Edison patented his "electric lamp" in 1880.

There's no doubt that the shoppers are here. And there is no doubt that Nebraska Furniture Mart has grown from the single-store brainchild of Rose Blumkin—"Mrs. B," as she is reverently spoken of by Buffett himself—to a three-store midwestern home furnishings powerhouse. But why, Chris and I wonder, is the Nebraska Furniture Mart not a national phenomenon?

Warren Buffett purchased the fabled Nebraska Furniture Mart in 1983, when this local institution was the largest home furnishings store in the United States generating an astonishing $100 million in sales from a single store.

That same year, a Minneapolis electronics retailer called Sound of Music opened its first "superstore" in Burnsville, Minnesota, and changed its name to Best Buy. Sales that year were just $28 million.

Today, Nebraska Furniture Mart has three stores with estimated combined annual sales of $1.2 billion. Best Buy has more than 1,000 stores, with sales exceeding $40 billion.

Looking around at this once groundbreaking operation, I wonder how it is that one small Midwestern retailer could grow to be almost 40 times bigger than the other in the same span of time. One had the desire and the capacity to grow, while the other, it would seem, did not.

I recall something Charlie Munger said late in today's meeting, "If a business is good, it will carry a lousy management."

How long, I wonder, can a good business carry an owner who does not reinvest in that business?

Could Warren Buffett be too "thrifty" for his own company's good?

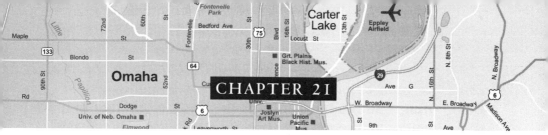
"This Is a Very Rational Place"

I t's time to go; it has been a long day. The air outside the Mart is cooling down thanks to the threatening dark clouds that are looming on the horizon.

We drive out of the parking lot and head downtown on Dodge Street. I'm hoping that whatever those clouds are going to bring, it won't happen early tomorrow morning when our flights are taking us home.

After the crowds at the Qwest Center and the Furniture Mart, the hotel feels deserted. There are some people waiting near the main door, dressed for dinner, and a few more in the bar. Chris and I split up for some down time before dinner.

My room is still quiet, and the giant sign for Sol's Pawn Shop is still there outside my window, vaguely calling to mind the giant eyes of Dr. T. J. Eckleburg, an advertisement overlooking the ash heaps in F. Scott Fitzgerald's *The Great Gatsby* that symbolized whatever the hell it was supposed to symbolize.

I just think that "Sol's Pawn Shop" looks interesting, given what we come to Omaha to celebrate. It's also a reminder of just how unique Buffett's "wiring" is. Northwest of Sol's, and just a few miles from Buffett's house, is the birthplace of another famous Omaha native son, Malcolm Little.

Born five years before Buffett, Malcolm Little's particular individual "wiring" and circumstances took him on a different route from that of his white counterpart: he would change his name to Malcolm X and die of gunshot wounds in New York City just three months before Warren Buffett took control of Berkshire Hathaway in 1965.

I had planned to take some photographs in Sol's direction after our excursion to the furniture mart, but a cop at the Qwest Center discouraged it. "Don't go north," he said, nodding in the direction of Sol's when I asked if there were any areas of town to avoid.

Chris and I meet up for dinner, intending to walk the few blocks from the Doubletree to Old Market, but those clouds look ready to break, so we decide to drive, even if it means going through the convoluted rental-car-door-opening routine. Three blocks into the drive, the clouds open up. We reach the restaurant, not too soaked and feeling oddly vindicated, having sized up the situation and à la Buffett "tried to see things that haven't happened" even if in our case it merely applied to a little rain.

> "We're looking for someone who doesn't only learn from things that *have* happened, but can envision things that have *never* happened. This is our job in insurance and investments. Many people are very smart, but are not wired to think about things that haven't happened before."

The restaurant is packed with other badge-wearing shareholders, and getting a table will take too long, so we sit at the bar. We eat, drink, and review the day, while behind the bar, waiters and waitresses bring back trays filled with empty water glasses, beer mugs, and martini glasses. One of the two bartenders keeps feeding glasses into a small Hobart dishwasher, which seems overloaded.

Chris and I feel overwhelmed ourselves.

ENVISIONING THINGS THAT HAVE NEVER HAPPENED

In 1979, the Iranian revolution triggered the second great oil shock to hit Western economies in a decade. Investors wanted to own oil stocks, and Wall Street firms needed oil analysts quickly, and that's how I got hired without any experience in the real world, and without knowing much more about investing than the fact that oil stocks always went up.

Gray-haired money managers listened to my opinions for no reason other than that I worked for Merrill Lynch and seemed to know something about a handful of oil companies. People asked me for tips on the elevator. Headhunters called, offering me more money than my father had ever earned until late in his career.

It was quite a heady experience.

Meanwhile, a heretofore successful investor out of Omaha, Nebraska, had begun accumulating a large position in General Foods, the predecessor of today's Kraft Foods and owner of such stalwart brands as Maxwell House, Birds Eye, Post, and Kool-Aid.

These brands seemed such dull, slow-growing businesses that stocks like General Foods were considered suitable only for value-investing chumps and coupon-clipping widows and orphans, not performance-hungry fund managers.

Outside of Warren Buffett's then-small band of loyal followers—250 investors, nearly 10 percent of the shareholders, attended the 1985 shareholder meeting—few people understood Buffett's infatuation with General Foods. The question around some parts of Wall Street was a jaded and cynical, "What is Buffett *thinking?*"

What Buffett was thinking was shelf space.

General Foods's key asset, he recognized—all on his own out there in Omaha—was the supermarket shelf space commanded by its Maxwell House coffee, Birds Eye frozen foods, Post cereals, and Kool-Aid brands. Since no supermarket could do without them, General Foods would be able to price those products high enough to earn a superior return on investment, even in a time of high inflation.

So strongly did Buffett feel this way that Berkshire eventually accumulated just under 9 percent of the giant food company.

In time, high oil prices triggered a recession. Oil prices collapsed, and so did oil stocks, as well as the demand for oil analysts. By the time Wall Street got around to realizing the inherent value of shelf space, General Foods was being acquired at a very high price by Philip Morris, to the enormous benefit of Berkshire Hathaway's bank account, Warren Buffett's reputation, and his growing base of worshipful shareholders.

Even young oil analysts began to understand why people called him the "Oracle of Omaha."

"WHETHER THEY WEIGH 300 POUNDS OR 325 POUNDS, IT DOESN'T MATTER: THEY'RE FAT"

To buy General Foods in the late 1970s and early 1980s, as Buffett did, was to *"envision things that have never happened."*

Yet Buffett was no clairvoyant. He had not predicted the future. He had not forecast the takeover by Philip Morris.

What he had done was much simpler but at the same time far harder: he had correctly identified a company's key asset, measured its worth, and judged it vastly underpriced in a stock market that was still looking backward at recent history, rather than forward at things that hadn't yet happened.

The result was such a clear investment opportunity that Buffett didn't need to precisely calculate the exact value of those General Foods brands or to worry about how quickly he would get paid for owning 9 percent of the company's shelf space. As Buffett himself said when asked his opinion of hurdle rates and other such sophisticated valuation techniques, "If somebody comes to the door, whether they weigh 300 pounds or 325 pounds, it doesn't matter: they're fat. We don't need to know more."

Munger put the inexact nature of their methodology a little differently: "We have no system for estimating the correct value of all businesses. We put almost all in the 'too hard' pile and sift through a few easy ones."

Still, a large portion of the investment world thinks that Warren Buffett is irreplaceable—a genetic mutation of sorts, never to be seen again on earth; a scary-smart, self-confident, supremely logical, and highly disciplined thinker who not only cornered the market on value-based investing, but was "wired at birth" with a preternatural ability to do precisely what he and his partner, Charlie Munger, seek in his eventual successor at the helm of Berkshire Hathaway: "envision things that have never happened."

But the heart of Berkshire Hathaway's success is not simply the prodigious brainpower of a unique human being. It is also the fact that, as Charlie Munger put it, with characteristically profound simplicity: "This is a *very* rational place."

Since what needs replacing at the head of Berkshire Hathaway is the extraordinarily rational behavior of an extraordinary human being—not the mystical powers of a genetic mutation—I'm beginning to think that Warren Buffett might, in fact, be replaceable as the chief investment officer of Berkshire Hathaway.

Charlie Munger, too.

"We'll find some people," Warren Buffett told his shareholders at the meeting.

They seem to believe him, and so, for the moment, do I. *Somebody* out there must be wired like Warren Buffett.

But Chris isn't convinced. "Look at the track record," he says. "You know any others out there like it?"

He's even more worried about the business itself. "He told us it's getting worse. He told us in plain English the insurance business was going to get worse. But nobody believes him."

It's that cult thing he witnessed the last time he came.

At the end of the day, he points out, with or without Warren Buffett at the helm, Berkshire Hathaway's value is the value of its businesses.

And as we have both seen with our own eyes, some of those businesses might be getting a little long in the tooth. Chris doesn't say so, but I suspect he'll sell his Berkshire shares.

And I may have to buy the stock for myself if I want to go back to the meeting next year.

We head back to the hotel and part ways.

The trip, as Chris had promised, was worth it—even more than I could have imagined, for it is impossible, I think, to completely understand Warren Buffett and Berkshire Hathaway without making a pilgrimage to Omaha.

It is not enough that Buffett himself is smart. There is a reason why Charlie Munger is his partner, confidant, and closest advisor: he is every bit Buffett's peer in the realm of the mind. Buffett's own son, Howard, has said he considers his father to be the *second* smartest human being he knows, behind Charlie Munger.

Yet it is not merely being scary-smart and partnering with a like-minded individual that has enabled Buffett to make Berkshire Hathaway a market-beating, efficient market theory-confounding enterprise for nearly 40 years.

Being in Omaha has a lot to do with it too.

"WE JUST HAD TO READ AND THINK EIGHT TO TEN HOURS A DAY"

Omaha sits very nearly smack in the middle of the country, both geographically and metaphorically. Even with jet travel, it is not all that easy to get to. Insurance companies and railroad head-quarters—not investment bank towers—dominate what skyline there is. The streets are wide and quiet except during rush hour.

This quiet environment allows Warren Buffett to "sit and think," which is how he describes his most cherished activity, other than reading. "I really had no idea what he did," his son Peter said in a 2008 interview. "But he read a lot. I know that."

During today's shareholders' meeting, Buffett had discussed his and his partner's actions during the 1998 worldwide financial panic this way: "We knew during the Long-Term Capital Management crisis that there would be a lot of opportunities, so we just had to read and think eight to ten hours a day."

Not many people on Wall Street—or in any other financial capital around the world—were "reading and thinking" during those fear-crazed days when a highly leveraged hedge fund nearly brought down the entire financial system.

Being thus removed from what he calls the "electronic herd," Buffett can ignore the short-term distractions of Wall Street and focus on the long-term opportunities for his shareholders. And by "long term," Buffett doesn't mean one year or even three years out: "You need to see five to ten years out," he told us at one point during the session.

Of course, Berkshire's shareholders are willing to wait. Some have been waiting four or five *decades*, and they have been amply rewarded for doing so. Being in Omaha and having perhaps the most patient shareholder base in the world allows Buffett to wait, and to eventually act on those visions of fatness when they appear in the doorway.

HEADING HOME

It is early Sunday morning, and time to head home.

Outside, it is still dark and wet. The storm clouds that broke last night on our way to dinner were part of a heavy weather system that spawned tornadoes elsewhere in the state and other parts of the Midwest overnight. One destroyed an entire town in Kansas, I find out when I turn on the Weather Channel. Getting home is looking tricky.

Instead of waiting for the hotel shuttle, I split a cab to the airport with a man who does not appear to be a member of the older, paunchier, more relaxed Berkshire Hathaway shareholder crowd. This guy is young, fit, and quite impatient to get to the airport.

It turns out he works for Warren Buffett.

More precisely, he works for an insurance business that was recently acquired by Berkshire Hathaway. And he knows quite a bit about Ajit Jain, Buffett's "super-cat" insurance man and one of those frequently identified as a successor to Buffett in his chief executive role.

Jain handles the supercatastrophic insurance policies that Berkshire Hathaway makes a specialty of underwriting, at great profit. Mike Tyson's life, Alex Rodriguez's health, billion-dollar Pepsi contests, and expensive offshore drilling rigs are the stuff of Ajit Jain's territory, and he is a legend in the business, thanks in no small part to Buffett's frequent mentions of him in the

Chairman's Letters, as well as Berkshire's reputation as the insurer of last resort.

I ask my fellow cab rider his impression of Jain, and he gives me a two-word answer: "scary-smart." Then he shakes his head. "Ajit never writes anything down. But he remembers every number you ever gave him."

He could, of course, be describing Warren Buffett.

The trip to the airport is brief, so our conversation ends quickly. He leaves for his gate, and I for mine. Outside, the sky lightens as the sun rises, and the rain mutes to a drizzle. My flight to Chicago leaves on time, lifting off over the muddy Missouri River and the brown, flooded fields, up into the clouds.

The trip home is smooth and—as much as a commercial airline flight with connections in Chicago can be these days—without incident.

Maybe the airline business isn't so bad after all.

"Many annual meetings are a waste of time, both for shareholders and for management. Sometimes that is true because management is reluctant to open up on matters of business substance. More often a nonproductive session is the fault of shareholder participants who are more concerned about their own moment on stage than they are about the affairs of the corporation. What should be a forum for business discussion becomes a forum for theatrics, spleen-venting and advocacy of issues. . .

Berkshire's meetings are a different story. The number of shareholders attending grows a bit each year and we have yet to experience a silly question or an ego-inspired commentary. Instead, we get a wide variety of thoughtful questions about the business. Because the annual meeting is the time and place for these, Charlie and I are happy to answer them all, no matter how long it takes."

WARREN BUFFETT
FEBRUARY 25, 1985

PART

II

[*Return to*]

[*Omaha*]

2008

Family Reunion

⟶

OMAHA, NEBRASKA, SATURDAY, MAY 3, 2008

I t is one year later, almost to the day, and the world has changed. The nation's largest mortgage lender, Countrywide Financial Corp., has collapsed after 38 years of making home loans—a victim of its own aggressive lending practices, soaring loan losses, and a credit squeeze that forced it to sell out at a fire-sale price.

One of the country's largest housewares retailers, Linens 'n Things, has filed for Chapter 11 bankruptcy after 33 years in business, unable to pay interest on the debt its owner, a private equity firm, incurred when it bought the company just two years earlier.

Most shockingly of all, Bear Stearns, one of the top investment banks in the United States, virtually disappeared *overnight* after 85 years on Wall Street. The firm—which had survived the Great Crash of 1929 without firing a single employee—collapsed in March after a run on the bank triggered by huge losses on subprime mortgages. Only an eleventh-hour rescue by JPMorgan Chase and the U.S. Treasury prevented what might have become a worldwide financial meltdown.

And 31,000 people have converged on Omaha to hear what Warren Buffett thinks will happen now.

It is 7:30 a.m., and I am in line outside the Qwest Center in Omaha. The skies above eastern Nebraska are bright, crisp, and cold—unlike yesterday, when severe weather from the Rockies to the Midwest disrupted the travel plans of nearly every person streaming into the large, gleaming Qwest Center complex for the Berkshire Hathaway annual meeting.

In fact, the only reason I made it here is, in a way, thanks to Warren Buffett.

"YOUR CAR IS HERE"

Not quite 24 hours ago I was in the United Airlines terminal at Chicago's O'Hare Airport, and everything seemed fine as I boarded the late-morning flight to Omaha along with dozens of other Berkshire shareholders.

There were, of course, many comfortably dressed older couples and sporty young men in blazers, chinos, and loafers. But this year there was also one casually dressed father with his daughter, and several more fathers with their sons. Everyone was talking about the coming weekend—some with British accents, South African accents, or German accents—and all were eager to get to Omaha. Our plane pulled away from the gate right on time, and I was starting to think good thoughts about the commercial airline industry.

Then the plane stopped a few hundred yards from the terminal and just sat there. We were waiting, the pilot told us, for thunderstorms to blow through. When the skies finally cleared up, the plane moved out into a long line of planes, and we stopped again.

An hour or so later we started moving . . . back toward the terminal.

"You've probably noticed we left the line," the pilot said. "Our weather radar isn't working. We've called maintenance, and we're heading back to the gate."

Then he added the single most alarming sentence—short of *"Assume crash positions"*—that any airline passenger can expect to hear: "It shouldn't be too long."

Another hour later, and nearly three hours since we'd left the gate, the pilot finally gave up. "This plane is broken," he said. "We're gonna get you off and try to find another plane."

Now, United Airlines is not exactly knocking the lights out when it comes to operational excellence, yet it seemed determined to not merely screw up the travel plans of 150 or so passengers who needed to get to Omaha *that night*, but also to create as much fear, doubt, and uncertainty as possible while we considered our options. The only thing the gate agent would tell us was that there were no flights until 8:30 a.m. Saturday morning.

I recalled what that young man said out loud last year at this time when a few of us were temporarily bumped from the American flight to Omaha: "I'm *screwed*." And I knew how he felt. It was then that I saw a fellow hedge fund manager and longtime Berkshire owner, who, it turns out, has been coming to these meetings off and on for more than 20 years. He was talking on his cell phone, with his young son nearby. I assumed he was renting a car. He waved me over. "I'm saved," I thought. It's 500 miles to Omaha from Chicago, and we could easily share the driving. It might take seven or eight hours, but at least we'd get there.

As it turned out, it took not much time at all, because he has a Marquis NetJets card.

That Marquis Jet Card card was good for 25 hours of air travel on NetJets, for him and anybody else he chooses. He calls NetJets—usually with more notice than he was giving them now—and they set him up with a plane, a pilot, and a flight plan. And he can take anybody he chooses.

A brief cab ride later, my hedge fund friend, his son, and I were walking through a small, nondescript building at a regional airport just north of Chicago. The terminal was calm and quiet. Two pilots walked past, talking shop. On the walls were photographs of celebrity pilots, including Jimmy Stewart and Johnny Carson. Nobody was running to catch a plane. And there was no security line either: NetJets had already cleared me.

One of our two pilots met us at the desk, told us about the weather—"should be fine"—and introduced us to a South

African couple from the same United Airlines flight, who were coming too. We all walked across the tarmac and climbed into the plane, a Citation Sovereign with plenty of headroom, leather swivel seats, and a stocked bar. With barely enough time to buckle our seat belts, we were wheels up and on our way to Omaha, the shores of Lake Michigan disappearing quickly behind us.

An hour later we were landing. It was cloudy, and there was some rain and a rough wind as the plane touched down, but we were actually in Omaha—not Chicago.

The plane taxied to the private terminal, and we unbuckled and got out. Sleek white jets and smaller propeller planes were scattered all around the tarmac, and more were landing. A woman with a clipboard and a harried but friendly look on her face greeted us. She was from NetJets, and she was making sure we had our bags and found our transportation. I asked her how to go about getting my Hertz rental car at the main terminal.

"Your car is here," she said, pointing behind me.

Sure enough, parked right there on the runway was a Toyota Corolla. NetJets had picked it up for me from Hertz. It's no wonder Warren Buffett liked NetJets so much he bought the whole company.

I thanked my friend profusely and drove off.

So thanks to NetJets, I'm now inside the Qwest Center and walking around the floor of the arena, getting a look at the heart of the Berkshire Hathaway family, up close and personal, before I take my seat up near the rafters. The talk is not about yesterday's weather or plane troubles in Chicago. It is about the man who has been expecting, and saying he expected, just such a crisis as the one that triggered the end of Bear Stearns. "Some day," Warren Buffett told us last year, "you will get a very chaotic situation." He was right. And soon the man who sits on top of one of the largest piles of cash in corporate America—"Fort Knox," he likes to call it—is going to speak about the state of his company, the state of his country, and the state of the world.

The "Oracle of Omaha" is in the building.

I am on the floor, near the stage where Warren Buffett and his partner, Charlie Munger, will sit down to take questions for nearly five hours. There are shareholders, professional investors, and the friends, family members, and employees from the dozens of Berkshire companies, talking, laughing, shaking hands, hugging, whispering, and yakking. It feels like a family reunion.

One, big, *happy* family reunion.

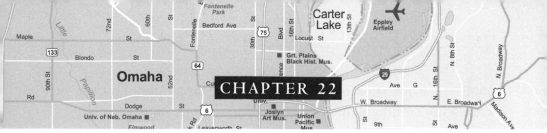

CHAPTER 22

Armageddon Avoided

"Someday, you will get a very chaotic situation. As to what could trigger this and when—who knows? Who had any idea that shooting an archduke would start World War I?"

—WARREN BUFFETT ON DERIVATIVES

"As sure as God made little green apples, this will cause a lot of trouble. This will go on and on, but eventually will cause a big dénouement."

—CHARLIE MUNGER ON DERIVATIVES

One year ago almost to the day, Warren Buffett and Charlie Munger warned of the dangers posed to the financial system by derivatives—the complex financial instruments at the heart of the sub-prime crisis now threatening to engulf the world—in no uncertain terms.

And while neither man gave a timetable for the financial Armageddon they envisioned ("I find it easy to predict what will happen and very difficult to predict when," Buffett has said), what followed their gloomy warnings is something that almost no hedge fund manager, bond trader, mutual fund manager, or small stock investor has experienced in his or her lifetime: a worldwide credit collapse.

Financial institutions from mighty Citigroup here at home to giant Union Bank of Switzerland have been laid low by massive credit losses—$350 billion in total, and counting—that were not only unforeseen by most investors, but have never been experienced on so large, broad, and deep a scale since the Great Depression.

"I think you might see an exogenous event," Buffett had told us last year when he was asked what might disrupt the worldwide economic boom, "a shock to the system that causes a huge widening of credit spreads and a cheapening of equities."

That "shock to the system" began almost as soon as those words were spoken.

"STARS ARE ALIGNED"

"The private equity world is in its golden era right now. . . . Stars are aligned."

—HENRY KRAVIS

The high-water mark of the globalization-driven, worldwide economic boom of the new century—at least for now—may have been June 22, 2007.

On that day, the Blackstone Group, one of the world's largest private equity firms, sold shares to the public in the wake of a private equity frenzy that caused *Fortune* magazine to label Blackstone CEO Steve Schwarzman "The New King of Wall Street," while Schwarzman's chief rival, KKR founder Henry Kravis, was making fin-de-siècle-style pronouncements of his own.

That kind of chest-thumping alone should have given the eager buyers of Blackstone's public offering pause. It did not.

So eager was the public to get in on the private equity mania, they ignored the fact that Blackstone's public offering was only for an interest in Blackstone's management fees from buying and selling companies, *not* in the actual companies Blackstone owned.

It was like buying a share of Warren Buffett's salary instead of all the companies that make up the Berkshire Hathaway "family." Of course, since Warren Buffett's salary is only $100,000 a year, nobody would have thought of doing that. No matter, the deal was a hit. Blackstone's initial public offering turned out to be the *sixth largest* in U.S. history. Shares soared on the first day of trading, from the $31 offering price to a peak of $38.

What nobody knew—although some professional investors suspected—was that Blackstone's IPO would mark the beginning of the end of the private equity boom, and of much more. The shares closed at $35.06 the first day of trading and never again reached their opening-day peak.

It was a signal that most of Wall Street understood, even if the public did not: the "stars" aligned in the private equity heavens were about to shine a little less brightly.

Even as Blackstone's "New King of Wall Street" was counting his windfall from selling shares to the public, money was getting tight around the world. The easy credit that had fueled speculative buying of everything from second homes in Naples, Florida, and Valencia, Spain, to entire companies on the New York Stock Exchange was becoming harder to scrape together.

When newly public Blackstone announced a fee-generating $26 billion takeover of Hilton Hotels—at a 40 percent premium to the market price—the evening before the July 4 holiday, the company's shares briefly traded higher, then resumed their decline as investors digested the jaw-dropping price and the deteriorating conditions in the credit markets.

By late July, word had begun to filter out that the bankers for Henry Kravis's firm, KKR—the original and one of the largest and most aggressive of the empire-building private equity firms—were having trouble getting commitments from junk-bond buyers for its $26 billion buyout of First Data Corp.

The stars began coming unglued.

A $25 billion buyout of student loan giant Sallie Mae soon fell apart amid squabbling and threats of lawsuits. An $8 billion deal for audio-system maker Harman International, a $6.5 billion bid for Alliance Data Systems, and a $4 billion takeover of equipment company United Rentals all collapsed.

And while the First Data deal would eventually get done—at a reduced price—the debt provided by investment banks would not find a home with investors for some time. More than $300 billion worth of debt committed by bankers to private equity buyers quickly piled up on the balance sheets of banks around the world.

As the subprime crisis had spread from Main Street to Wall Street, it now began to spread from Wall Street to London and Paris.

In mid-September, thousands of depositors lined up at the branches of Northern Rock, a fast-growing bank based outside Newcastle-upon-Tyne, to withdraw all their funds, after news leaked that the bank had gone "cap in hand" to the Bank of England for emergency funds.

It was the first run on a British bank in nearly 150 years.

Four months later came news that a young trader at Société Générale, a large, old-line French bank, had secretly accumulated $70 billion in trading positions over a two-year period. The bank lost $7 *billion* cleaning up after him.

"Some day," Warren Buffett had warned us last year, "you will get a very chaotic situation."

That day is at hand.

NO LONGER "THE BEST OF ALL WORLDS"

Along with the collapse of Northern Rock and Bear Stearns, the near failure of Countrywide Credit, and the staggering losses at giants such as Société Générale, Citigroup, Merrill Lynch, and Fannie Mae—not to mention yesterday morning's bankruptcy filing by Linens 'n Things—a few other things have changed in the last year.

And several of them were anticipated by Warren Buffett.

"We're following policies in this country that will lead to a decline in the dollar," Buffett had told us last May.

And the value of the U.S. dollar has indeed dropped 10 percent since then.

"Corporate America is living the best of all worlds," Buffett had said last year. "And history has shown this is not sustainable."

And total profits of U.S. companies declined $53 *billion* in the fourth quarter of 2007, thanks to the spectacular collapse of the housing, banking, and finance sectors, not to mention rising energy costs, healthcare costs, and raw material costs and cautious consumer spending.

Even profits at Berkshire Hathaway have declined, as forecasted, since last year—the result of tougher conditions in the insurance business and the many housing-related companies in the Berkshire family.

"It couldn't get any better than it was last year," Buffett had told us. Berkshire's profits are "going down." And they did.

One more thing Buffett told us to expect: if a financial Armageddon *were* to happen, Berkshire could move very quickly to take advantage of the opportunities.

While Armageddon has, thus far, been avoided, Buffett has indeed been busy during the crisis. Just this week he announced that Berkshire would provide $6.5 billion to help finance a $23 billion takeover of the Wrigley chewing gum company by the privately held, secretive maker of Snickers Bars—Mars.

And later in the day we will hear about a few more examples that Buffett did not *announce* to the public.

ADVISING ALEX RODRIGUEZ

Some things, on the other hand, have not really changed since last year.

Berkshire's "Corporate Performance" table shows yet another increase in Berkshire's economic value, its forty-second in the 43 years since Buffett took control.

And the price of Berkshire Hathaway stock has climbed again, to $133,600—precisely 22.3 percent higher than last year at this time. Warren Buffett's shares alone make him worth $62 billion, according to *Forbes* magazine—the world's richest man. The Dow Jones Industrial Average, meantime, has fallen 1.6 percent.

Unchanged, too, is the fact that despite Berkshire's continued prosperity, some of the Berkshire companies continue to struggle, if not downright deteriorate. Dairy Queen is being sued by franchisees; Fruit of the Loom is fighting off low-cost overseas competitors; and Berkshire's newspapers—the *Buffalo News*, which Berkshire owns entirely, and the *Washington Post*, in which Berkshire has a large interest—continue to fight the technology revolution that is making their core business obsolete, as Buffett himself will readily admit.

The newspaper business is so bad, in fact, that Buffett's favorite childhood baseball team, the venerable Chicago Cubs, recently was put up for sale by the struggling newspaper chain that owns it.

Speaking of baseball, third baseman Alex Rodriguez, whose hitting and fielding abilities Berkshire once insured, is back with the New York Yankees after calling Warren Buffett for advice when a disastrous negotiating ploy left him without an offer. (According to press reports, Buffett advised Rodriguez to simply go around his agent and deal directly with the Yankees.)

There is, however, one important event that Warren Buffett did *not* foresee at last year's meeting, and it is a far less welcome development for Buffett and the Berkshire Hathaway family than a global credit crisis or a short-term decline in Berkshire's profits. Four executives of Berkshire's General Re division—including its former CEO, who Buffett once lauded for his "integrity, professionalism and leadership"—have been convicted on charges including conspiracy, securities fraud, and making false statements in helping insurance giant AIG conduct what the government called a "sham transaction."

"HE TOLD ME TO SELL"

Here in Omaha, meanwhile, the changes since last year have been less dramatic, if entirely predictable.

The sheer numbers attending the Berkshire meeting have increased: 31,000 people have reportedly descended on Omaha this year, up from 27,000 last year.

And despite the presence of several new hotels in the area, the ripple effect of 4,000 extra Berkshire shareholders has pushed me several miles out of downtown Omaha to a hotel on the western fringe of the city, out beyond Warren Buffett's quiet neighborhood. The crowd of shareholders, too, is slightly different this year: the "Newspaper Generation" of Berkshire faithful is inexorably being replaced by the BlackBerry Generation. Nearly everyone on the airplane in Chicago seemed to be using a BlackBerry while we waited for the thunderstorms to blow through, and here on the floor of the arena, two young men are engrossed in their iPhones, scrolling through e-mails and reading news items. iPhones hadn't even been on the market at the time of last year's meeting.

And while he hasn't yet appeared, Warren Buffett himself seems to have changed—outwardly, at least.

No longer merely the world's most quotable billionaire, he has become a media celebrity and a regular on CNBC, which now has a "Warren Buffett Watch" news page on its Web site. The cable news channel even sent a correspondent with Buffett on a trip to South Korea and China last October, providing breathless stories about his reading habits, his eating habits, and how much sleep he got on the plane.

Also, for the third time in his life, Buffett made a cameo appearance on a TV soap opera, and for at least the second time in his career, he testified before Congress. His appearance before the Senate Finance Committee in November was not, however, to discuss wrongdoing on Wall Street, as in the old Salomon Brothers days, but to urge Congress to keep a "meaningful estate tax" on the wealthy.

One other thing has changed since last year's annual meeting: it has been learned through a DNA analysis that Jimmy Buffett, the laid-back "Margaritaville" singer and Berkshire shareholder, is no relation to Warren Buffett, the richest person in America.

Oh—and Chris Wagner is not coming to the meeting. Chris, as I suspected, sold his long-held shares after last year's meeting. His reasoning was simple: "He told me to sell," Chris said, referring to Buffett's warning last year that Berkshire's insurance profits were "going down."

"Besides," Chris said, echoing Buffett's words of warning that the derivatives market had become too popular, "Berkshire is a crowded trade."

To come back this year, I need to either buy Berkshire stock or find another shareholder with an extra pass to the meeting.

Now there are actually two ways to buy Berkshire stock. One is to buy the famously high-priced regular shares, called "A" shares, which were selling at $133,600 each on the stock exchange yesterday. The other is to buy B shares, which are worth one-thirtieth of the A shares and were selling at $4,448 each yesterday.

Buffett issued the cheaper shares in 1996 precisely so less wealthy investors could have a shot at owning a piece of Berkshire Hathaway. Kindly, Berkshire provides any shareholder—A or B—with four passes to the annual meeting.

So in early 2008 I decided to buy Berkshire stock for my personal account (not for my hedge fund). I bought the less expensive B shares because, well, they're less expensive, plus they'll still entitle me to four passes to the meeting. With the financial system looking so fragile following the collapse of Bear Stearns, I've decided that Berkshire might be the best-positioned company in the world to take advantage of it.

And I'm here to see if I'm right.

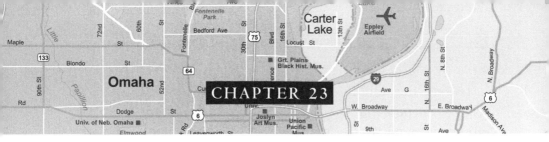

CHAPTER 23

The 1 Percent

"If you're in the luckiest 1 percent of humanity, you owe it to the rest of humanity to think about the other 99 percent."

—WARREN BUFFETT

ill Gates is signing autographs. Warren Buffett's children are greeting friends, family, and directors. And Mario Gabelli is fishing for stock ideas.

I am standing on the arena floor of the Qwest Center, ground zero of Warren Buffett's "Woodstock for Capitalists," and it does indeed feel like a rock concert is about to begin—not some annual meeting. And not just any rock concert, but a reunion of some supergroup, long hoped for and highly anticipated.

The VIP area is, as it was last year, staked out between the stage and the main seating area, where most of the seats are reserved for Berkshire subsidiaries. Signs have been taped on chairs where executives from Wesco, GEICO, and General Re will sit. Even the seats that slope up from the floor on either side of the stage are reserved in large blocks—Helzberg Diamonds, Nebraska Furniture Mart, Borsheim's, and many other Berkshire companies whose names also flash on the electronic display ringing the upper levels of the arena.

Toward the middle of the arena floor, where the seating isn't reserved, I notice a few rows where young women are sitting at either end with several empty seats between them. They are college students, hired as squatters by some of the older shareholders who do not want to get up early enough for a good seat. As the time for the movie approaches, the real shareholders will take their seats and settle in.

It really is like a rock concert.

But not many people around me are sitting just yet—the movie isn't going to start for another 15 or 20 minutes, and people are *talking*.

Money managers are talking to insurance executives; insurance executives are talking to each other. Elderly couples are reuniting with hugs and handshakes. And all those eager young men who got here early enough to get a chair on the floor are watching, gawking, and talking among themselves.

I spot Mario Gabelli nearby, deep in conversation, and instantly recognizable with his shock of white hair. He is one of the original value-investing greats and a longtime Berkshire owner. I met Mario years ago at a lunch with the financial officers of a privately held cable television company who were reluctant to provide information about their business. Mario said to me, "We can figure this out!" and in five minutes, after tossing out numbers while the cable guys reluctantly nodded or shook their heads, he had indeed figured out their company's revenue, operating margins, and cash flow.

This morning he is talking to a casually dressed man who, it turns out, is not only a veteran Berkshire investor but an Omaha native. Mario being Mario, he stops long enough to introduce me to his acquaintance. Then he continues grilling the man about a local company that's publicly traded. Mario never stops.

There is a commotion at the VIP railing: Bill Gates is there, signing autographs, and people are gaga. They thrust pieces of paper at him to sign, with their shareholder's badge—it is round this year, with a blue-green island theme—underneath.

For all his public persona as the world's richest computer geek, Gates is surprisingly personable. He listens earnestly as people lean over the railing to tell him things, or to request a particular dedication on the autograph. An African American woman hands him something to sign and a pen. "Thank you for what you do for education," she says fervently. He smiles, blushes, and signs. She is the thirteenth African American I have seen just in the first hour today, which is more than I saw all day at last year's meeting.

But she will also be the last.

Behind Gates, in the VIP section near the stage, other directors are gathering. There are handshakes, hugs, and kisses as with old, old friends. Tom Murphy, the Capital Cities legend, tall, thin, and conservatively dressed, stands out. So does Susan Decker, now 45 and recently promoted to president of Yahoo!; she is younger than most of the other directors and their wives by a good 30 years. Blonde and petite, she smiles broadly and moves among the knots of people, introducing members of her family who have come along for the day.

She does not, however, approach Bill Gates. It's not because he's still signing autographs; it's probably because Gates's company, Microsoft, is in the midst of a hostile takeover attempt for Decker's company. In fact, unbeknownst to probably everybody in this arena except Decker and Gates, Yahoo!'s two founders are secretly flying to the Seattle airport just about now to meet with Gates's longtime partner, Steve Ballmer. They will try, unsuccessfully as it happens, to hammer out a deal.

"I'M GOING TO BE THE RICHEST MAN IN THE WORLD"

One by one the Buffett children have emerged from behind the stage.

Peter Buffett, the youngest of the three children and the one who most completely abandoned his father's formidable center of gravity, is shaking hands and saying hello to friends, directors, and their wives.

Peter sold his Berkshire shares early and became a musician. "When I heard *Tubular Bells*, it completely blew my mind," he says on his Web site, referring to an offbeat instrumental work that was wildly popular in the 1970s. "I decided right then what I wanted to do with my life."

There is, in his manner, no sign of the family turmoil that erupted following the release of *The One Percent*, an 80-minute documentary by a Johnson & Johnson heir examining the "wealth gap" in America. (Its title refers to data indicating that 1 percent of Americans control as much as half of all wealth in America.)

The turmoil erupted because Peter Buffett's adopted daughter, Nicole, appeared in the film.

Despite speaking warmly of her experience in the Buffett household—"I feel very fulfilled and happy in my life," she said at one point—Nicole's participation in the film and later appearance on Oprah earned her Warren Buffett's rarely seen wrath.

"I have not legally or emotionally adopted you as a grandchild, nor have the rest of my family adopted you as a niece or a cousin," he wrote, chillingly, to the girl according to a February 23, 2008, *Wall Street Journal* account.

As the article pointed out, Buffett's disavowel of Peter's adopted daughter did not square with the actions of his late wife, Susan. Warren's first wife, Susan Thompson Buffett, who died in 2004, named Nicole in her will as one of her "adored grandchildren" and left her $100,000. She wrote that Nicole "shall have the same status and benefits . . . as if [she was a child] of my son, Peter A. Buffett."

Warren's cold reaction to Nicole's appearance in *The One Percent* compared to Susan's warmth toward her adopted granddaughter is less surprising than it might appear on the surface.

Susan Thompson Buffett left Warren Buffett and Omaha 25 years into their marriage and moved to California. She was, by most accounts, the polar opposite of her husband: outgoing, devoted to causes, and more interested in helping others than in accumulating wealth.

In a bittersweet interview with Charlie Rose shortly before her death, she described her first encounter with Buffett, who had greeted her with a sarcastic quip: "I thought, 'Who is this jerk?'"

Buffett began courting Susan through her father. "My dad fell in love with him," she told Rose. "We had fun dancing, which never happened after we were married."

"He would go around saying 'I'm going to be the richest man in the world.' I thought, 'Oh, okay.'"

"I always thought I'd marry a minister or a doctor or somebody else doing some valuable service to human beings. The fact that I married somebody who makes just piles of money is really the antithesis of what I ever thought."

Susan nevertheless described her husband as "phenomenal" in the same interview, telling Rose "there is no finer human being," and the couple remained married despite their physical separation. Susan encouraged Astrid Menks, a local Omaha friend, to look after Buffett, and Menks eventually moved in with Buffett. Still, Susan often traveled with her husband, and returned to Omaha each year for the annual meeting. She was a Berkshire board member until her death in 2004.

Buffett and Menks married two years later.

Susie Buffett, the oldest of Susan and Warren Buffett's three children, now appears in the VIP section, moving through the crowd of "1 percents."

With a big smile and an energetic personality, Susie looks remarkably like her mother. After her mother left her father, Susie returned to Omaha, to help look after him. She once told her mother about Buffett—whose mind was usually on investments— "I knew when I talked to Dad I had to hurry up, because pretty soon I'd lose him."

Susie carries on her mother's charitable works, chairing two Buffett-related foundations and serving on the board of DATA (Debt, AIDS, Trade, Africa) along with U2 lead singer Bono, who cofounded the organization to lobby Western countries on behalf of poor African nations. Bono sang two songs, including "Forever Young," at her mother's funeral.

Finally "Buffett" himself shows up with the other VIPs, shaking hands, and saying hello to directors and friends. But it is not Warren Buffett—it is his middle child, Howard.

Now 53, Howard looks startlingly like pictures of his father at that age, with a shock of hair, oversized glasses, and a stocky, heavyset build. With a ruddy complexion and big hands, he looks like the farmer he professes to be at heart. Yet Howard is also a noted conservationist, photographer, and author, and is active in land-use issues around the world. His wildlife photographs hang in Berkshire's offices.

Shaking hands and chatting up the well-dressed men and women near the stage, he is as gregarious as his sister.

The announcer's voice comes over the loudspeaker: "The movie will start in five minutes." Security men with earphones who have been standing guard near Bill Gates now open one of the metal barriers. "Please clear a path!" one says sharply. Gates finishes his autographs and moves away, to take his seat with the other VIPs.

Cameras start flashing, and now Warren Buffett in the flesh appears from the tunnel behind the stage, smiling and shaking hands. He follows the security men through the opening in the gate into the main seating area, and walks, smiling but slightly dazed, behind the security detail as they push through the knot of people trying to get near him. Howard Buffett follows his father, glad-handing as he goes. "Please clear a path!" the security men say as they brush past, marching briskly down the aisle.

"The movie will start in two minutes," intones the voice from the PA system, and the lights go down. Buffett sits in his chair at center court to watch the movie, a can of Cherry Coke in hand, while the security men try to move everyone away. "Please clear the aisle! Please return to your seats!" they shout. "Please keep this area clear!" I manage to take a picture before I go.

The sound of U2's "Beautiful Day" begins to fill the Qwest Center as I head back to my seat. I walk out through the tunnel at the far end of the arena, climb three levels of stairs, and make my way to a seat in the upper mezzanine, same as last year.

With the "newspaper generation."

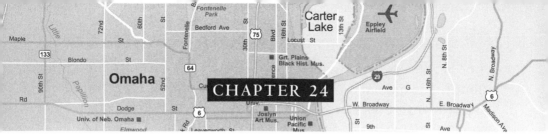

CHAPTER 24

It's a Beautiful Day

"I can't do without Berkshire."

—WARREN BUFFETT

The movie starts with a bang. It is a fast-motion video of the entire preparation for the Berkshire meeting, and the soundtrack is U2's upbeat song, "Beautiful Day." The video shows everything, from the stage being assembled to the chairs on the floor being set up, to the eager young shareholders lining up outside the Qwest Center door in the early-morning darkness, to Warren Buffett himself doing a sound check on the stage playing the ukulele. When the Qwest Center doors open, people pour in and the arena fills up in seconds. It's terrific.

The cartoon "documentary" that follows, unfortunately, is a whole lot slower. Its theme is the presidential election, and its story line is that Charlie Munger has been roped into running for president, with Warren Buffett as campaign manager.

Slogan: "A man who knows how to *make* money, not *spend* it."

A cartoon Walter Cronkite narrates the "documentary," intoning, "And so the Financial Independence Party was born," with a voice no doubt familiar to the gray-hairs in the crowd, but probably baffling to anyone who came of age after Cronkite retired from television 27 years ago. In the end, Munger is elected president, and appoints Warren Buffett head of the U.S. Treasury Department, the Commerce Department, and the Federal Reserve Board, to the delight of the shareholders around me.

The rest of the movie seems a little less insular than last year. Gone are the obscure University of Nebraska football highlights and the "Mean Joe Greene" Coke commercial.

In their place, a funny and quite long video clip that circulated on the Internet last year is shown, of two British comedians lampooning the banks and brokers who gave us the subprime crisis. This is interspersed with television commercials for Helzberg Diamonds, GEICO, and Fruit of the Loom, as well as Buffett's Senate testimony on the Salomon Brothers scandal:

"Lose money for the firm and I will be understanding. Lose a shred of reputation for the firm and I will be ruthless."

I realize now—after seeing how many of those seated in this arena represent the 76 companies within the Berkshire family— that Buffett does not include his Salomon Brothers testimony every year merely to play up to his investors. That single sentence is the guts of the Berkshire culture, and it is played in this arena to infuse that culture in every manager and every employee of every one of Berkshire's companies seated in this place.

The movie-within-the-movie that winds up this year's film is less Buffett-worshipful than last year's, but annoying in its own right. Buffett is shown in his simple, wood-paneled office, picking up the phone and calling Charlie in great excitement. "I just got this computer," he says. "And this Internet thing, it's gonna be *big*. I wanna buy!" Munger, filmed in his own Los Angeles office—which is every bit as drab and non-technology-oriented as Buffett's—listens to his overeager partner with disgust, rolling his eyes behind his thick glasses and shaking his head. "No no, *no*," Munger emphatically barks and slams down the phone.

Buffett, rebuffed, makes another call. The camera cuts to a room at the Beverly Hilton, where actress Jamie Lee Curtis is lying in bed, the covers pulled up to her naked shoulders. Why Warren Buffett is calling Jamie Lee Curtis is not clear, but she's ready to do whatever Buffett asks. "I'll do *anything* for you, Warren Buffett," she coos.

At Buffett's request, Jamie Lee then calls Charlie Munger, whom we see hanging up on his wife to take the call. Jamie Lee pushes Buffett's idea of buying Internet stocks on a weakening Munger, then tells him she plans to have him in her next movie, where they'll have "carte blanche" on the set. "I'll do *anything*," she coos.

Munger dreamily hangs up the phone and calls out to his assistant the funniest line of the movie: "Who was I on the phone with before her?"

Old-fashioned and out of place as it is in the year 2008, the women-as-sex-objects business gets some laughs in this crowd. Nor is it new territory for Buffett, who regularly employs hoary jokes about "gorgeous blondes" in his shareholder letters. The 2006 Berkshire holiday card was a photograph of Buffett, Munger, and the rest of the Berkshire board of directors outside a Hooters restaurant, surrounded by a gaggle of Hooters waitresses. "Berkshire directors are only paid $900 per year. Yet we get 100% attendance at meetings. I wonder why? Happy Holidays! Warren."

Buffett himself would probably never doubt that his deeply held "meritocratic" ideals are fair to women. One of the mainstays of the original "Sainted Seven" Berkshire companies, Nebraska Furniture Mart, was founded and run by a female Russian immigrant; while several Berkshire companies are managed by women: Borsheim's, Business Wire, and Pampered Chef. And he received loud applause at last year's meeting when he said that he believed that federal abortion law would have been quite different from the start if all nine Supreme Court justices had been women.

Of course, if all 11 members of the Berkshire board of directors were women, it is unlikely they'd be stopping at Hooters to take the holiday card photograph.

It is also unlikely that the film clip with one vixen would be followed by another—but it is. Buffett's recent cameo with Susan

Lucci, on the soap opera *All My Children* is shown. When it ends, a CNBC anchor breaks the news to shareholders that Buffett is stepping down from Berkshire Hathaway to join the cast of *All My Children*.

The lights come up and Charlie Munger walks out from behind the curtain on the stage, but he is alone.

There is applause followed by a pause as we wait for Buffett himself. The curtain rustles and the real Susan Lucci comes out instead, all tight clothes and big hair. She sits in Warren's place at the table next to Munger and announces, "I'm going to be taking over."

Munger looks Lucci over and says dryly, "Well you've certainly got some important qualities that Warren lacks." It gets laughs.

The vixen then tells Munger that she's going to do everything Buffett has refused: Berkshire is going to pay a dividend, give earnings guidance to Wall Street, and "pay the directors more than $900." At this last, the directors all stand and cheer, which brings down the house.

Finally, Warren himself walks out on stage. "*All My Children* can't do without you," he says to Lucci, ripping up his contract, "and I can't do without Berkshire."

Truer words may never have been spoken.

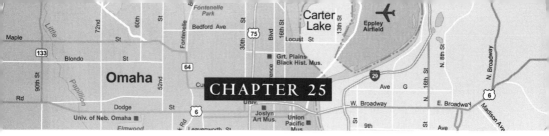

The Usual Procedure

"Hanging around with Charlie, you get the sunny side of life."

—WARREN BUFFETT

Warren Buffett takes his seat next to Charlie Munger. The applause dies down, and the arena goes quiet. The atmosphere is expectant. Like last year, the only master of ceremonies is Warren E. Buffett. Unlike last year, there is no review of the first quarter's earnings report. We go straight into the Warren and Charlie show.

Buffett begins matter-of-factly. "We'll follow the usual procedure," he says in his gruff but friendly voice. "We answer your questions—whoever is at the microphones. We don't screen them ahead of time. Our best estimate is we have around 31,000 people here today."

He shuffles papers on the table. "Somewhere I have a map here," he says, to keep track of the questions. Thirteen microphones are placed around the arena, including one in an overflow room, he tells us. "We'll just mark 'em off as we go along." He looks up from his pad. "Let me introduce our directors. Charlie Munger—he's the one that can hear; I can see, so we work together."

The joke works as well as last year. So does his standard applause line after introducing the directors: "The best directors in America."

Buffett settles in and looks at his watch. "Charlie and I will take a break at noon," he says. "I'd appreciate it if you'd limit your questions to one question, not a three- or four-parter. It's not necessary to make an opening statement."

"Post one," he calls out. We're underway, and we're very quickly in familiar territory.

"IF WARREN HAD GONE INTO BALLET, NOBODY WOULD EVER HAVE HEARD OF HIM"

The first shareholder has come all the way from Bombay, India, to be here, and he begins by praising Buffett in an odd but earnest way: "What touches me most is what you've achieved all these years—100 percent honesty."

The young man then hurries through his question, which has to do with the vast proportion of investors who act like "lemmings," and how, in the midst of this, he can achieve the appropriate investing "mindset."

When the young man has finished, Buffett is still cupping his ear while Munger is nonchalantly reaching for a piece of candy from the box of See's on the table between their two microphones. "Can't seem to hear the question," Buffett says to Munger, who by now has a mouthful of chocolate.

The crowd collectively chuckles while Munger takes his time swallowing. Finally, Munger says in his driest, most succinct manner, "He wants to invest less like a lemming."

Munger's ability to hear each question and condense it into the most economic form possible will be on display throughout the day. So, too, will the easy, respectful relationship between the two partners—Munger the erudite, judgmental, supremely rational phrase maker; Buffett, the earnest, numbers-oriented, eager-to-please, supremely rational wisecracking machine.

Munger, to a high school student from Bonn, Germany: "You'll do better if you develop a passion for something for which you have a particular aptitude. If Warren had gone into ballet, nobody would have heard of him."

Buffett, dryly: "Well, they'd have heard of me, but not in a positive way."

Munger—who has donated Berkshire stock to Stanford University Law School and funded a humanities research center at Huntington Library in San Marino, California—to a New York University professor: "It's a real pleasure to have an educator come, someone who is doing something simple and important instead of something foolish and unimportant."

Buffett: "I hope Charlie's not gonna name names."

Munger, to a shareholder asking advice on donating money: "I would predict that if you have an extreme political ideology, whether on the left or the right, you're liable to make a lot of dumb charitable gifts."

Buffett: "Hanging around with Charlie, you get the sunny side of life."

Asked how to evaluate the drug pipelines at pharmaceutical companies, Buffett says, "We don't try to assess it. What we feel is we have a group of companies bought at reasonable prices, where we have a reasonable chance at success. I would not know how to pick a specific winner."

Munger, dryly: "We've demonstrated our knowledge of pharmaceutical companies."

Buffett, chuckling: "He gets cranky late in the day."

After lunch Munger, the normally dour and extremely conservative "abominable no-man," responds favorably to a shareholder who asks about the notion of investing in small regional banks:

"I think the questioner is on to something," Munger says thoughtfully. "So many of our large banks here and in Europe have cast a pall of disgrace over the industry, and *that* has cast a pall over many smaller banks, so you're prospecting in a good area. . . . Yes. Yes. It is a territory that has some promise."

Buffett reacts to this stunning display of optimism by waving his arms: "*That* is a wildly, wildly bullish statement from Charlie." This brings down the house.

"THEY'VE GOT IT ASS-BACKWARD"

The Warren and Charlie Show has its repetitive moments. Buffett uses the same joke as last year, almost word for word, when a question on executive pay brings the now-familiar Buffett warning on envy: "Charlie has always said envy is the worst of the seven deadly sins, because y*ou* feel worse, and the other guy doesn't know it. Rule out envy. But gluttony—*that* has some upside to it," he says, picking up a See's chocolate, to laughter.

Munger, on the other hand, does not so much repeat the same jokes as he repeats his darker view of human behavior.

Discussing the speculative excess that came close to causing financial Armageddon recently, Munger, a long-standing Republican, says, "There's a lot that goes on in the bowels of the market that aren't pretty. Part of the trouble came from some of the prominent members of the Republican Party—*my* party. They kind of overdosed on Ayn Rand. One of them headed the Federal Reserve. I think Alan Greenspan did a very good job averaged out, but I think he overdosed on Ayn Rand. I think *some* things should be forbidden."

Munger will also continue his habit of making extraordinarily politically incorrect comments: "I think the stupidity involved in this mess," he will say when asked whether complex credit instruments could result in a subprime mortgage-style crisis, "is not as extreme as sweeping bums off skid row to give them sub-prime mortgages, but it's pretty bad."

And neither man will resist frequent wisecracks at the expense of graduate schools, despite the fact that Munger graduated from Harvard Law and Buffett, who was famously rejected by Harvard Business School, speaks to dozens of graduate classes each year. Asked about Berkshire's heavy concentration in stocks, which flies in the face of what most investors are taught—to diversify their holdings in order to reduce risk—Munger will get in the first digs early:

"Students of America go to these elite business schools and law schools and learn how this is taught, and they say 'the *whole* secret of investment is diversification.' They've got it ass-backwards. Diversification is for the know-nothing investor."

It is 58 years since Buffett was rejected by Harvard Business School, and although he has since claimed that it was the "luckiest thing that ever happened to me"—because it led him to enroll at Columbia, where he met his mentor, Ben Graham—he also manages a dig in that direction.

"I can't help you with MBAs," he says to one shareholder looking for advice on hiring better managers for his business. "They've learned how to fool you by that point—what answers to give in the interview." Later in the day, Buffett will repeat a favorite joke about MBAs: "I always tell the kids that come to see me to work for an *organization* you admire or a *person* you admire. Of course, that usually means they become self-employed."

Discussing the use of stock options as a method of enhancing financial returns, Buffett will declare the entire field of study a waste of time. "The amount of time spent in business schools teaching options—it's *nonsense*. You need two things: how to value a business, and how to think about stock market fluctuations."

He then compares teaching options and other complex financial theory to the teaching of religion. "If you were teaching religion and you'd spent all this time reading all these tomes, you'd hate to admit it all comes down to the Ten Commandments," he says. "And all investments come down to Chapters 8 and 20 of *The Intelligent Investor.*"

Yet for all that Buffett exudes the same self-assuredness, quick wit, and clear-eyed pragmatism, there seems to be a bit more mellowness this year on his part.

A question shortly before lunch about advising children on their finances will prompt him to reflect on the relationship between parents and children with some sensitivity. "If you already have money saved up, who's to say you shouldn't take your children to Disney World?"

There is a poignancy to his answer. By his own admission, Buffett's wife Susan raised their children while he worked. Susan told Charlie Rose, "Physical proximity to Warren doesn't always mean he's there with you. We were two parallel lines."

Perhaps his personal legacy, and especially the succession issue, is more at the forefront of Buffett's mind. It certainly seems to be at the forefront of his investors' minds. The two men will be asked several questions about the future of Buffett and Berkshire—and, indeed, about the direction of the United States and even the dangers of nuclear proliferation around the world—before the day is over.

But for now, with Buffett cupping his ear and Munger summarizing for his partner the first question of the day, we are in familiar territory.

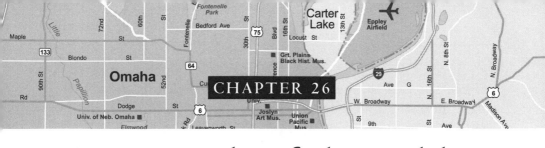
In Search of the Oldest Living Manager

"Events like this make our managers feel appreciated, not just by Charlie and me, but by the people here."

—WARREN BUFFETT

"He wants to invest less like a lemming," Munger says, repeating the first shareholder question. His hard-of-hearing partner nods and begins to speak.

"I believe in reading everything in sight," Buffett says, with the same force and enthusiasm as if the idea had only recently crossed his mind.

"For about eight years, I wandered around with technical analysis," he continues, referring to the practice of buying and selling stocks based strictly on price and volume patterns in stock charts. "And then I read a book, *The Intelligent Investor*, when I was 19."

The words are almost identical to the ones he spoke at last year's meeting, although in his enthusiasm for Ben Graham's book that famously changed his life, Buffett this year recommends the two chapters that most influenced him—Chapter 8, "The Investor and Market Fluctuations," and Chapter 20, "'Margin of Safety' as the Central Concept of Investment."

"It's as great a book now as when I read it in 1950," he says flatly. "You can't get a bad result if you follow the lessons Ben Graham taught in that book."

Buffett then digresses, plugging an entirely different kind of book: "My cousin has written a book," he says, "about my grandfather's grocery store: *Foods You Will Enjoy—The Story of Buffett's Store.*"

The Buffett grocery store is one of the many local touchstones of Buffett's career. He and Charlie Munger each worked there as children, although they didn't meet at that time. Also, it was at that store that Buffett—at the age of six—began buying six-packs of Coca-Cola and reselling the individual bottles for a profit. Open for 100 years, it was the last independent grocery store in Nebraska when it closed in 1969.

"My grandfather," Buffett says wryly, "was very negative on the stock market and big on hard work at the grocery store, so we stopped paying attention to him." This gets a laugh, but Buffett does not want to end without coming back to the young man from India's question.

"There are three big lessons in Graham," he says. "You're buying part of a *business*; you use the market to *serve* you and not to *instruct* you; and you want to have a margin of safety. You'll never be a lemming if you do that."

BREACH OF ETIQUETTE

The second question of the day is from a native of Cologne, Germany—the first of *eight* shareholders from Germany out of the 63 who will ask questions over the course of the day. This will be not only by far the most from any single country outside the United States, but more than from any state inside the United States, including New York (four), New Jersey (four), and the most heavily represented state, California (seven, not including three Native Americans here to discuss the Klamath River situation).

In fact, it will be a German shareholder who asks what might be the most perceptive question of the day, but this comes later in the morning. For now the question concerns a Berkshire reinsurance subsidiary in Cologne, and the discussion proves so bland that while Buffett talks, Munger busies himself opening a can of Coke and pouring himself a glass, over ice.

The third question of the morning proves more interesting. It is the first from a U.S. shareholder, who hails from Fort Lee, New Jersey, the backyard of CNBC—the stock market cable news channel that helped to turn Warren Buffett into a worldwide media star. He wants to know something that, as it so happens, CNBC and its hundreds of thousands of viewers around the world probably want to know.

"You commented this week on the recession," the man begins, referring to a statement Buffett made at the time Berkshire's financing of Mars's acquisition of Wrigley was announced: that the recession will be "longer and deeper than most people think."

The shareholder says, "Then the stock market was up in April," as if the stock market proved Buffett wrong. This draws some chuckles and a few outright laughs from the audience. Buffett, after all, pays no attention to the stock market on a day-to-day or even month-to-month basis, as most of the 31,000 people here already know. He doesn't even have a stock quote machine in his office.

"You use the market to *serve* you and not to *instruct* you," he told the young man from India.

Still, the shareholder from CNBC country forges ahead: "Can you expand on where the market's going this year?" he asks.

The chuckles turn into outright laughs at this breach of Berkshire etiquette—asking Warren Buffett for short-term stock market predictions.

If it bothers him, however, Buffett doesn't show it. "Well I could expand, but I couldn't answer," he says. "Charlie and I have no idea whether the market is going up next week, next month, next year. That's not our game," he says, as if anybody here needs a reminder.

What *is* their game is looking at businesses: "We see thousands and thousands and thousands of companies priced every day . . . we ignore 99.9 percent of what we see," he says. "We look at the *business*, not the stock."

Then he makes his favorite investment analogy—farmland in Nebraska. "If you were to buy a farm out here in Omaha, you wouldn't look at the price every day . . . you'd look at the value of what the farm produced relative to your purchase price. That's *exactly* what we do with stocks."

This concise summation of Berkshire's entire investment philosophy concluded, Buffett turns to Munger. "Charlie?"

"Nothing to add," Munger says in his dry, thin voice.

"He's been practicing for weeks," Buffett cracks. Then he checks off on his pad and calls for the next question.

MAKING THE MANAGERS FEEL APPRECIATED

"I am very bad hiring managers," says a man with an Indian accent hailing from Seattle, who lays himself bare before Warren Buffett, Charlie Munger, and the 31,000 people gathered to listen. "Some of decisions I make, I think, *'What was I thinking?'*"

How, he asks, do Warren Buffett and Charlie Munger find good managers?

"We cheat," Buffett says. "We *buy* businesses with great managers." He relates the problem of evaluating potential managers to the graduate student classes that come out to Omaha to visit Buffett:

"I've had about 30 schools come out this year, about 100 students in each class. I no more could take those 100 students and rank them from 1 to 100 in their future achievements—it would be impossible for me."

"We buy businesses with management already in place; we've seen their record, and they come with the business. *Our job is to retain them*," he says. "To make sure they have as much enthusiasm, *passion* as they did before they got the check" from Berkshire.

"It can't be done by contracts," he adds. "They *love* their businesses," he says of the families who sell to Berkshire. "The businesses are a work of art to them; they've been in their families for generations."

And then Buffett says in words what I had perceived only after seeing dozens and dozens of chairs here at this meeting reserved for the men and women who work for the many different Berkshire Hathaway companies, and after watching the replay of the Salomon Brothers testimony—that this meeting is as much for Berkshire's managers as for the shareholders:

"Events like this make our managers feel appreciated, not just by Charlie and me, but by the people here."

"I've learned to look at passion, integrity, good communicators," Buffett continues. "I like our game: we look for '.400 hitters' and put them in the lineup."

"Mrs. B worked for us until she was 103, and then she died the next year," he says, invoking, as he often does, the legendary founder of the Nebraska Furniture Mart, Rose Blumkin. After a pause, he delivers the punch line. "And *that* is a lesson to our managers."

This gets laughs, but Buffett is not really joking.

"My God," he told Carol Loomis of *Fortune* in a 1988 article on his skill at running the Berkshire businesses: "good managers are so scarce I can't afford the luxury of letting them go just because they've added a year to their age."

In Loomis's account:

> Louis Vincenti, chairman of Wesco until shortly before he died at age 79, used to periodically question whether he should not be training a successor. Buffett would turn him off with a big smile: "Say, Louie, how's your mother feeling—these days?"

Thinking back to my visit to the Nebraska Furniture Mart last year, I wonder at what point does an old manager become an old-timer?

Rose Blumkin was certainly a legend. She built an enormously successful business—so successful that national chains would not even try to compete against it. Yet she left the company in a huff six years after Berkshire bought the business, after run-ins with her grandsons over her management of the carpet business. She set up a competing store across the street, said some nasty things about Warren Buffett, and came back to the fold only after Buffett brought her roses and a box of See's. Is it possible she did not understand what the Mart could become?

Other Berkshire managers have likewise demonstrated a resistance to change.

In 2000, Jeff Comment, the CEO of Berkshire's Helzberg Diamonds jewelry retailer, told author Robert P. Miles that he didn't see the future in online sales. "People like to look at the diamond," said Comment, then 57 years old. "We're not going to try to do a lot of business on the Internet per se." Today, however, Internet retailer Blue Nile sells over $300 million of high-end diamonds annually, primarily in $5,000-and-up engagement rings, exclusively over the Internet.

Other Berkshire managers may not have gotten the most out of their businesses. For many years, Buffett sang the praises of Chuck Higgins, who ran See's Candies from the time Buffett and Munger bought it in 1972 until Higgins retired in 2005.

Yet in his 2007 letter, he boasted that the profitability of See's Candies had "increased more than 50 percent" in just two years under Higgins's successor. The fact that See's suddenly, somehow, 35 years after its purchase, became dramatically more profitable under a new CEO, Buffett did not discuss.

Nevertheless, if Warren Buffett had his way, none of his managers would retire until they died.

And neither, it is clear, will he.

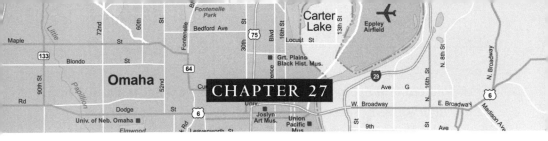
What Would Warren Do?

"I worship Mr. Buffett . . ."

—BERKSHIRE SHAREHOLDER FROM INDIA

I t's a subtle change from last year, but it's perceptible. Not one shareholder has prefaced a question by first offering profuse thanks to "Warren" or "Warren and Charlie" or even "Mr. Buffett and Mr. Munger" for the money they have made as longtime shareholders of Berkshire Hathaway.

And the reason doesn't appear to be because Buffett had said at the start, "It's not necessary to make an opening statement." He said the same thing last year, as I recall—yet most of the shareholders began by thanking him anyway.

More likely the reason is that so many of the shareholders asking questions are so new to the Berkshire family.

"HE'S A HERO IN CHINA"

Perhaps they first heard of Buffett five years ago, when he shared a press conference directed toward fighting AIDS with U2 singer and political activist Bono, at the University of Nebraska, or two years ago when he made the largest charitable donation in history—$37 billion, most of it toward addressing world health issues. Or maybe they watched his testimony on the estate tax before Congress last year, or his long, folksy indictment of U.S. tax policy with Tom Brokaw.

Or perhaps they watched the breathless televised coverage of his trip to China last year, with a CNBC reporter in tow.

However it was that they learned of Warren Buffett and came to make the pilgrimage to Omaha, many of the shareholders in this arena haven't known about Berkshire long enough to make a significant amount of money on Berkshire stock, let alone retire on it.

They have, instead, come to worship the man himself.

I'd gotten a hint of this last night at a dinner gathering in a big, noisy restaurant in Old Market. A reporter from Asia who'd followed my blog series on last year's annual meeting began grilling me about the blog and this book. "Are you going to publish the book in China?" she asked.

I hated to admit it, but, the notion of publishing a book on Warren Buffett in China had literally never crossed my mind.

The globalization of my world happened right then and there.

"Well, you should," she said. "He's a hero in China. People *worship* him." They admire Buffett's straightforward personality, his emphasis on integrity and long-term investing, and especially his respect for family-run businesses. Something in Buffett's philosophy of a "meritocracy" strikes a deep chord wherever there is a growing economy.

And many of today's "opening statements" are not expressions of thanks; they're outright hero worship.

From that first shareholder from India ("Where it touches me the most is what you've achieved over all these years—100 percent honesty") to the woman from Bonn, Germany, asking for advice on the pitfalls of giving away money ("Both of you are generous persons"), their words are suffused not with thanks for what Buffett and Munger have done for shareholders in the *past*, but for what Warren Buffett represents to the world today. "I worship Mr. Buffett for his philanthropy," says an earnest young man from India.

The reporter had been right. Warren Buffett is worshipped, and not just in Omaha, Manhattan, and other parts of the United States, but in Bonn, Singapore, Bombay, and Mexico City. And that hero worship will continue throughout the day.

At the moment, however, there is one constituency that has not come to worship Warren Buffett, as we learn as soon as he calls for the next microphone.

"WE WERE REALLY DISRESPECTED HERE"

"I fasted for 10 days driving over here to speak to you," the speaker says sharply into the microphone. It is a good bet that nobody has ever started off a question for Warren Buffett and Charlie Munger this way, and it certainly gets everyone's attention.

The speaker is Leaf "Chook-Chook" Hillman, a member of the Karuk Tribe and a Klamath River Basin tribal leader. Unlike last year's quiet, emotional speech by Wendy George, the Hoopa Valley Indian representative who came with four other Native Americans in traditional dress, Hillman pulls no punches.

"We really were disrespected here last year," he says, launching into an emotional criticism of the Klamath River dams owned by Berkshire's PacifiCorp, and then winds up with a flourish: "I come here with a principal agreement where you and I will sit down and resolve the issue in a way that saves *you* money and saves *our* culture!"

But instead of disclosing what's in his "agreement," Hillman unloads directly on Buffett: "I am an indigenous American and *you* are a guest as a European American."

The crowd stirs. This is *not* the way to get a deal done. This could get ugly.

Buffett responds quickly. "Last year we read the order," he says, reminding everyone about the affidavit he read from. "I am prohibited from making decisions." He then seems to distance Berkshire from the establishment of the dams themselves: "I think the first dam was built in 1907, and we bought it just a couple of years ago."

"I don't think we meant to be disrespectful," he says; "We may have differences of opinion . . ."

Then he calls on David Sokol, chairman of the Berkshire energy holding company, to speak.

This is significant, for reasons that go beyond the Klamath River dams.

Sokol has done a spectacular job of building Berkshire's energy holdings from nothing in 1999 to the largest noninsurance business at Berkshire today, and he is thought to be in line to take Buffett's job overseeing the 76 or so Berkshire companies.

Sokol speaks calmly and respectfully from a microphone midcourt of the arena. "It would be inappropriate for Mr. Buffett to respond," he begins. "He specifically agreed not to interfere. These four dams that we operate on the Klamath River," Sokol explains, involve "a whole series of issues. There are 28 parties," he says, and "four different directions these parties wish to go."

"We have met with each of the four tribes. Hopefully over time a cooperative resolution will be met."

The shareholders applaud sternly, and Buffett calls on the next shareholder.

"WE COUNT OUR BLESSINGS BECAUSE THEY'VE BEEN MANY"

It is, thankfully, a friendly and enthusiastic young man from California, who happens to have a thick Indian accent. "How do you maintain your mental and physical health?" he asks the two men, to some laughter.

"Well you start with a balanced diet," Buffett says, picking a See's candy out of the box. "Some Mars, some See's, some Wrigley, some Coke . . . "

More laughter from the audience helps restore the mood. Buffett then turns serious and somewhat philosophical.

"If Charlie and I can't maintain a healthy physical and mental balance, who can? We're forced to do virtually *nothing* that we don't want to do. How could you be sour about life, being blessed in so many ways? Great partners, great managers, you know, great families. No reason to focus on the minuses of life. We count our blessings because they've been many."

"From the moment we get up 'til we go to bed at night," Buffett says, "we're associating with wonderful people. . . . I mean, we think we live in the best country in the world. We could have stayed in my grandfather's grocery store, and it would have been *hell*."

The good mood lingers as Buffett calls for the next question.

Before the day's end, however, two more Klamath River activists will speak, prompting Buffett to actually cut off the discussion, perhaps the first time he has had to do so.

"YOU COULD JUST *TALK* TO THEM"

In his 1984 Chairman's Letter, Warren Buffett discussed why Berkshire meetings weren't like other corporate annual meetings:

> Berkshire's meetings are a different story. The number of shareholders attending grows a bit each year and we have yet to experience a silly question or an ego-inspired commentary.
>
> Instead, we get a wide variety of thoughtful questions about the business. Because the annual meeting is the time and place for these, Charlie and I are happy to answer them all, no matter how long it takes.

And it *was* true.

My friend with the NetJets Marquis card talked wistfully about those days as we flew to Omaha.

It was a very casual affair back then, he said, held at the Joslyn Art Museum just up the hill from the Qwest Center, which hadn't yet been built. There were only 200 or so investors—"75 from New York, maybe 50 from California, and 75 from Omaha."

"Warren and Charlie just walked in and sat down," he said. No bodyguards shouting "*Clear the aisle, please!*" The questions were all about the businesses, and about investing. "And Warren and Charlie hung around afterwards," he said, "You could just *talk* to them."

In that 1984 Chairman's Letter, Buffett wrote somewhat prophetically:

> Many annual meetings are a waste of time, both for shareholders and for management. . . . What should be a forum for business discussion becomes a forum for theatrics, spleen-venting and advocacy of issues. . . . Under such circumstances, the quality of the meeting often deteriorates from year to year as the antics of those interested in themselves discourage attendance by those interested in the business.

Today's questions have included a fair share of theatrics and some spleen venting, but mostly they have veered toward idolatry.

From high school students to middle-aged doctors, people have been asking, "What would Warren do?"

Far from being "a forum for business discussion," as Buffett wrote, *not a single shareholder* has even asked about the business.

And it doesn't look like the kid at the next microphone is going to either.

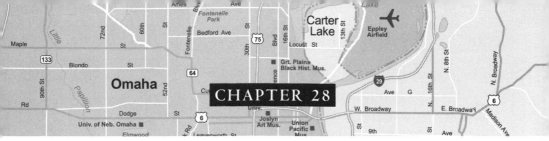
A Convulsion That Makes Enron Look like a Tea Party

"We're going to have this turmoil as far ahead as you can see."

—CHARLIE MUNGER

They have come from Bombay, Fort Lee, and Cologne to ask Buffett not only how to avoid becoming an investment "lemming," where the stock market is going, and how he maintains his health, but also what they should do with *the rest of their lives.*

"I attend high school," the next shareholder says. He is a soft-spoken young man from Bonn, Germany, and he is wondering "what to do with the rest of my life." (When *I* was in high school, some of us were wondering what to do with the rest of the *afternoon.* This meeting is beginning to scare me.)

"If you were about to start all over again," the young man asks Buffett, "what profession would you choose, and why?"

"I'd choose what I do," Buffett says immediately. "A, I'm good at it. B, I meet interesting people, no heavy lifting." He asks rhetorically, "What's your *passion* in life? I mean, unless Shirley MacLaine is right, this is your only life."

"I was very lucky," he continues over the laughter. "My dad was in business with a bunch of books in his office"—Buffett's father was a stockbroker before running for Congress—"so I'd go down there and read a bunch of books, and it turned me on. If he was a minister, I'm not so sure I'd be so enthused about visiting the office." This gets more laughs.

"Go to work for an organization or a person you admire," he adds. "And be sure to get the right spouse." Buffett has always spoken warmly of his first wife, Susan, and although he does not mention her by name, her presence looms large for many in the audience; she was a Berkshire director until her death in 2004. Buffett has called himself "very, very, very lucky" to have married her. Her death, people who know Buffett say, was devastating to the man, although he does not show it now.

Instead, he follows up his sober advice on marriage with a joke: "Charlie tells the story of the fellow who spent 20 years looking for the perfect woman and found her, but *she* was looking for the perfect man."

"THE ABILITY TO WRITE AND COMMUNICATE ORALLY IS OF *ENORMOUS* IMPORTANCE"

Next up is a teacher from New York University who tells Buffett that she has "something off the investing path" to ask Buffett and his partner. She may not know it, but she is going to touch a nerve.

Speaking of students who are too shy to participate in her classes, she asks, "What advice would you give to the *quieter* half of the population to raise their visibility in their careers?"

The question animates Buffett. "When I was in high school and college, I was terrified of public speaking," he says. "I avoided classes requiring them, got physically ill if I had to do them." He tells how he signed up for a Dale Carnegie course when he was living in New York, but lost his nerve: "I paid them $100 and then went home and stopped payment on the check."

After moving back to Omaha, Buffett recovered his nerve, and this time he paid the $100 Dale Carnegie fee in *cash*, so that he could not back out.

> I took that course, finished that course, and went right out to the University of Omaha and volunteered to start teaching.

> The ability to write and communicate orally is of *enormous* importance. If you can communicate well, you have an enormous advantage. It's important to get out there and do it while you're young. Force yourself into situations where you have to develop yourself. Be around people with the same problem. That's what they did at Dale Carnegie.

People have come from around the world to ask Buffett for advice on what to do with their lives and how to make shy students more forceful.

They've also come for advice on how to run their own businesses.

"WE'VE ONLY CREATED FROM SCRATCH *ONE* BUSINESS"

"I have a good successful small business," a shareholder from Fort Lauderdale with an Indian name and accent says. "But I can't seem to grow it to the next level." What, he wants to know, would Warren do?

"Berkshire was a small business at one time," Buffett says. And he means it. On May 10, 1965—the day Buffett took control of the aging New Bedford, Massachusetts, textile maker— Berkshire reported first-quarter earnings of $1,139,714 on revenues of $13 million. Now, 43 years later, almost to the day, Berkshire has reported first-quarter 2008 net income of $940 million on revenues of $25 *billion*.

"It just takes time. Charlie and I have never tried to do some masterstroke to convert Berkshire into something bigger," he says. "We will have more businesses a few years from now, as well as all the businesses we have presently. Most will do better; some will not. We've got 76 or so, in the most cases, wonderful darn businesses."

Buffett then repeats a line he has used many times. "Gypsy Rose Lee once said, 'I have everything I had five years ago, but it's all two inches lower.' . . . We want to have everything two inches *higher*." It gets a few chuckles.

Munger, of course, supplies the voice of grim reality. "You've got to remember most small businesses don't become big businesses, and most big businesses lapse into mediocrity," he cautions, before making a startling observation:

"We've only created from scratch *one* business I can think of that became a big business—the reinsurance business—out of thin air."

And it is true. Just about every single business at Berkshire Hathaway has been acquired, except for the business of taking on huge risks from other insurance companies—known as reinsurance—that Ajit Jain runs out of a small office in Stamford, Connecticut. Buffett concurs with Munger's observation. "Ajit did it," he says. "We just sat there cheering."

"Somebody asked once the best decision we ever made," Munger adds. "I said it was the fee we paid to the executive recruiter to get Ajit Jain."

And for once Charlie Munger is not being ironic. Unlike Apple, or Google, or Microsoft, or IBM or even GE, Berkshire Hathaway has become one of the world's largest companies without creating a single—to use Apple CEO Steve Jobs's favorite expression—"insanely great" product. Just a business insuring billion-dollar Pepsi lotteries, sporting events, office buildings, oil platforms, and much else.

"I put a heavy weight on certainty," Buffett has said, and this applies, it would seem, to nearly everything in his life, from the house he lives in to the stocks he buys to the investments his companies make.

Explaining his distrust of the computer industry, Buffett once wrote:

> Why, then, should Charlie and I now think we can predict the future of other rapidly-evolving businesses? We'll stick instead with the easy cases. Why search for a needle buried in a haystack when one is sitting in plain sight?

Certainly, Berkshire shareholders can be justifiably proud of their chairman's track record of buying when everyone else is selling—whether it involves stocks, bonds, or currencies. But they will never find themselves sharing stories of how their chairman saw the power of the Internet and used profits from, say, the *Buffalo News* to invest in the next Google. Nor will Berkshire ever fund the next iPod.

Shortly after buying Dairy Queen, Buffett said, "The Dilly Bar is more certain to be around in 10 years than any single software application."

And he is right, of course.

But that doesn't mean that the world would be what it is today—globally connected and relentlessly innovative—if Warren Buffett ran it.

"I HAPPEN TO BE A POLITICAL JUNKIE"

A 12-year-old from Philadelphia—who will *not* be the youngest to ask a question here today—wants more advice on life. "There's a lot they don't teach in school," he says. "What kind of things should I be reading?"

"I'd be in the habit of reading a daily newspaper," Buffett says. "I happen to be a political junkie," he adds. "The more you learn, the more you *want* to learn."

The boy's question delights Munger, who likes to say that his children probably think of him as "a book with legs sticking out of it." "My suggestion would be that the young person who just spoke has already figured out how to succeed in life," he says, to applause.

"WE WANT A BUSINESS WITH A DURABLE COMPETITIVE ADVANTAGE, MANAGEMENT WE TRUST AT A PRICE THAT WE UNDERSTAND"

Buffett fields questions on everything from Swiss chocolate companies ("We've probably looked at every confectionary company we can over the last 20 years") to the direction of the U.S. dollar ("If I landed from Mars on a UFO with a billion of Martian currency, I don't think I'd put all the billion in U.S. dollars") and where a small investor could find opportunities outside the stock market ("If I were working with small sums of money, it would just open up *thousands* of possibilities").

Along the way, Buffett reiterates the simple, long-standing approach that has made Berkshire so successful: "We want a business with a durable competitive advantage, management we trust at a price that we understand."

Munger, for his part, starts slowly, passes on the early questions, and begins to warm up only as the morning goes on. He positively comes alive when the subject of private, family-held companies that sell out to the highest bidder comes up, and his sense of probity is offended:

"I watched a man who created a wonderful business," he says indignantly, "And he sold it to a *known crook* just to get a slightly higher price. I think that's a crazy way to sell a business. I think you sell to a known steward."

By "known steward," he means, of course, Berkshire.

"WE HAVE HAD A CONVULSION THAT MAKES ENRON LOOK LIKE A *TEA PARTY*"

The last of the Klamath River questions has been asked and answered, and aside from that controversy, the questions have been uniformly friendly and of the "What would Warren do?" type—no matter what age or nationality or gender has done the asking. But when Buffett calls on the twenty-fourth question of the day, the pleasant mood quickly changes.

"I'm Dr. Silber of the Infertility Center of St. Louis," the man starts off, in a bright, friendly voice. The arena collectively freezes. *Here we go: the abortion question.*

He continues, "Everybody is looking very closely at what Charlie Munger and you are going to be saying. Everybody wants to know what you think." And everybody in the arena is now expecting a doozy of a statement, or question, or harangue, or *something*, on abortion.

But the doctor isn't going there at all. "We have three candidates, all of whom seem to be pandering to voters," Dr. Silber says, referring to the presidential election campaign now in full swing. "What would *you* do as president?"

The relief is palpable. Buffett—the self-described "political junkie"—seems relieved, too.

"I think we have three pretty good candidates this time around," he says. "The pandering—I'm afraid that's just part of a very long process. I think two of the three are pretty smart on economic policy." (Buffett, of course, has advised both Barack Obama and Hillary Clinton on economic policy.)

"You wanna buy a stock in a business so good any idiot can run it, because eventually one will," he says—a line that he has used for years, and one that he now applies to the entire country. "I think we have three very good candidates."

Munger speaks up in his crisp, didactic fashion. "I'd like to address the recent turmoil and its relation to politics. After Enron totally shocked the nation . . . ," he says, referring to the fraud-ridden energy company that collapsed in 2001, "our politicians passed Sarbanes-Oxley [regulations designed to make public companies more financially transparent].

"And it now turns out they were shooting at an elephant with a pea shooter."

Munger lets that sink in briefly, before hammering the main point home. "We have had a convulsion that makes Enron look like a *tea party*," he says. "Human nature always has these incentives to rationalize and misbehave. We're going to have this turmoil as far ahead as you can see."

The "convulsion," of course, is the subprime mortgage crisis that led to the sudden collapse of Bear Stearns.

How close this convulsion came to spreading around the world is something that Warren Buffett will discuss shortly, in vivid detail.

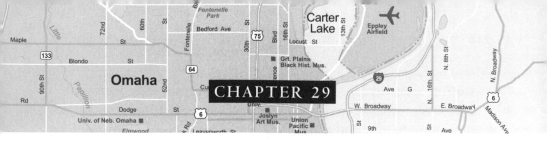

CHAPTER 29

Crying Wolf

⌐⁓

"There is absolutely *no question that returns for owners of Berkshire shares will be less than in the past."*

—WARREN BUFFETT

I t's time to break for lunch. Actually, there are still five minutes to go, but if you want to spend less time in line getting lunch than eating it, it's best to cut out early. You won't miss anything either: there are television monitors near all the concession stands.

Greek salad from Katie's in hand, I find an electric wall outlet near a stairwell, plug in the computer, and begin to eat while the battery recharges. I'm going to need it for the afternoon session.

On the monitor next to the burger counter across the way, Buffett is finishing up the last question of the morning, which is about the kind of financial advice that Buffett thinks parents should give to their children. He says that children will follow their parents' example. And while he has always been a fan of "living within your means," Buffett cautions against being too tough on kids, or they'll "go crazy" later in life.

"I do not advocate extreme frugality," says the man who is so frugal that he still refers to major expenses—such as his first wife's wedding ring—as a percentage of his net worth. (It was 6 percent.)

Buffett looks at his watch and adjourns the morning session.

Swarms of people begin to surge out of every tunnel and stair-well in the place. People shuffle by, glassy-eyed, looking at their watches, and making plans. Lines quickly form outside the bath-rooms and at the concession stands. The crowd at the burger counter goes from five deep to a line 20 yards long in a minute.

Those with food wander past, looking for a place to eat. Some lean against the railings overlooking the giant atrium, while oth-ers carry their lunch down the escalators, looking for some place in this building to sit. Many simply take their lunch back inside the arena.

Male and female, young and old, they all look very much alike. I have seen no more African Americans since the movie started.

"If you're in the luckiest 1 percent of humanity," Buffett said at a political fund-raiser after last year's meeting, "you owe it to the rest of humanity to think about the other 99 percent."

As near as I can tell, 31,000 members of the "luckiest 1 per-cent" are here today—standing in line for cheeseburgers, or heading downstairs to the exhibition hall to check out the NetJets display and the Clayton house, or filling up a See's Candies shopping bag with goodies.

If Buffett is thinking about that other 99 percent, as he says we all should, you wouldn't know it from this crowd.

"ANYBODY THERE SEEM BOTHERED?"

I have an e-mail from Chris Wagner. Chris, of course, sold his stock after last year's meeting. But like any good investor, he keeps an eye on things, and he has sent along a story from the *Financial Times* on Berkshire's first-quarter earnings, which came out yesterday, in case I hadn't seen the numbers.

Warren Buffett's Berkshire Hathaway was hit by a $1.6bn first-quarter non-cash loss on derivatives contracts—an asset class he once described as "financial weapons of mass destruction."

The surprise investment loss, announced on the eve of Berkshire's annual meeting in Mr Buffett's native Omaha, caused a 64 percent plunge in first quarter profits to $940m, from $2.6bn in the same period last year.

In a statement, Mr Buffett blamed the fall in profits on accounting rules that force companies to mark down un-realised gains or losses on derivatives.

Quoting an excerpt from Berkshire's annual report, Mr Buffett said he and his long-term associate Charlie Munger were not "bothered by these swings even though they could easily amount to $1bn or more in a quarter and we hope you won't be either".

Chris highlights the last paragraph. "Anybody there seem bothered?" he writes me.

So far, nobody seems to be bothered, although unlike last year, Buffett didn't start the meeting with a review of the earnings. Looking at the numbers, which I hadn't seen, it's clear why he didn't. They're pretty lousy.

Not that Buffett didn't warn us last year that this would hap-pen. "Profits are going down," he had said right up front at the meeting. But a two-thirds drop in Berkshire's first quarter earn-ings is probably more than most of the 27,000 people who watched him deliver that message might have expected.

Looking at details, I see that not only did the larger, more volatile reinsurance business earnings decline, but even profits at GEICO, the direct-to-consumer auto insurance company with the omnipresent advertising, fell hard.

Yet not a single person asked about it this morning.

"WE'RE GONNA GET DECENT, NOT *IN*DECENT RESULTS"

Of course, Buffett has never tried to hide the fact that growth gets tougher as Berkshire gets larger. "There is *absolutely* no ques-tion that returns for owners' shares of Berkshire will be less than in the past," he told an Australian shareholder.

"We operate now in a universe of marketable stocks," he said, "with market values of maybe $50 billion and up. Well, that universe is not as profitable as if you have the *entire* universe of thousands and thousands of companies."

He ran through an example of what would happen if Berkshire made a 10 percent investment in a $5 billion company—simultaneously demonstrating why Berkshire needs *huge* investments to make an impact and also how quickly Warren Buffett can do math:

"If that $500 million investment *doubles*, we pay a 33 percent tax on that gain, so that's a $335 million profit. It amounts to only 2/10 of 1 percent to Berkshire's assets."

"Anyone that expects us to come close to replicating the past should sell their stock, because it isn't gonna happen," he concluded. "We're gonna get decent results—we're not gonna get *in*decent results."

Munger agreed with his partner emphatically: "If you have a small amount of money and lots of time to examine thousands of companies, you should do that. We like to buy first-class businesses with first-class managements and just sit there. It's a formula that works for us."

But not many people actually believe what they have just been told. Buffett has been crying "wolf"—telling investors that his returns will go down—for many years:

> We have a number of important negatives operating on our future and, while they shouldn't add up to futility, they certainly don't add up to more than an average of quite moderate profitability.

That was contained in a letter written to investors in Buffett Partnership Ltd. on January 22, *1969*. It's no wonder that nobody seems to pay attention when Buffett warns about a less rosy future.

The lunch break is nearly over. The garbage cans fill too quickly for the workers to clear, and people begin piling trash creatively wherever they can. My computer battery is charged up enough to make it through the end of the afternoon session, so I head inside the arena.

The crowd here in the upper mezzanine has thinned out, as it did last year. Many have moved down closer to the floor, as they did last year. Also, like last year, only fewer than half the VIPs have returned to their seats in front of the stage.

Still, the after-lunch crowd is distinctly larger than last year, thanks to the extra 4,000 people who came this year. One day soon the Qwest Center may not be big enough to hold the Berkshire annual meeting.

Of course, one day in the future the Qwest Center may suddenly prove to be far *too* big.

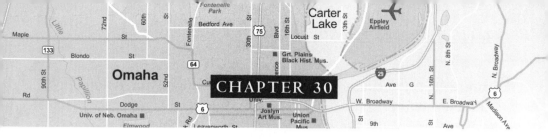

CHAPTER 30

A Particularly Foolish Mess

"It's crazy to let people get so big and so important to be too big to fail. It's knavery."

—CHARLIE MUNGER

I t is 12:55 p.m., and Warren and Charlie return to the stage and take their seats. "Okay," Buffett says, "we're going to get back to work here."

Before he calls on the first question, however, he wants to make an announcement. "We've had three questions on the Klamath River situation, which is more than proportional."

Buffett's rational, unemotional phrase—"more than proportional"—manages to shut off discussion without being offensive even to the activists he's telling to shut up, and it generates the first applause of the afternoon, but not the last.

The first shareholder called on is from Salt Lake City. "Are investment banks too complicated?" he asks.

"Exceptionally good question," Buffett says, the first time I've heard him commend a shareholder. "Probably yes," he states flatly. "When we bought General Re, it had 23,000 derivative contracts. And I could have spent *full time* on that and not got my mind around it."

For Warren Buffett not to be able to get his mind around something, that's a big deal.

"I don't want to have the chances of having something go wrong *slim*, I wanna have it *none*. There's no way I can assign that to a risk committee." Buffett lets that sink in briefly. "I think the big investment banks and big commercial banks are almost too big to manage effectively from a risk standpoint."

"The way they've conducted their business, you don't see the risk," he says. "If you have a 1-in-50 chance the place will go broke, the chief executive who is going to retire soon doesn't have the incentive to worry." Jimmy Cayne retired as CEO of Bear Stearns just two months before that company collapsed.

"I worry about *everything* at Berkshire."

Munger speaks up. "It's crazy to let people get so big and so important to be too big to fail. It's *knavery*." He decries "this crazy culture of greed and overreaching and overconfidence and trading algorithms. It's quite counterproductive to the country."

"It was *demented* to allow derivative trading to become embedded in the system. It was just *so* much easy money." Yet the wealth tied up in derivatives, Munger observes, turned out to be illusory: "It was in the category of assets that I call *'good until reached for.'* The assets are there until you *reach* for them."

He makes a motion of grasping for something and coming up empty-handed; then sits back, to laughter and applause, while Buffett follows up.

"When we first got to Salomon," Buffett says, going back to the early 1990s when he and Munger briefly abandoned their hands-off approach to management and stepped in to rescue that firm, "we noticed they were trading with Marc Rich, who had fled the country, and we told them they should stop trading with him."

Infamous even on Wall Street, Marc Rich was indicted in 1983 for trading oil with Iran during the Iranian hostage crisis, among other charges. He was pardoned by President Clinton following numerous White House visits by his ex-wife, Denise Rich. The pardon shocked the Street and made *Time* magazine's list of "10 Most Notorious Presidential Pardons."

Buffett continues, "And they said, 'We're making money with him, and what the hell do *you* know?'" He sounds offended by the memory more than 15 years later. "And it was only by *total directive* that we stopped it."

"IF BEAR STEARNS HAD FAILED SUNDAY NIGHT—WHICH THEY *WOULD* HAVE, BY SIX O'CLOCK THAT NIGHT . . . "

The near-collapse of Salomon Brothers brings Buffett to the implosion of Bear Stearns and the Federal Reserve rescue.

The Fed backstopped $29 billion of Bear Stearns debt so that JPMorgan could buy the firm without itself being at risk of failing. Bear Stearns's shareholders, however, were nearly wiped out. The shares had traded as high as $170 in early 2007. JPMorgan paid $10 a share in 2008.

"I think the Fed did the right thing with Bear," Buffett says. "If Bear Stearns had failed Sunday night—*which they would have*," Buffett says emphatically, "by six o'clock that night, they would have walked to a bankruptcy judge." He pauses to let that sink in, and then says, "There were $14.5 *trillion* worth of derivative contracts."

"We had four to five years to unwind the $400 *million* of derivative contracts at General Re," he reminds us. "And when we reached for them," he says, evoking what Munger called "good until reached for assets" with a hand gesture, "they weren't there."

"At Bear it would have been four or five *hours*" to unwind $14.5 trillion of contracts.

Then, in no uncertain terms, Buffett declares: "Another investment bank would have gone under in another day or two." "When the world doesn't wanna lend you money," Buffett says, "10, or 20, or 50 basis points doesn't do it," he says, meaning that merely paying a higher interest rate won't attract lenders. And if you're dependent on borrowed money, you have to wake up every day hoping when you wake up, people are gonna think well of you."

Bear Stearns—which had been in business since 1923 and had laid off no employees during the Crash of 1929—woke up one day in March 2008 . . . and virtually disappeared. It was later revealed that at the height of the crisis, Buffett had been approached about rescuing Bear Stearns. He declined. "I couldn't get my mind around that situation in the required time," he said.

> Over time, markets will do extraordinary, even bizarre, things. A single, big mistake could wipe out a long string of successes. . . . Certain perils that lurk in investment strategies cannot be spotted by the use of models commonly employed today by financial institutions.

Warren Buffett wrote those words one year before the collapse of Bear Stearns.

If the financial world had forgotten the perils that lurk and how close it came to Armageddon on Sunday, March 14, it has just been reminded.

Munger concludes with a simple, Mungerian observation: "It was a particularly foolish mess."

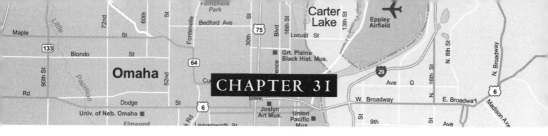

CHAPTER 31

Like Breathing

"Those are great times to make unusual amounts of money."

—WARREN BUFFETT

N

ow, as it turns out, Warren Buffett was wrong at least twice last year. First, he said that the private equity phenomenon was "not a bubble" and wouldn't burst soon; in fact, for all practical purposes, it *was* a bubble, and it burst almost as soon as the meeting was over.

At least $50 billion in announced transactions soon collapsed. And any investment bankers in the audience who took comfort from Buffett's sanguine view of the private equity mania last year are regretting it; they're stuck with over $200 billion worth of loans for private equity deals they can't get rid of. To make matters worse, just yesterday, Linens 'n Things, one of the larger private equity deals in recent years, hit the fan, unable to pay the interest on the massive debt load taken on by a private equity firm.

The bubble exploded. Private equity, for now, is quite, quite dead.

Second, Buffett told us that he didn't think the subprime crisis would cause a recession. "I don't think it'll be a huge anchor on the rest of the economy," he had said.

Yet the subprime crisis has become just that, and even Buffett himself is now saying that we are, in fact, in a recession, spawned largely by the real estate collapse and the ensuing credit crisis.

> "In my lifetime, I can't remember one where this residential real estate bubble has sent out shock waves like this one,"

> "Stupid things were done that won't be done soon again, but variations will pop up. There are these sort of *primal urges* in terms of getting rich and using leverage and wanting to believe in the tooth fairy, and sometimes they pop up on a big scale."

Still, Buffett was right in one crucial way, for both he and Munger had, in no uncertain terms, foreseen that a dislocation—something out of the blue—would occur, and that the complex financial derivatives that ultimately helped bring down Bear Stearns would be at its core.

"Someday, you will get a very chaotic situation," Buffett had said. "As to what could trigger this and when—who knows? Who had any idea that shooting an archduke would start World War I?" Whatever was to come, Berkshire was prepared: "We have good businesses, deal from strength, always have a loaded gun, and have the right managers and people and an owner-oriented culture."

Those words were spoken on May 5, 2007. And one year later, a Berkshire shareholder from Germany wants to know what Warren and Charlie have done to "take advantage of these market dislocations."

THINKING FAST AND ACTING RESOLUTELY

"There have been some really important dislocations," Buffett says, shuffling through some papers on the table. "I've brought along for your amusement a few figures on things we've done recently . . . it does illustrate just how dramatic the changes were."

He sounds almost giddy as he begins leafing through pages and calling out the tax-exempt money market funds—so-called auction-rate securities—that Berkshire bought heavily when the markets dried up early in 2008.

"Here's one, backed by the Los Angeles County Museum of Art," he says, his excitement picking up. "January 24 they were priced at 3.15 percent . . . January 31, at 4.1 percent . . . February 14, at 10 percent! Now they're back to 4.2 percent."

Now, these percentages may not seem like much, but anybody who bought these when they were yielding 10 percent, and held them while the price recovered and the yield dropped back to 4.2 percent, could have nearly *doubled* their money. In only a couple of months. Buffett shuffles through the papers and picks out a different set of securities. "On one page we bought 'em at 11.3 percent. On another page, somebody bought them at 6 percent—same day, same broker!"

He looks up from the sheets, smiling. "Those are great times to make unusual amounts of money. We have about $4 billion of this right now," he says, meaning the kind of auction-rate securities whose price movements he just described.

This is a guy who *loves* to make money.

Buffett has been talking like a kid finding quarters under a soda machine as he reviews the way Berkshire took advantage of a panicky breakdown in an obscure segment of the bond market. Munger, however, adds an analytical and philosophical note:

"What is interesting is how brief these opportunities frequently are," he says. "Somebody bought these on margin and had to dump them. . . . The dislocation was very brief, but very extreme, so if you can't think fast and act resolutely, it does you no good."

And *that's* how Berkshire has been taking advantage of the market dislocations.

DOUBLE-LAYERED PROTECTION

When people think of Warren Buffett, they think of the "Oracle of Omaha," the world's greatest investor, the man whose unparalleled 43-year track record, sage advice, and earnest deliberation attracts tens of thousands of people from around the world to Nebraska each spring for the chance to hear him speak.

Yet that is only one of the *two* roles that will need to be filled when Warren Buffett is no longer at the helm of Berkshire Hathaway. The other role is Warren Buffett, the chief executive officer, who oversees the managers in charge of the 76 or so Berkshire companies.

Most outsiders view this as Buffett's less important job, because he lets the companies run themselves. Besides, Buffett has said he has a successor as CEO lined up, even though the name hasn't been made public, and nothing should change for the Berkshire companies. And so the questions about succession focus on the four people who have been selected as candidates to succeed Buffett the *investor.*

A shareholder from Chicago asks, "What were the criteria you used to select the four people who could replace you as chief investment officer?"

"The criteria, I think, we laid out in the 2006 annual report," Buffett says, picking up the report itself and leafing through it as he speaks. "A good track record is important. Human qualities are *enormously* important. We made a qualitative judgment on four for their ability."

He finds the right page and begins reading his own carefully crafted words:

> Over time, markets will do extraordinary, even bizarre, things. A single, big mistake could wipe out a long string of successes. We therefore need someone genetically programmed to recognize and avoid serious risks, *including those never before encountered.*

"I think that proved rather prophetic," he says somewhat proudly. "You really need in the investment world someone very solid, someone you trust, with reasonable analytical skills, but also someone who can contemplate problems that haven't cropped up yet. That's a rare quality. That inability to envision something that doesn't show up can be painful."

Munger stirs in his chair. "You can see how risk-averse Berkshire is," he says. "You try and behave in a way so that no rational person is going to worry about your credit. Then you do this for a number of years and get to the point where *you don't notice* when someone does worry about your credit."

"That double-layering of protection—that's like *breathing* around Berkshire," Munger says. "The alternative culture is just the opposite. The 'chief risk officer' is the guy who makes you feel good while you do dumb things."

Buffett chimes in over the laughter from Munger's wise-crack. "We really wanna run Berkshire so that if the world is working tomorrow the way nobody thought it would work, we don't notice."

"Obviously, we could have run Berkshire with a lot more leverage—but we wouldn't have slept as well," he says, adding "We have a lot of people in this room with all their net worth in Berkshire. It would expose us to ruin and disgrace and a lot more things."

It is an unexpectedly touching and deeply personal admission.

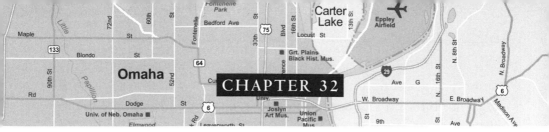

CHAPTER 32

Secrets in Plain Sight

"The most important thing to invest in is yourself . . . Very few people get the horsepower out of their life that they possess."

—WARREN BUFFETT

The "secrets" to Warren Buffett's success are hidden in plain sight. He talks about his methods freely with anybody who asks—not just here at the annual shareholders' meeting, but in his office and on the road, with student groups and television reporters, and, of course, each year in the detailed Chairman's Letter to Berkshire shareholders.

Entire *books* are devoted to the subject of how to invest like Warren Buffett.

Yet out of the roughly $12 trillion that is currently managed by American mutual funds, the amount that is managed on the rational, straightforward basis that Buffett and Munger have hewn to, with abnormal success, for the past four decades is insignificant.

As Charlie Munger observed at last year's meeting, "Our system ought to be more copied than it is."

And Munger is right, although it is no doubt far easier to make only a handful of big, rational investment decisions each year when you are sitting in a quiet room in Omaha, Nebraska, "reading and thinking" a good portion of each day than when you are sitting in a noisy trading room in Boston, New York, London, or Shanghai and feeling pressure to get with the program and trade stocks like the pros.

Still, throughout the course of the day, Buffett does his best to provide a blueprint that anyone can use.

EVALUATE THE BUSINESS FIRST, BEFORE YOU LOOK UP THE STOCK PRICE

An investor from San Francisco wants to know whether the story behind Berkshire's very profitable—and, outside this arena, controversial—investment in PetroChina, a subsidiary of the state-owned China National Petroleum Corporation, is completely true.

The story goes like this: Buffett read the PetroChina annual reports and decided that the company was dramatically undervalued. So in 2002 and 2003, he acquired 1.3 percent of PetroChina for $488 million, without visiting the company or even calling the management. "All you did was read the annual report?" the shareholder says with disbelief. "How could you make an investment based only on the annual report?"

"It was a straightforward report, just like Chevron and ConocoPhillips," Buffett answers quite matter-of-factly. "It was 2002, 2003, and I read it. I didn't talk to anybody. What I *did* do," he says, "was evaluate PetroChina's different businesses."

"It's not hard to understand their crude oil and refining and chemicals—I do that for Exxon and others. And I concluded it was worth $100 billion, and it was selling for $35 billion in the stock market. What is the point of talking to management?"

What indeed. By turning the normal method of investigating a stock on its head—looking at the business first and the price of the stock second—Buffett takes the emotion out of the decision. If the value of the business is far greater than the stock price, Buffett acts quickly.

If it isn't, he moves on.

DON'T SWEAT THE DETAILS

After Buffett determined that PetroChina was worth triple the current stock price, the next step was simple: to buy the stock.

"There's no *reason* to refine your analysis," he says. "Any further refining of analysis would be a waste of time when you should be buying the stock. If you have to carry it out to three decimal places, it isn't a good idea."

Buffett repeats a line from last year, although he uses a different weight scale this time: "If somebody walked in the door here, and they weighed somewhere between 350 and 400 pounds, I'd know they're fat."

Buffett was right, of course, that PetroChina was dramatically undervalued when he invested $488 million for Berkshire. In 2007, Buffett sold the entire position for $4 *billion.*

DON'T WORRY ABOUT THE ONES YOU MISS

"You need to be able to act quickly and decisively," a shareholder from Munich, Germany, says, and asks how Buffett determines which ideas to pursue and which not to pursue.

"There's a go/no-go signal," Buffett says, when callers pitch an idea. "Charlie and I are often thought to be rude where we cut them off in midsentence and say 'no,' but we're just trying to save their time and ours. We don't worry about the ones we miss."

"We wanna make sure we don't waste time thinking about anything where, when we're done thinking, we still can't make a decision. We can make a decision in five minutes very easily; it's just not that complicated."

STICK WITH WHAT YOU KNOW

"There's a variety of things we know about, and it's nice if we can expand that universe of knowledge," Buffett says. "But the important thing is, if we get a call, or if I'm reading a paper or an annual report or a 10-K and there's a significant difference in value, we'll move *right then.*"

"The answer to your question is, we can make a decision very quickly," Munger adds. "The reason we're able to is that there are just an *enormous* amount of other things we don't think about at all. I have a phrase I use—'We don't do start-ups.'"

"WE TEND TO PREFER THE BUSINESSES THAT *DROWN* IN CASH"

A New Yorker asks, "If you couldn't talk with management or read an annual report, but were only allowed to look at financial statements, what metric would you look at?"

"I think there's one metric that catches a lot of people," Munger says. "We tend to prefer the businesses that *drown* in cash."

"There are other businesses, like the construction equipment business," he says, telling of an old friend in that business who complained, "I work all year and there's my profit, sitting in the yard."

"DIVERSIFICATION IS FOR THE KNOW-NOTHING INVESTOR"

"Mr. Buffett, it's great to be here," an investor from New York City says. "I've read that when you were young, you were confident enough to have 25 percent or more of your net worth in one idea. Could you talk about any of those times?"

In fact, Buffett put *two-thirds* of his net worth in shares of GEICO—"my first business love," he has called it—after that famous Saturday visit with Lorimar Davidson at the company's otherwise deserted Washington, D.C. headquarters in January 1951. And his convictions haven't changed in 57 years.

"Charlie and I have been confident enough—if we were running only our own money, there have been a lot of times we'd put *75 percent* of our net worth in one idea," Buffett says.

Munger stirs. "Warren, there are times when I've put more than *100 percent* of my net worth in an idea."

"That's because you had a friendly banker," Buffett jokes, then says, quite seriously: "You will see ideas when it will be a mistake to have too little in. There will be some *extraordinary* things that will happen in a lifetime."

"You could have bought Cap Cities with Tom Murphy running it in 1974 at one-third its net value and gotten the best manager in the business," he says by way of example. "You could have put 100 percent of your net worth in Coca-Cola when we bought it and not have to worry."

"There are quite a few people in this room who've had 100 percent of their net worth in Berkshire for 40 years," Buffett adds, paying homage to the individuals who invested in Berkshire early on, "although Berkshire was not in the cinch category."

Munger can't help himself. "Students of America go to these elite business schools and law schools and learn how this is taught, and they say 'the *whole* secret of investment is diversification.' . . . they've got it ass-backwards. Diversification is for the know-nothing investor."

Buffett sums it up: "We try to load up on things."

"YOUR BEST ASSET IS YOUR OWN SELF"

Buffett gives perhaps his best advice to a teacher at an Orlando community college who asks what she should be teaching her students about financial matters.

"The most important thing to invest in is *yourself*," he says. "Very few people get the horsepower out of their life that they possess. Just imagine you're 16 and I was going to give you any car you wanted—but with one catch: it's the only car you'll get, has to last you the rest of your life."

"How would you treat it?" Buffett asks rhetorically. "You'd read the owner's manual five times; you'd change the oil twice as often as you do now. . . . And I tell students they should treat their body the same way now. It pays off in an extraordinary way."

"Your best asset is your own self," he repeats emphatically. "You can become the person you want to be. I ask classes, if you can invest in *one* of your classmates, who would you invest in? It's not the best looking, smartest—it's the most effective person."

"The habits they have today will follow them throughout life."

Buffett's own most noteworthy habits—frugality and rationality—have certainly followed him throughout his life. And they have made him, for the moment, the richest human being in the world.

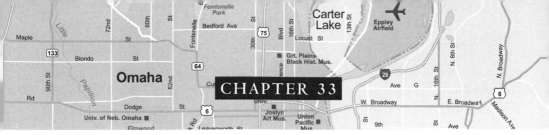

Buffett's Radar

"Warren Buffett told me, 'Don't appeal to the conscience of America, appeal to its greatness, and I think you'll get the job done.'"

—Bono, U2 Singer, on his African AIDS initiative

Not only does Warren Buffett know how to manage an investment portfolio; he also knows how to manage a crowd.

A shareholder from Oregon asks perhaps the ultimate "What would Warren do?" question: What three major problems would Warren and Charlie solve to make this a better country?

Munger reacts immediately with astonishment. "Three major problems solved in a few minutes?" he says in disbelief. "We just barely manage to stagger through *life*, and I don't think we're up to it."

As Munger sits back in his chair, to laughter and some applause, Buffett steps in to tackle the question and soothe any ruffled feathers.

Now, it is no secret that Buffett would radically alter the tax code if he suddenly found himself—as in this morning's cartoon—the secretary of the Treasury as well as the head of the Federal Reserve. In real life, he's testified before Congress, calling for a "progressive and meaningful estate tax." And he told Tom Brokaw on national television that tax policy has "tilted toward the rich and away from the middle class," and "I think it should be addressed."

But you wouldn't know that today.

Here, in front of old friends and new, Buffett tones down the fiery rhetoric and avoids all mention of "lucky sperm," his most frequently invoked pejorative for his wealthy counterparts. "I would change the tax system," he tells the Oregonian mildly, "so that the super-rich pay a little more and the middle class pay a little less."

And that's it.

Having managed not to offend *anyone*—even, I suspect, the substantial number of "lucky sperm" here in this arena who inherited either their Berkshire shares or their position running one of the many family businesses owned by Berkshire—Buffett moves on to the next question.

It's no wonder that rock stars seek his advice on how to influence American public opinion: Buffett's radar is extraordinary.

It homes in on possible rifts within the Berkshire family, senses when "Charlie" is pushing the envelope of political correctness, and distinguishes the odd fanatic from the mere eccentric.

When a disturbed shareholder from Illinois begins a rambling statement urging Buffett to "get out your copy of the U.S. constitution—everything that's going on today has to do with our constitution," Buffett quickly interrupts.

"Do you have a question?" he asks.

"Yes," the man says, pausing. "Well, no."

"I didn't think so," Buffett says, calling for the next question.

When a teacher starts with a long, rambling description of the things she has been teaching her students, however, Buffett lets her speak. As she continues talking, the crowd grows impatient, restive, and finally annoyed enough to applaud over her, to try to get her to shut up.

It is unspeakably rude, and entirely out of place here. The teacher, however, seems to misinterpret the applause as genuine approval and keeps going, but Buffett gently interrupts her: "Could you move on to your question, please?"

"Okay," she says, quietly, "what else should I be doing?"

"I'm ready to hire your entire class right *now*," Buffett says enthusiastically. This gets a laugh from the crowd and no doubt makes the teacher feel great.

"THERE'LL BE SOME CONSEQUENCES"

Sometimes Buffett's radar seems overly sensitive.

In the afternoon, Charlie Munger tells a shareholder from China, "Well, I hope you'll go back to China and tell them that you met at least one fellow who really appreciates the Confucius reverence for elderly males."

Nobody in the arena appears to take offense; Munger, being one of the most elderly males in the arena, is merely cracking a joke at his own expense.

But Buffett's radar detects a snub. "I think you should dig yourself out of that by adding *females*," he grumbles to his partner.

Munger does not see how anybody could be offended. "Well, it was Confucius's idea," he says matter-of-factly.

"No reason you can't modify it," Buffett says, moving on to the next question.

Concerned as he is about his shareholders' feelings, Buffett is also remarkably solicitous of Munger's stature.

A discussion on why the world does not have spare oil capacity leads Buffett to ask, "Charlie, what's your over/under for world oil production 25 years from today?"

This will be interesting. The arena goes quiet while Munger pauses with a far-off look and considers his partner's question for a few seconds. He finally says firmly, "Oil in 25 years, *down*."

This response provokes a kind of knee-jerk laughter from some people in the audience who were expecting a specific number, not just an "up" or "down" response. They seem to think that Munger has been holding us in suspense only to give a flip, "Charlie-being-Charlie" type of answer.

Buffett won't let the misunderstanding linger.

"That's *not* an insignificant forecast," he says quickly and firmly, signifying that his partner has just given us a serious and

considered response. The laughs die down. "China's gonna produce 10 million cars this year, so 'down in 25 years' is significant." Buffett adds, "There'll be some consequences."

Munger's partner's stature is intact.

Buffett's respect for his longtime partner's opinions runs
deeper than making sure that Charlie is not misunderstood
before a crowd of 31,000 people. When the two men happen to
disagree on a subject, Buffett will earnestly engage his partner in
dialogue to draw out why Munger thinks as he does.

It occurred once during last year's meeting, on global warming:

MUNGER: "It's not clear that it would be a disaster for all
humans, but the dislocations would be hard."

BUFFETT: "You don't think it would be a problem if the sea level
rose 15 or 20 feet?"

MUNGER: "With enough time, these things can be adjusted to."

And it happens today, when the men are asked to "share two
or three educators who influenced you."

Buffett answers the question without a pause: "The biggest educator was my father; I think Charlie would say the same thing."

Munger, however, says no such thing. "I would argue that different people learn different ways," Munger answers thoughtfully. "I learned by reading. I learned the things I wanted at the
speed that worked for me."

Buffett is obviously surprised—his eyebrows go up—and he
engages Munger on this: "You probably learned more from your
father than all the things you read, don't you think?"

"Well, yes," Munger finally says grudgingly, "but in terms of
conceptual stuff, I learned more from books."

"DO YOU KNOW JESUS CHRIST?"

Remarkable as their relationship is, it is Buffett's response to a
slim young man wearing a baseball cap who asks the most dramatic question of the day—and, potentially, the most danger-

ous—that demonstrates his extraordinary sensitivity to the collective thread that binds everyone in this large family together.

The young man stands at the microphone in the spotlight of Area 10, quietly states his name, and where he is from. It turns out he is from Norman, Oklahoma, which, as many here know, is home to the University of Oklahoma football team, a fierce rival of Nebraska.

Buffett, ever the diehard Cornhusker's fan, quips: "We won't hold that against you," But the young man does not share in the laughter. He does not even acknowledge the joke.

Instead he launches straight into his question: "Do you know and believe in Jesus Christ, and do you have a personal relationship with God?"

It is as unexpected as it is out of place, and the arena goes quiet.

Now, Buffett's religious skepticism is no secret, even though it may not be well known to many of the people in this arena. Buffett's biggest influence—his father—was deeply religious, and the family regularly attended a Presbyterian church. But the lessons backfired: Buffett famously calculated the ages of the composers of various hymns in an attempt to figure out if a religious calling led to a longer lifespan.

He concluded that it did not.

Still, Buffett does not talk much about religion publicly. Answering the question here risks opening the floodgates on the kind of "theatrics, spleen-venting, and advocacy" that mar most annual meetings—and that Buffett himself had warned against in his Chairman's Letter more than 20 years ago.

Also, we've already had three questions on the Klamath River alone, and shareholders are getting tired of the distraction. If Buffett declined to answer the young man from Norman, and instead called for a moratorium on questions that are unrelated to Berkshire, he'd probably get a standing ovation.

Surely Buffett senses this also.

But he does not decline to answer, nor does he express any rancor, aggravation, or annoyance with the question. Instead, he responds quickly and firmly. "No, I'm an agnostic," he says. "I grew up in a religious household. . . . But I'm an agnostic."

It is a remarkable moment, as unexpected as the question, yet Buffett does not leave it at that. He seems to want us all to understand him *precisely*—and at the same time make certain that *everyone* in the arena is comfortable. "And when I say, 'I'm an agnostic,'" he says, cutting the air with his hand as if to indicate that he is straight down the middle of the subject, "I'm a true agnostic. I'm not closer to one side or the other."

Buffett sits back and offers the floor to his partner. "Charlie?"

Munger is plainly annoyed by the question and comes closer to capturing the mood of the majority of the crowd. "I don't want to talk about my religion," he says flatly, and nothing else, to some rather surly applause.

Buffett, however, wants to leave the issue on a friendly, upbeat note. "Being an agnostic, I don't *have* to talk about my religion," he says, getting a few chuckles. "I wish everybody well in their own."

The crowd seems to exhale at once; the room relaxes, and Buffett calls on the next shareholder, his radar at the ready.

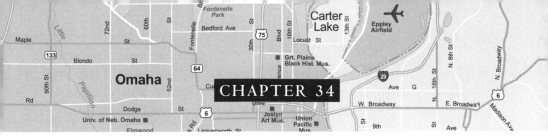

CHAPTER 34

A Family Affair

"We would like more family owners of . . . businesses, who, when they feel some need to monetize their business, think of Berkshire Hathaway."

—WARREN BUFFETT

uffett's ability to sense controversy and then work around it is extraordinary. It is also extremely important for the future of Berkshire Hathaway. After all, controversy is bad for any business, but it is doubly bad for Berkshire.

First, it is bad for Berkshire's huge reinsurance business, which provides Berkshire with much of its earnings and the "float" to invest. In the reinsurance business, a firm's reputation counts almost as much as its financial strength. Anything that tarnishes that reputation puts the business at risk.

As Buffett once wrote:

> When it's Berkshire promising, insureds know with certainty that they can collect promptly.

Second, and as Buffett himself has said, controversy is bad for his ability to attract new companies to the Berkshire family.

In many areas, including acquisitions, Berkshire's results have benefited from its reputation, and we don't want to do anything that in any way can tarnish it.

Indeed, in just a few weeks after this meeting, Buffett is going to make a highly publicized trip to Germany, Switzerland, Spain, and Italy to spread the Berkshire gospel.

Buffett's trip is on the mind of a German shareholder, who says: "May I ask what are your reasons for coming to Germany?"

"It's simple," Buffett answers. "We would like more family owners of German businesses, who, when they feel some need to monetize their business, think of Berkshire Hathaway."

"We want to be on their radar screen," he says, getting more specific as he speaks, "when they have some reason . . . to convert their ownership of a company about which they care a great deal, to think about calling us."

Anything that might cause a family owner to decide that perhaps she doesn't want to be associated with Berkshire Hathaway—such as the fraud conviction of a former CEO of a large reinsurance company that Buffett once hailed—would be bad indeed for the future of Berkshire Hathaway.

"QUALITY, INTEGRITY, PROFESSIONALISM"

Companies—especially ones owned by strong-willed individuals who care passionately about their business, not to mention want to avoid having it sold to pay estate taxes—often seek to be purchased by Warren Buffett. Some of them he buys; others don't interest him.

Those that he bought include Business Wire, NetJets, Shaw Industries, and ISCAR. The head of each of those companies wanted to sell to Warren Buffett—and *to nobody else.*

Some family-controlled companies are so eager to sell to Warren Buffett, in fact, that they accept a lower price than they might have gotten in a more public auction. These included International Dairy Queen and Benjamin Moore.

Clearly, if anything were to tarnish Berkshire's and Buffett's sterling reputations, it might give pause to families that were thinking of doing what others have done: selling their cherished business to Warren Buffett.

And just such a controversy has been on the front pages of business sections for the last year. In fact, it's the worst thing that ever happened in the Berkshire family, and it involves the company's largest acquisition: the General Re Corporation.

General Re is a reinsurance company—it insures *other* insurance companies. Usually this happens when an insurer like Allstate, which might be exposed to a catastrophic event such as a large hurricane or earthquake, decides it doesn't want to bear all the risk.

Buffett described two examples in his 1996 Chairman's Letter:

> We wrote a contract with Allstate that covers Florida hurricanes, and though there are no definitive records that would allow us to prove this point, we believe that to have then been the largest single catastrophe risk ever assumed by one company for its own account.

> Later in the year, however, we wrote a policy for the California Earthquake Authority that goes into effect on April 1, 1997, and that exposes us to a loss more than twice that possible under the Florida contract. Again we retained all the risk for our own account.

Buffett purchased General Re 10 years ago for $22 billion worth of Berkshire stock, with high hopes—but reportedly without input from Charlie Munger. Buffett rhapsodized over the purchase in his 1998 Chairman's Letter:

> For many decades, General Re's name has stood for quality, integrity and professionalism in reinsurance—and under Ron Ferguson's leadership, this reputation has been burnished still more. Berkshire can add absolutely nothing to the skills of General Re's . . . managers. On the contrary, there is a lot that they can teach us.

Pretty much everything Buffett wrote in those lines has proved wrong.

First, Berkshire spent several years and more than $400 million untangling General Re's 23,000 troublesome derivatives contracts.

Second, in February of 2008, Ron Ferguson was one of four General Re managers convicted of fraud in an alleged scheme to help another insurance company look better to Wall Street.

Third, federal prosecutors reportedly pressured Buffett to remove Ferguson's successor, Joe Brandon, as CEO shortly after the convictions. The company is on its third CEO since the acquisition.

Buffett wrote a self-critical review of General Re in his most recent Chairman's Letter, although he did not mention the scandal:

> For decades, General Re was the Tiffany of reinsurers, admired by all for its underwriting skills and discipline. This reputation, unfortunately, outlived its factual underpinnings, a flaw that I completely missed when I made the decision in 1998 to merge with General Re. The General Re of 1998 was not operated as the General Re of 1968 or 1978.

It seems hard to fathom Warren Buffett buying a company based on his impression of the business from one or two decades prior to the acquisition. But what must especially gnaw at Buffett is not that he misjudged General Re's business but that he also misjudged the *people*.

And not only that, but the actions for which those people were prosecuted took place on Buffett's own watch.

"THE WORLD NOW TURNS TO HIM"

Buffett might have done far better by simply sticking with Berkshire's homegrown reinsurance business. Known as Berkshire Hathaway Reinsurance, the business is run by Ajit Jain, a publicity-shy native of India who was working as a consultant for McKinsey & Company when Berkshire hired him in 1986.

Buffett wrote this year:

> Since joining Berkshire in 1986, Ajit has built a truly great specialty reinsurance operation from scratch. For one-of-a-kind mammoth transactions, the world now turns to him.

Those mammoth transactions provide Berkshire Hathaway Reinsurance equally mammoth premium payments, and it is the float from those premiums that makes Jain's reinsurance operation so important to the success and growth of Berkshire Hathaway.

This is the business that Charlie Munger was referring to when he said, "We've only created from scratch *one* business I can think of that became a big business—the reinsurance business—out of thin air."

Oddly enough, Ajit Jain does not live or work in Omaha. He runs the business out of a small office in Stamford, Connecticut. Yet he is probably responsible for more of Berkshire's growth in value in the last two decades than any individual except Warren Buffett.

As Buffett wrote after 9/11, "It's impossible to overstate his value to Berkshire."

He's not kidding. Buffett spent $22 billion to buy General Re, and virtually nothing to hire Ajit Jain. Yet in 2007, Jain's business generated nearly three times the profit of General Re and $23.7 billion in float compared to General Re's $23 billion.

The contrast between Ajit Jain's phenomenal success and the front-page controversy surrounding General Re couldn't be greater.

And by tarnishing Berkshire's reputation for upright behavior and Buffett's reputation for high moral standards, the General Re controversy has the potential to become bad for *future* business. As Buffett once wrote,

> At Berkshire, our carefully-crafted acquisition strategy is simply to wait for the phone to ring. Happily, it sometimes does so, usually because a manager who sold to us earlier has recommended to a friend that he think about following suit.

Yet not one shareholder has asked about the General Re convictions, or the CEO change, or the disappointing earnings, or the fact that Buffett paid $22 billion in shares of precious Berkshire stock—which now have a value close to $37 billion—for a poorly run company in a business Buffett knows better than almost anyone alive.

I can't wait to tell Chris.

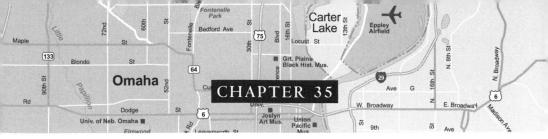

CHAPTER 35

The Berkshire
Flea Market

—⌒—

"*I'm your bank.*"

—Warren Buffett

I

t is Saturday afternoon, just a minute or two before 3
o'clock, and the Berkshire shareholders' meeting is
now over.

Buffett concluded nearly five and a half hours worth of questions and answers on a reflective, almost emotional note, and
then he and Charlie received a standing ovation from everybody
in the Qwest Center. Even the directors in the VIP area right in
front of the stage stood and cheered.

Buffett, Munger, and the directors, of course, have to stay
around for the brief business portion of the Berkshire board
meeting. The rest of us are stretching our legs, packing up our
gear, and making our way out of the arena doors, onto the escalators and down to the street level of the Qwest Center.

Shareholders from overseas, meanwhile, are lining up at a special desk set up in the lobby outside the exhibition hall to have

their credentials checked before their 4 p.m. meet-and-greet with Buffett and Munger.

I head into the exhibition hall to buy a keepsake of the meeting.

BOOTS, BRICKS, AND BENJAMIN MOORE

It is, not surprisingly, full of men and women buying Berkshire Hathaway T-shirts at the Fruit of the Loom store, trying on a pair of Justin Boots, and having their picture taken in front of a giant, colorful portrait of Warren Buffett that was painted this morning by an artist who used only Berkshire-owned Benjamin Moore paints.

Nearby is the tail of a long line that snakes in between the various exhibits, seemingly halfway around the hall. I follow it to its conclusion at a Wrigley booth, where packs of gum are being given away to celebrate Berkshire's investment in Mars's acquisition of Wrigley earlier this week. You'd have thought Buffett himself was giving away stock tips—the line is that long.

The Wrigley gum might just be the first and only freebie ever provided to Berkshire shareholders in the entire history of the Berkshire shareholders' meeting—outside, of course, Warren and Charlie's question-and-answer session.

Nevertheless, the product of that remarkable partnership is Warren Buffett's flea market made visible here inside the exhibition hall .

Products and services from Berkshire Hathaway's "76 or so, for the most part, wonderful darn businesses," as Buffett described them today, are on display, stretching to all four corners of the hall.

They range from the quaint and outdated, such as *World Book Encyclopedia*, to the modern and self-indulgent, such as NetJets.

The scope of these businesses is staggering to contemplate.

- MidAmerican, Berkshire's energy business, owns natural gas pipelines, electric utilities, and those infamous dams on the Klamath River.

- Acme makes bricks; Benjamin Moore, paint; Clayton, manufactured housing; Forest River, recreational vehicles; Fruit of the Loom, underwear; Johns Manville, insulation; Justin Boots, footwear; Kirby, vacuum cleaners; the Pampered Chef, kitchenware; See's, candies; and Shaw Industries, carpets.

- International Dairy Queen sells ice cream, NetJets sells air travel. McLane sells groceries, and ISCAR sells machine tool components.

- Nebraska Furniture Mart, Jordan's Furniture in New England, R.C. Willey of Utah, and Star Furniture of Houston sell mainly home furnishings. Borsheim's, Ben Bridge, and Helzberg Diamonds sell jewelry.

Near the center of it all sits a GEICO insurance counter, where shareholders are lined up to get discounted rates on their car insurance.

So too does the insurance business sit at the center of Berkshire Hathaway.

And just as all these companies here in the exhibition hall offer their wares from separate booths, they all operate independently of one another, almost exactly as they did before Buffett bought them.

"THE CEOS DON'T KNOW ONE ANOTHER."

In fact, only one thing changes when Berkshire acquires a company, and it changes overnight: all the cash, except what the company needs to run its business, goes to Berkshire's bank account. As the Helzberg Diamonds CEO, Jeff Comment, told Robert P. Miles, author of the excellent book *The Warren Buffett CEO: Secrets from the Berkshire Hathaway Managers*:

> The only change that really took place happened the day after we were purchased. Warren called me up and said, "Guess what you get to do today." And I said, "What's that?" And he said, "Start breaking all your banking relationships, because from now on I'm your bank."

Now, Warren Buffett is not going to buy a company without keeping an eye on it. And the way he keeps an eye on the Berkshire companies is through a simple statement of figures the companies send him each month.

They do not report through a chain of command. They report to Warren Buffett. And the different Berkshire companies, even those in the same business—don't talk much among themselves.

Indeed, author Miles included a remarkable note in his preface to *The Warren Buffett CEO*:

> In addition to wanting to produce a book that would appeal to as many readers as possible, I felt some pressure to provide a book that each Buffett CEO would enjoy reading. In general, the CEOs don't know one another.

He isn't kidding.

In August 2000, Barry Tatelman, the CEO of Jordan's Furniture—one of four Berkshire home furnishings retailers—told author Miles:

> The other stores hadn't been doing anything as a group. They'd never even gotten together for a meeting.

"A WIDELY USED TERM TO EXPLAIN AN ACQUISITION THAT MAKES NO SENSE"

Now, more meetings don't necessarily make better companies. In fact, for strong-headed, independent businesspeople of the type Warren Buffett wants running his companies, the opposite holds true. Meetings lead to consensus building, and consensus building often leads to a kind of group-think that Buffett himself calls "the institutional imperative."

"The institutional imperative" is a label Buffett created to describe the tendency of big corporations to do stupid things out of simple inertia, regardless of whether the end result is actually good. Buffett wants no hint of an "institutional imperative" in his family.

And don't even get him started on "synergies," which he calls "a term widely used in business to explain an acquisition that otherwise makes no sense."

Ironically, Buffett violated his own tenet when he bought General Re, enthusiastically playing up the notion in the press release announcing the 1998 transaction:

But the main attraction of the merger is synergy, a word that heretofore has never been used in listing the reasons for a Berkshire acquisition. In this transaction, however, there are at least four areas of powerful synergy, which Charles Munger, Berkshire's Vice Chairman, and I believe justify the premium price that Berkshire is paying.

While General Re may have proved Buffett's original point about synergies—they're no reason to acquire a company—it doesn't mean that businesses shouldn't *talk* to one another for the sake of sharing ideas. Especially when, like Berkshire's furniture retailers, they share the same business.

And in fact some of the Berkshire retail companies wouldn't mind a little back and forth. In *The Warren Buffett CEO,* Borsheim's CEO, Susan Jacques, cited almost a dozen:

> There are synergies for buying, credit card processing, and extension of credit. There are also inventory and inventory management, compensation, and appraisals, shop repairs, and industry-related issues. I think there is a tremendous amount we could do together.

The companies here at the exhibition hall don't seem to be doing much *together*, but they're certainly doing a lot of business, which is all that matters to my fellow shareholders.

I don't find anything worth buying, and I'm not going to stand in line for a pack of *gum*. I leave the hall and get in my Toyota—with automatic door locks; no climbing over the seat required—and drive west.

It's time for a follow-up visit to the flagship location of one of Warren Buffett's favorite companies in the world.

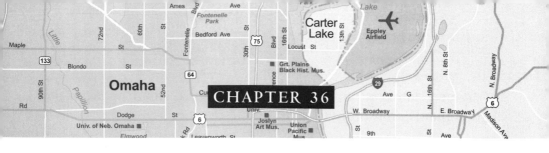

CHAPTER 36

Decline and Fall of the Sainted Seven

"Do you want to have a company with high profitability but okay growth, or a global company with okay profitability?"

—Shareholder from Germany

If the shareholders asking questions today knew more about Warren Buffett than they did about Berkshire Hathaway's 76 different companies, it's a certainty they couldn't name which seven of those companies made up Berkshire Hathaway's core noninsurance business 20 years ago.

For the record, those seven companies were World Book Encyclopedia, the *Buffalo News*, the Kirby vacuum cleaner company, the Fechheimer work uniform company, Scott Fetzer Manufacturing (Ginsu knives, among other things), See's Candies, and what was probably Buffett's pride and joy: Nebraska Furniture Mart, which called itself "The Largest Home Furnishings Store in North America."

In 1987, Buffett dubbed them the "Sainted Seven."

A year later, earnings from those seven companies were so good that Buffett proudly wrote:

In 1988 the Saints came marching in.

After buying Borsheim's in 1989, Buffett changed the title of "this divine assemblage" to "The Sainted Seven Plus One." It was the last time Buffett would mention these companies as a group in his letters.

This is partly because they soon became overshadowed by the many billions of dollars worth of increasingly large companies he would acquire.

Mainly, however, it is simply because several are in decline. Of the original seven, only See's Candies earns enough money to even be *mentioned* in the "Management Discussion" of Berkshire's financials, and World Book Encyclopedia has almost disappeared entirely.

See's Candies aside, as a group, "The Sainted Seven" has not come marching in for years.

And it is in the cavernous electronics superstore on the grounds of the Nebraska Furniture Mart that I begin to understand why.

"WE THINK THEY ARE ABOUT THE BEST THERE IS."

If Buffett's 1967 purchase of National Indemnity demonstrated the value of owning an insurance company for its float, and Buffett and Munger's 1972 purchase of See's Candies demonstrated the value of paying up for a great business, then Buffett's 1983 purchase of Nebraska Furniture Mart probably demonstrated the value of owning a business run by a maniacally customer-focused proprietor—in this case, the remarkable Rose Blumkin—and leaving it alone.

Nebraska Furniture Mart under "Mrs. B" and her children struck awe in competitors—so much so that Dillard's department store chain actually decided *not* to sell furniture when it first came to Omaha. "We don't want to compete with them," Buffett delightedly quoted the Dillard chairman as saying in his 1988 Chairman's Letter. "We think they are about the best there is."

The Blumkins not only struck fear in the hearts of their competitor but also helped Warren Buffett build Berkshire's large home furnishings business by identifying for him other choice acquisition candidates in the field. R.C. Willey of Utah, Star Furniture of Texas, and Jordan's Furniture of Massachusetts all came to Buffett, in one way or another, at the suggestion of Irv Blumkin.

Today, the original Nebraska Furniture Mart still thrives in its original location at 72nd Street and Rose Blumkin Drive, a jumble of huge buildings that is now surrounded by strip malls and other "big-box" retailers, including a Best Buy and a Target.

And Buffett would be happy to know that the Furniture Mart complex looks every bit as busy today as it did after last year's shareholders' meeting, but with one big difference from last year: the electronics store has been refurbished.

Gone are the giant warehouse-club-style metal racks of big-screen televisions and the long, straight, bland rows of music CDs, digital cameras, and appliances. In their place are sleek, angular fake-wood displays holding digital camcorders and notebook computers, with wide aisles curving past Dyson vacuum cleaner displays, sound rooms, and tricked-out designer kitchens. High-end boutiques house Apple, Bose, and Sony gear, while at the far end of the store digital television screens cover one entire wall, flashing bright, crisp images.

What seemed like a crowded, out-of-date store when Chris Wagner and I walked through it last year is now bright, clean, airy, and modern.

In fact, it looks a lot like a Best Buy.

About the only thing that hasn't changed is what the sales clerk is using to look up inventory: the old-fashioned computer screen with the blinking white cursor and block letters, the same as Chris and I saw here last year. "It's our own system," the salesman says proudly, when I ask him about it. "We developed it in 1992."

"That's a long time ago," I observe.

"Yeah, but it's stable!" he says cheerily.

"A MANAGERIAL STORY YOU WILL NEVER READ ELSEWHERE"

One more thing that hasn't changed from last year: the banners in the parking lot. Heading to my car, I notice the old, faded Compaq and Kenmore signs that we saw, and mocked, last year.

Chris won't believe it when I tell him.

Or maybe he will. Students of Buffett know the story of R.C. Willey, a home furnishings store based in Utah, acquired by Berkshire in 1995.

Willey is run by Mormons and does not open on Sundays. Bill Child, the CEO, wanted to open a store in Boise, Idaho, but Buffett resisted. Buffett wrote about it in his 1999 Chairman's Letter, "A Managerial Story You Will Never Read Elsewhere":

> I was highly skeptical about taking a no-Sunday policy into a new territory where we would be up against entrenched rivals open seven days a week. . . .
>
> Bill then insisted on a truly extraordinary proposition: He would personally buy the land and build the store—for about $9 million as it turned out—and would sell it to us at his cost if it proved to be successful.

The Idaho store was a success and Child sold it to Berkshire. Mormon or not, Bill Child subsequently opened more R.C. Willey stores outside Utah, including one in *Las Vegas*.

To Warren Buffett, the R.C. Willey story is a wonderful demonstration of personal integrity in the business world.

To anybody else reading the story, it is also a demonstration of how hard it must be to spend Warren Buffett's money. As Buffett wrote of the Berkshire managers in his 1990 Chairman's Letter:

> In the past five years they have funneled well over 80% of their earnings to Charlie and me for use in new business and investment opportunities.

And while he declared in that same letter that "this does not mean that our managers are in any way skimping on investments that strengthen their business franchises or that promote growth," it is no wonder, I think, that the Nebraska Furniture Mart of 2008 is only now getting up to speed with Best Buy in its electronics store.

In the 25 years since Buffett acquired the business, Nebraska Furniture Mart has opened precisely two new locations—Kansas City and Des Moines. And while all three stores pack them in— sales per location averaged $400 million in 2007—the business is a shadow of what it might have been in different hands.

Today, while Best Buy is doing $40 billion in sales from over 1,000 stores, busily expanding in Canada, and experimenting in China, Nebraska Furniture Mart is doing a bit over $1 billion in sales from three locations and has been busy refurbishing its original electronics store to look more like, well, Best Buy.

THE GREAT, THE GOOD, AND THE GRUESOME

If shareholders were not going to bring up the recent troubles at General Re at today's meeting, there were certainly not going to ask Warren Buffett whether his frugal spending habits discourage Berkshire businesses from realizing their full potential.

After all, who in their right mind would want to debate the "Oracle of Omaha" on his capital allocation decisions in front of 31,000 people? Yet the subject did come up, in a subtle way, thanks to one of those many Germans who packed the microphones this morning.

"I have a question regarding the chocolate industry," this particular man said. "I cannot buy See's candy in my hometown of Bonn, Germany," he explained, so instead he buys chocolate made by a Swiss company called Lindt & Sprüngli.

He said he doesn't understand why See's remained a small chocolate company while "Lindt went global."

"Do you want to have a company with high profitability but okay growth" like See's, he asked Buffett, "or a global company with okay profitability" like Lindt?

It was easily the most insightful question of the day.

See's Candies has been enormously lucrative for Berkshire, as Buffett highlighted in several rapturous paragraphs in this year's Chairman's Letter, within an essay on businesses titled "The Great, the Good and the Gruesome."

See's, of course, was an example of "the Great" kind of business, producing $1.35 billion in profits since Berkshire acquired it in 1972, and requiring only $32 million to expand its buildings and buy equipment. Of the $1.35 billion, Buffett exults:

> *All of that*, except for the $32 million, has been sent to Berkshire . . . After paying corporate taxes . . . we have used the rest to buy other attractive businesses.

As the German shareholder implied, what has been good for Berkshire Hathaway's shareholders—sending all its spare cash to the world's greatest investor—may not have been good for See's Candies.

Just as Nebraska Furniture Mart is now hemmed in by the rapid growth of other well-managed big-box retailers, See's is hemmed in by global chocolate companies such as Lindt & Sprüngli, a small, Swiss chocolate maker that has grown into a $3 billion global force.

It's no wonder that the German shareholder can't buy See's in Bonn, Germany: only two of See's 200 U.S. stores are east of the Mississippi River.

"We want a business with a durable competitive advantage, management we trust, at a price that we understand," Buffett answered, repeating his well-worn mantra, but not answering the question. "We've probably looked at every confectionary company we can over the last 20 years." It was the only time all day Buffett has dodged the heart of the question.

And it's a shame, because it was a bloody great one.

FAMILY MATTERS

I begin writing up the day's notes at a Starbucks down the street from the Furniture Mart.

Starbucks was not in existence when Berkshire bought See's in 1972. The coffee chain did not even expand outside Seattle until 1987, the year Buffett anointed his "Sainted Seven." Yet Starbucks today has more than 15,000 stores around the world and generates more pretax income every three *months* than See's does in a year.

If a small, regional coffee brand from Seattle, Washington, can become a worldwide brand, I wonder as I swig my coffee, why not See's chocolates?

It could have something to do with the fact that Berkshire companies send their spare cash to Warren Buffett.

It could also have something to do with Buffett's hands-off management style, which leaves most decision making to the longtime managers of the Berkshire companies. In some cases, these managers include second and third generations of families—Nebraska Furniture Mart being a prime example.

Buffett's fondness for family-run companies is as exuberant as it is vocal. In his 1983 letter he praised Rose Blumkin—"Mrs. B"—and her children extravagantly:

> And what managers they are. Geneticists should do handsprings over the Blumkin family. . . . We are delighted to be in partnership with them.

With similar pride, after buying Borsheim's jewelry store from Ike Friedman, he wrote:

> All members of the Friedman family will continue to operate just as they have before; Charlie and I will stay on the sidelines where we belong. And when we say "all members," the words have real meaning. Mr. and Mrs. Friedman, at 88 and 87, respectively, are in the store daily. The wives of Ike, Alan, Marvin and Donald all pitch in at busy times, and a fourth generation is beginning to learn the ropes.

Yet this infatuation with family businesses seems to run counter to Buffett's own ideas about "meritocracy." As he said at the announcement of his gift to the Bill & Melinda Gates Foundation in 2006:

I can't think of anything that's more counter to the idea of a meritocracy than dynastic wealth. I mean the idea that you win the lottery the moment you're born if you come from the right womb, it
just strikes me as outrageous.

Is being from "the right womb" less outrageous if your family
happens to run a jewelry store or a furniture store?

Would Berkshire and its shareholders have been better off if
Warren Buffett had insisted on the kind of strict meritocracy in
his businesses that he would like to see in *all* companies?

Did a family-run big-box furniture store from Omaha miss the
chance to become a dominant national business because it was
family run?

I finish writing up the day's notes at Starbucks and get a call
from Jim, a longtime Berkshire investor who made the pilgrimage to Omaha this year at my suggestion. He is calling about dinner. "Anthony's Steakhouse," he tells me. "They say that if we
get there by 6 o'clock, we should be okay."

That's good, because I'm hungry, and we have a lot to discuss.

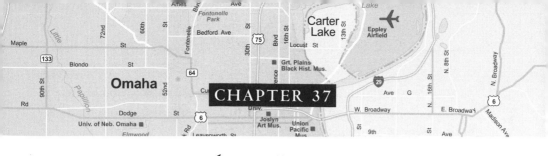
The "Yes" Won't Change

> "The $6.5 billion [Berkshire financing for Mars's purchase of Wrigley] will be available whether a nuclear bomb goes off in New York City, or whether Ben Bernanke runs off with Paris Hilton."
>
> —WARREN BUFFETT

I meet Jim outside Anthony's Steakhouse a little after 6 p.m., and the parking lot, which seems endless, is packed as far as the eye can see. Same thing inside. "It's an hour wait," the lady tells us, "unless you want to eat in the bar."

We do.

The service is quick and friendly, and we get a chance to review the day.

"Were we really that close to a financial meltdown?" Jim asks.

Jim is a dentist. I run a hedge fund. But we're both a little shocked at Buffett's matter-of-fact account of how close we had come to some kind of financial Armageddon in March:

"If Bear Stearns had failed Sunday night—which they *would* have, by six o'clock that night . . . Another investment bank would have gone under in another day or two."

Jim shakes his head. He can't get over Buffett's ability to simplify any investment concept down to its absolute essence, and make it clear for anyone to grasp. He mentions one in particular: "how television expanded the baseball field."

When Buffett was asked by a nine-year-old boy, the youngest shareholder of the day, whether he might buy the Chicago Cubs baseball team, he first explained why owning a baseball team like the Cubs became so profitable after the advent of television and cable TV:

"In effect, television has expanded the *field*. You had 40,000 seats available when I went to my first baseball game there in 1949, and then television came along and then cable television came along, and that expanded the *stadium*. Now, a lot of that money went to the players, but some of that stuck to the owners."

And it was like that for the better part of five hours. Buffett stripped down concepts ranging from investing for beginners to nuclear proliferation to their bare essence:

WHAT IT MEANS TO INVEST

"What we're doing in an investment is we're laying out money *now* to get *more* money back in the future."

WHAT HE LOOKS FOR IN A BUSINESS

"We want a business with a durable competitive advantage, management we trust, at a price that we understand."

WHY HE DOESN'T HIRE AUDITORS WHEN HE BUYS A BUSINESS

"If you think the auditors know more about making an acquisition than you do, you ought to take up accounting and let the auditors run the business."

ON EGREGIOUS CORPORATE COMPENSATION

"The idea that you have to pay some guy a $10 million retention bonus to keep him around—I don't know of a CEO in America that wouldn't gladly do the job at half the price or a quarter of the price."

HOW TO CHANGE EGREGIOUS CORPORATE COMPENSATION

"If the half dozen largest institutions would simply withhold their votes and issue a short statement why they're doing it, it would work. Big shots don't like to get embarrassed."

WHAT A SMALL INVESTOR SHOULD DO TO START INVESTING

"Put it all in a low-cost index fund, like Vanguard."

WHEN "YES" WON'T CHANGE

"We got a call [from Mars, to finance the purchase of Wrigley] and we said 'yes.' I can tell people 'yes,' and that won't change. The $6.5 billion will be available whether a nuclear bomb goes off in New York City, or whether Ben Bernanke runs off with Paris Hilton."

WHY THE DERIVATIVES MARKET GOT OUT OF HAND

"You had to read 750,000 pages to evaluate one security, and that was madness."

WHEN REGULATION FAILED

"We had this organization called OFHEO [Office of Federal Housing Enterprise Oversight] whose sole purpose was to oversee two companies, Fannie Mae and Freddie Mac . . . They had 200 people going to work at nine every morning, whose sole job was to oversee Fannie Mae and Freddie Mac, and they had two of the biggest financial scams ever, so they were two for two."

WHY MASS TRANSIT ISN'T USED

"The American public doesn't like mass transit. I used to be involved in bus companies, and you can make all kinds of rational arguments to people about mass transit. But one person per car seems to be an enormously popular method of moving around."

WHY THE CHINA OLYMPICS SHOULDN'T BE BOYCOTTED

"We didn't let women vote in the U.S. until the 1920s, and I would say that was a great human rights violation, and I would have hated to see the U.S. banned from the Olympics prior to 1920."

WHY NUCLEAR PROLIFERATION IS STILL A THREAT

"The genie is out of the bottle. . . . That's the problem of mankind. You've got 6.5 billion people in the world, so there are close to twice as many people that wish ill on other people as you had when the population was 3 billion."

THE MOST IMPORTANT JOB IN LIFE

"I tell students the most important job you have is your children. You provide warmth and food, and they're learning about the world . . . and you don't get any rewind button."

As it turns out, Jim and I made a good move eating here in the bar. The food was great, and tables in the dining room are turning *very* slowly.

I get the check and almost laugh out loud: my club soda cost $1.50. In New York it would have been $5.00. No wonder Buffett lives here.

Jim looks around the crowded room and wonders what percentage of the customers here are Berkshire shareholders.

I guess one-third. Jim guesses 50 percent. We ask the waitress. She tells us it's probably more like 80 percent.

The Berkshire shareholder meeting is more than a pilgrimage for 31,000 investors: it's big business here in Omaha.

CHAPTER 38

Yesterday I Died

"Warren doesn't plan to leave very early. I always say, when people ask what Warren Buffett wants said at his funeral: 'that's the oldest looking corpse I ever saw.'"

—CHARLIE MUNGER

W arren Buffett has been planning his death for years. "I've already sent out a letter that tells what should be done," he told an audience of students at the University of Washington a decade ago, when he was in his late sixties. "And I've got another letter that's addressed that will go out at the time, and it starts out, 'Yesterday I died,' and then tells what the plans of the company are."

First and foremost among those plans, no doubt, is replacing Buffett as the head, heart, and soul of Berkshire Hathaway, if such a thing can be done. His role, as he has said many times, will be split in two: a chief investment officer, to make investment decisions; and a chief executive officer, to oversee the operating businesses.

Buffett and the board have identified the candidates for both roles, but they are not naming names until the time comes.

In addition to naming his replacements, Buffett also wants to maintain Buffett family control over Berkshire affairs. "I'd view it as a tragedy," he told *BusinessWeek* in 1999, "if someone whose achievement was issuing the most junk bonds or having the silliest stock price took over the company and all that we've built evaporated."

Buffett's desire to protect what he has created is natural enough—but it is at odds with his own strong belief that companies ought to do what shareholders want. In the 2004 Chairman's Letter, he wrote with scorn of one public company board of directors—which he did not identify—that scuttled a takeover offer without disclosing it to shareholders:

> I have first-hand knowledge of a recent acquisition proposal (not from Berkshire) that was favored by management, blessed by the company's investment banker and slated to go forward at a price above the level at which the stock had sold for some years (or now sells for). In addition, a number of directors favored the transaction and wanted it proposed to shareholders.
>
> Several of their brethren, however . . . scuttled the proposal, which meant that shareholders never learned of this multi-billion offer.

Nevertheless, Buffett put his first wife, Susan, on the Berkshire board of directors in 1991, and their son, Howard, two years later, in order to maintain Buffett family control over Berkshire Hathaway.

Buffett had expected that his wife would outlive him, but she did not: Susan T. Buffett died of a stroke in 2004, less than a year after being diagnosed with mouth cancer, and only a few months after attending her last Berkshire Hathaway shareholders' meeting.

Asked by a New Jersey shareholder at today's meeting what safeguards Berkshire has against "a hedge fund or some activist" trying to break up the company after he is gone, Buffett appeared quite sanguine.

"My stock will be sold over a 12-year period after my death," he said, adding, "You'll still have large blocks held by people who have the same philosophy as I have. It'll be about as unlikely with Berkshire as any company I can think of."

It is not merely the influence of controlling shareholders that could stop a hostile run against Berkshire. "If you look out," Buffett said, "with compounding it would be a $600 to $700 billion deal."

As Buffett spoke those words, the market value of Berkshire was roughly $200 billion. If the price of Berkshire stock grew at 10 percent annually—less than half the rate of the last 43 years, but still staggering for such a large company—the value of Berkshire would reach Buffett's "$600 to $700 billion" deal size in about 12 years.

What might Berkshire look like in 12 years, besides being very, very big?

GOOD, *NOT* GREAT

For starters, Buffett could very well remain at the helm that long. Despite a famously atrocious diet—he reportedly salts his hamburger after every bite—12 years was the "expected lifespan" that Buffett gave himself in a letter to shareholders written early in 2007 before adding "(though, naturally, I'm aiming for more)."

With Buffett still running the company, Berkshire would probably look very much like it does today: an insurance giant with a growing set of industrial and energy businesses and a diminished collection of consumer brands, operating increasingly outside the United States.

The acquisition of ISCAR, an Israeli company, in particular, seems to have fired Buffett's appetite for foreign-based industrial businesses. "By the way," he volunteered during the shareholders' meeting, "I had very high expectations for ISCAR when we bought it, and they've been exceeded. It's been a *dream* acquisition."

Buffett's upcoming European tour, in fact, was planned in part by the CEO of ISCAR.

The outlook for Berkshire's nonindustrial businesses—other than Ajit Jain's insurance franchise—is probably mixed at best.

While Warren Buffett advises investors to buy companies with durable competitive advantages and strong brand names, the fact is that Berkshire doesn't own too many of them.

NetJets, for example, is an extremely well managed company—as at least one recent user can attest—but the private jet business will always be very sensitive to the business cycle. FlightSafety International, which Buffett held out as an example of a "Good"—but *not* "Great"—business in his recent letter, is somewhat dependent on the health of the notoriously unhealthy airline industry.

Carpet giant Shaw Industries appears to have underperformed its nearest, and best, competitor, Mohawk Industries, in the five years since Berkshire completed the Shaw acquisition. And Shaw is likely to remain at the mercy of the cyclical U.S. housing market, along with other Berkshire companies such as Acme (bricks) and Johns Manville (insulation).

Berkshire's retailing group, while it includes impressive individual brands such as Borsheim's and See's, may well suffer from the lack of reinvestment that appears to have stifled Nebraska Furniture Mart's potential over the last 25 years.

Dairy Queen, which is a terrific brand name and should be one of the "Great" businesses, has structural problems in its franchise arrangements that may never allow it to perform up to its potential. Fruit of the Loom and Russell Corporation, which together employed more people than any other Berkshire operation at the end of 2007 and are under extreme competition from low-cost overseas competitors.

So far, whatever problems might lurk beneath the surface at Berkshire have been more than made up for by Warren Buffett's seemingly uncanny ability to buy new companies and find profitable new investment ideas, mainly by staying rational at all times and having a partner whose judgment he respects to keep him that way.

Not to mention probably the world's best Rolodex. Who, after all, would refuse a phone call or a meeting with the "Oracle of Omaha"?

"IT'S LIKE A FATHER"

Without Warren Buffett, the picture in Berkshire in 12 years or longer becomes far less clear. "I can't do without Berkshire," Buffett said as he took the stage before the morning session began.

And Berkshire very likely can't do without Warren Buffett.

First, every one of the major companies in the Berkshire "family"—from National Indemnity in 1967 to Marmon Holdings in 2007—was acquired either by Warren Buffett and Charlie Munger or by Warren Buffett alone. Will Berkshire Hathaway be able to attract major new acquisitions without those men?

Second, most of the CEOs running Berkshire's "76 or so, in the most cases, wonderful darn businesses," report directly to Warren Buffett. Except at the annual meeting, they do not appear to mingle much with other Berkshire Hathaway managers.

And why would they? Those CEOs love having a direct relationship with Warren Buffett. NetJets founder Rich Santulli—often mentioned as a successor to Buffett in his role as chief executive officer—described it this way to the *Nightly Business Report's* Susie Gharib on "Working with Warren":

> We work for Warren Buffett, or at least I do. It's like a father. You just really want to show Warren that you really are capable of providing for him the returns that he expected when he bought your company. And . . . you feel good when he writes you a note saying great job.

Gone will be the handwritten notes for a job well done—unless Buffett, in his zeal for rational planning, has stockpiled a batch for his successor to dole out at the appropriate times.

Gone too will be the nifty private jet trip to Augusta National for the inaugural round of golf that Warren plays with the CEO of each newly acquired company.

Gone also will be the chance to pick up the phone and speak with one of the most perceptive minds in the world—and not merely the business world. "The fact that I can pick up the phone and talk to him is invaluable," Stan Lipsey of the *Buffalo News* told author Robert P. Miles.

And, depending on the man—for it is almost certainly a man who will replace Buffett as CEO—gone will be the ability to run your own company without budgets, without anything but "applause."

> At Berkshire, our carefully-crafted acquisition strategy is simply to wait for the phone to ring.

Will the phone at Berkshire still ring when Warren Buffett is no longer there to pick it up?

And will 31,000 people travel to Omaha to listen to Rich Santulli or David Sokol or Ajit Jain—the speculated successors to Warren Buffett as CEO—answer questions from shareholders?

The waitress at Anthony's Steakhouse certainly hopes so. And so do a lot of other people around Omaha.

CHAPTER 39

His Fondest Hope

⌐⌐⌐

"What is your fondest hope for Berkshire?"

—BERKSHIRE SHAREHOLDER, TO WARREN BUFFETT
AND CHARLIE MUNGER

I t is 7 a.m. on Sunday, May 4, at Eppley Airfield in Omaha, Nebraska, and what seems like a significant portion of the 31,000 people who attended the Berkshire Hathaway shareholders' weekend are attempting to leave right *now*.

In fact, the security line at the north terminal of Eppley is almost as long as the food lines at the concession stands at the Qwest Center yesterday. Or maybe it just seems that way because on my previous flight—NetJets, that is—there *was* no security line.

I don't particularly mind the wait, however. I bought a copy of *Barron's*, the weekly financial newspaper, at the Hudson's Bookseller—the one with the Warren Buffett books on the tables, in the windows, and on the counter. (There was even an auto-graphed copy of Roger Lowenstein's biography of Buffett for sale.) And the cover story of *Barron's* is about Warren Buffett.

Once through security, I see that our plane is at the gate; the sky outside is clear and blue, and United Airlines Flight 568 will be leaving Omaha for Chicago on time. So I settle down with a cup of coffee and the *Barron's* cover story, which was obviously timed for this particular weekend. "The Next Warren Buffett," it says. And the article inside minces no words:

> Who will fill the biggest shoes in Corporate America? *Barron's* believes the succession situation at Berkshire has become clearer in the past two months: The next CEO is likely to be David Sokol, chairman of MidAmerican Energy, the big Berkshire unit that owns electric utilities in the Midwest, Pacific Northwest and Britain, as well as two U.S. natural-gas pipelines.

According to *Barron's*, Sokol—who spoke three times at yesterday's meeting—is the likely choice because he is relatively young (51), smart, and a business operator as well as a deal maker. And Buffett, the article says, admires him greatly.

Two other frequently mentioned CEO candidates, NetJets founder Rich Santulli and GEICO CEO Tony Nicely, may be a little too old, according to *Barron's*. Buffett supposedly wants somebody who can be at the helm a long time.

The newspaper also writes off Ajit Jain, the scary-smart insurance ace who very likely has made more money for Berkshire than any individual besides Warren Buffett:

"He has never run a large organization, shuns publicity and may lack the temperament to run a huge company."

The speculation is, of course, interesting. It is also, I believe, misguided.

After Warren Buffett, everything at Berkshire will change, and probably not for the better.

Companies that might have sold out to Warren Buffett at a discount to what they'd fetch elsewhere might hesitate to sell to David Sokol or Rich Santulli or Tony Nicely or even Ajit Jain. After all, how could any one of those men possibly guarantee another 43 years of hands-off management at the top of Berkshire Hathaway?

Furthermore, the "76 or so" companies that are already part of the Berkshire "family" will come under a new, and possibly unwelcome, scrutiny. This is because every one of those companies is one of Warren Buffett's babies. Would a new CEO have the same attachment to—and patience with—Fruit of the Loom, say, or Dairy Queen, or any of the other underperforming members of the Berkshire family as Warren Buffett?

Finally, what happens at those companies if Warren Buffett's replacement as Berkshire's chief investment officer can't keep up Buffett's investment track record? Will they willingly send their cash to Berkshire if the Next Buffett doesn't invest it as brilliantly as Buffett himself did?

I stick the article in my ever-expanding Berkshire Hathaway folder. Buffett's response to the final question of the day—a question so fitting that it is easy to forget that the questions weren't screened in advance—comes back as I watch the United ticket agents get ready for boarding. His words now seem more poignant than prescient.

"WHAT WE'VE TRIED TO BUILD"

"What is your fondest hope for Berkshire?" a woman from California asks in a soft, earnest voice, and the arena goes very quiet.

"That the decent performance and the culture are maintained," Warren Buffett says crisply, but with a surprising amount of sentimentality in his voice. "That we're both shareholder- and management-oriented."

"I fully expect that what we've tried to build into Berkshire will live far beyond my tenure here," he continues. "We have a board and a group of managers who have seen that the system works. I think we have as strong a culture as exists in a company."

"My hope," he says, "is that 20 years from now, if someone has a fine business they've spent generations building, that they *immediately* think if they have to sell this business that Berkshire Hathaway is the home for that business."

Munger, who is not given to expressions of sentimentality, stirs in his chair and speaks:

"I would say that I would like to see Berkshire even more deserve to be an exemplar, and I would like to see it have more actual influence on changes in other corporations."

Buffett, as he always seems to do, ends the answer and the session on a light note, with a joke that draws laughter and then an ovation that brings the entire audience to its feet:

"We'd also like to see it have the oldest living managers."

To the casual listener, Charlie Munger's comment—that he would like to see Berkshire be "an exemplar"—might have sounded like a wistful thought, almost a throwaway line, even though there are no throwaway lines at this meeting. Or it might have seemed like the usually acerbic Charlie Munger trying to offer an upbeat comment to close the session.

I think, however, what Charlie Munger really did was put his finger on the one realistic hope that Berkshire Hathaway can live well beyond "The Warren and Charlie Show."

For whether David Sokol is indeed the rightful heir, as *Barron's* seems to think, or not; and whether families feel the same pride in selling out to a David Sokol or an Ajit Jain or a Rich Santulli as they do in selling to Warren Buffett and Charlie Munger, or not; and whether Fruit of the Loom and the *Buffalo News* and even Nebraska Furniture Mart go the way of World Book Encyclopedia, or not; and whether See's Candies can compete against Lindt & Sprünglin a world gone global, or not; and whether the family heirs who run many of Berkshire's businesses are truly the best at what they do, or not; and whether Warren Buffett gets his fondest wish and the Berkshire culture and performance live on well past his tenure or not—Charlie Munger is right in a very profound way: *all* companies should study Berkshire Hathaway, and try to understand how it is that two men from one Midwestern city could create so much economic value so consistently over such a long period of years.

I think every CEO and every director of every public company anywhere in the world should ask themselves how an enterprise with 76 companies, close to a quarter-million employees, and operations stretching from Omaha, Nebraska, to the United Kingdom, Israel, and China can operate with only 19 people at the home office, including a chairman who sits down every year and writes a 20-page letter explaining what he has done, and who has become the world's richest human being *not* by paying himself $200 million bonus packages or granting himself millions of shares of stock options or selling his company to the highest bidder but by buying shares of stock like everyone else, and holding onto them.

And they should make this pilgrimage to Omaha.

They should come here and watch two men sit alone on a stage, with no handlers, no lawyers, and no screened questions—just a box of candy and a Coke—and answer *anything that is asked of them*, from whether they have a personal relationship with Jesus Christ to what they would do to solve the healthcare crisis.

For almost five and a half hours.

We begin boarding the plane right on schedule.

Getting everyone settled, though, takes a little more time: everybody seems to have Berkshire paraphernalia—bags of See's Candies, boxes from Borsheim's—that they're trying to fit into the overhead bins. But unlike on most flights, everybody is friendly about it.

A man rearranging things right above my head calls out, "Whose bag is this?"

"Mine," another answers from a few rows down.

"May I move it over here?"

"Sure."

Even the overworked flight attendants get caught up in the spirit of things. A man asks for help with a shopping bag, and the nearest attendant comes down the aisle. She lifts the bag and starts to push it into a bin. "Is there anything *squishable* in here?" she asks.

"Naw," he says, "just some diamonds for my wife."

Laughter erupts around us. We're a family, even right here on the plane.

Beyond Buffett

In May 1956, seven of Warren Buffett's friends and family members invested in a partnership that would be managed by a self-assured 26-year-old Omaha investor. They would pay him no fee or salary, but he would keep a quarter of the profits he earned for them, provided they made at least a nominal 6 percent annual return.

The seven friends and family members invested $105,000. Warren Buffett himself put in $100.

Over the next 13 years, Warren Buffett grew Buffett Partnership Ltd. into a $100 million fund. Thanks mainly to his incentive fee, $25 million of the fund belonged to him.

Bereft of new investment ideas in the overheated stock market of 1969, Buffett disbanded Buffett Partnership Ltd. and focused on managing its largest investment: a troublesome textile company called Berkshire Hathaway. Forty-three years later, that company was worth nearly $200 billion, and Buffett's one-third ownership put him on the top of the Forbes 400 list of richest human beings in the world, with a net worth of $62 billion.

From $100 to $62 billion, Warren Buffett's investment legacy is, needless to say, secure around the world.

On Wall Street, however, it is a bit more mixed.

Buffett's influence among investment professionals ranges from "value" investors who have studied him for decades and run their own funds very much in line with Buffett's methods, to money managers who think the technology-phobic Buffett is brilliant but old-fashioned and out of date. There are even some downright cynics who regard Warren Buffett's eye-popping career as a statistical fluke, consider Berkshire Hathaway to be something of a cult, and view Buffett himself as a kind of Teflon-coated master of public relations.

Call the cynics victims of professional jealousy, if you like—there is, in fact, no person alive who can match Buffett's professional track record, and none that likely ever will. But they raise a few interesting contradictions between what Buffett says and what he does.

During the hostile takeover boom of the 1980s, companies like International Paper and Salomon Brothers sold preferred stock to Berkshire solely to prevent themselves from unfriendly takeovers. Warren Buffett, the implacable foe of clubby corporate boardroom behavior, appeared to be helping underperforming managers keep their companies intact and their jobs safe.

After the collapse of junk-bond king Drexel Burnham in the early 1990s, Berkshire purchased billions of dollars worth of junk bonds despite Buffett's own warnings that junk bonds were "a *kind* of bastardized fallen angel" and that, as he once warned shareholders, "The only time to buy these is on a day with no 'y' in it."

And just this year Berkshire announced it has taken in nearly $8 billion of premiums on 94 derivative contracts, those "financial weapons of mass destruction" Buffett has been warning about for years.

Of course, all these activities were quite profitable for Berkshire's shareholders. Just because Buffett casts a dim view on a particular investment class doesn't mean he shouldn't take advantage of a profitable opportunity when it appears within his famed "circle of competence."

More grating, and harder to rationalize, might be the sharper moral edge Buffett's always blunt voice has taken on recently—especially considering his own history.

Buffett criticizes hedge fund managers because they charge big incentive fees and receive favorable tax treatment compared to common folk. Yet, Buffett Partnership Ltd was structured like a hedge fund, providing Buffett with very large incentive fees and very favorable tax treatment.

Buffett also criticizes efforts to reduce the inheritance tax on rich families—"the lucky sperm club," he sniffs. Yet Buffett has, quite deliberately, made Berkshire a haven for family companies that want to keep their business and their own management intact, while avoiding the very estate taxes he encourages. In fact, Buffett has *advertised* the tax advantage of selling out to Berkshire in his own shareholder's letter:

> In making acquisitions, we have a further advantage: As payment, we can offer sellers [Berkshire] stock. . . . An individual or a family wishing to dispose of a single fine business, but also *wishing to defer personal taxes indefinitely* [emphasis added], is apt to find Berkshire stock a particularly comfortable holding.

Finally, Warren Buffett himself is dodging what must surely be the biggest estate tax bill of them all by giving away all his Berkshire stock instead of selling it.

These contradictions rankle in the quieter corners of Wall Street, although certainly not on Main Street, where Buffett has, in recent years, become a very public figure known literally around the world.

His higher public profile, of course, has a rational impetus: Buffett is engaged in a race against time to create a brand name for Berkshire that not only will attract family-owned businesses to become part of the Berkshire "family" but also will survive his death. The more exposure Buffett gets on CNBC and elsewhere—superficial as it may be—the better it is for Berkshire after Buffett's death.

Publicly, Buffett faces that inevitablility with his usual brand of sharp wit, as when he once described the very first of the instructions contained in the envelope that is to be opened upon his death:

"Take my pulse again."

While Buffett's passing is a certainty, the manner in which Berkshire Hathaway survives his passing is not.

Survive, however, Berkshire will. "Fort Knox," Buffett has called it, and Berkshire Hathaway is just that.

Whether or not Buffett's famous thrift has impaired some of Berkshire's companies, Berkshire's enormous financial strength has certainly been a boon for the Berkshire subsidiaries that depend on credit. At the end of the day, Warren Buffett has created one great enterprise and immense wealth for himself and the investors who came to Omaha, listened, and believed.

He has also, as Charlie Munger puts it, created an "exemplar" of corporate behavior that others might follow.

As for me, I'll keep my small investment in Berkshire stock, even though I don't expect much from it in the near term.

For one thing, Berkshire is, at its core, an insurance company, and, as Buffett told us last year, the best days of the insurance business may be past, for now.

Also, insurance companies have never fit within my own "circle of competence." Floods hurt them, hurricanes hurt them, and trial lawyers are forever trying to create new ways to extract money from them.

Of course, nothing so dramatic is going to cripple Berkshire Hathaway. "That double-layering of protection" that Charlie Munger said was "like *breathing*" around Berkshire will remain in place a long time, whatever happens to Buffett himself.

And there's a chance that Buffett and his successors can fulfill his own "fondest hope" for Berkshire Hathaway: "that the decent performance and the culture are maintained."

In the meantime, I'll keep getting four tickets to the Berkshire annual shareholders' meeting, and I'll keep going back to Omaha.

The only problem might be *getting* there, what with commercial airlines being so unreliable.

Of course, with three extra tickets to the meeting, I ought to be able to find somebody to go with me who happens to be a NetJets member.

Any takers?

NOTES

PART I

Chapter 1

p. 15 "What we have created . . . is, to some extent, a cult.": Janet Lowe, *Damn Right!: Behind the Scenes with Berkshire Hathaway Billionaire Charlie Munger* (New York: Wiley, 2000).

p. 19 "My name is Warren and I'm an airoholic": "The Sage of Omaha's Trans-Atlantic Game," *The Age*, September 24, 2002, http://www.theage.com.au/articles/2002/09/23/1032734111833.html.

Chapter 2

p. 29 "I never went back to the high-tech mode . . .": Lowe, *Damn Right!*, p. 59.

p. 30. "I could spend all my time thinking about technology...": Robert G. Hagstrom, *The Warren Buffett Portfolio* (New York: Wiley, 1999), p. 105.

Chapter 3

pp. 39-40 "In fact, in July 2006, he gave Loomis the first interview on his plan to give away his considerable fortune . . .": "Warren Buffett Gives It Away," *Fortune*, July 10, 2006, 154 (1):56-60, 62, 64 passim.

Chapter 4

p. 43 "We have a reverence for logic around here.": Carol J. Loomis, "The Inside Story of Warren Buffett," *Fortune*, April 11, 1988.

p. 44 "It is also true that a week before the 1987 stock market crash, Buffett sold stocks out of a Berkshire profit-sharing plan.": Roger Lowenstein, *Buffett: The Making of an American Capitalist* (Broadway Books, 1955), p. 303.

p. 44 "And that he bought nearly half a billion dollars worth of RJR Nabisco junk bonds . . .": Lowenstein, *Making of an American Capitalist*, p. 362.

p. 47 "Gates uses the name 'Challenger X,' while Buffett is 'T-Bone.'": *Wall Street Journal*, November 14, 2003.

Chapter 7

p. 63 "The first rule is not to lose. The second rule is not to forget the first rule.": Loomis, "The Inside Story."

Chapter 8

p. 67 "This is not the forum in which to address these comments.": *Nardelli, refusing to answer questions at his final shareholders' meeting;* Joe Nocera, "The Board Wore Chicken Suits," *New York Times,* May 27, 2006.

p. 73 "Assuming that Buffett worked 12-hour days over the course of 43 years . . .": Lowenstein, Making of an American Capitalist, p. 63: *He was working virtually all the time, and loving every minute.*

Chapter 9

pp. 76-77 "Andrew Kilpatrick, author of the massive Buffett hagiography—*Of Permanent Value* . . .": (Andy Kilpatrick Publishing, 1998).

p. 77 "Buffett does not advise . . .": Benjamin Graham, *Intelligent Investor,* 1949.

Chapter 10

pp. 79-80 "I sat down with seven people who gave me $105,000 . . .": Warren Buffett speaking at Bill and Melinda Gates Foundation, June 26, 2006.

Chapter 13

p. 105 "I don't think we want to be in the candy business.": Lowenstein, *Making of an American Capitalist,* p. 164.

Chapter 14

P. 115 "We can afford to lose money—even a lot of money. . .": *Buffett letter to Berkshire CEOs;* Robert P. Miles, *Warren Buffett CEO* (New York: Wiley, 2001), p. 357.

Chapter 15

p. 120 "If we hadn't bought See's...": Lowe, *Damn Right!,* p. 133.

p. 121 "There Munger fields questions solo . . . ": *Poor Charlie's Almanack: The Wit and Wisdom of Charles T. Munger,* (3d ed., Donning Company, 2005).

Chapter 17

pp. 128-129 "In 1969, Buffett personally crusaded to open his downtown eating club to Jewish members . . ." Lowenstein, *Making of an American Capitalist,* pp. 115-116.

Chapter 20

pp. 149–150 "Buffett and his sisters . . . 20 years?": Lowenstein, *Making of an American Capitalist*, passim.

p. 150 "He said if you let yourself be undisciplined on the small things, you'd probably be undisciplined on the large things, too.": David Elsner, *Chicago Tribune,* December 8, 1985.

p. 152 "That same year, a Minneapolis electronics retailer . . .": Laura Heller, "Best Buy," in *DSN Retailing Today* (January 2006), ch. 21.

p. 158 "So strongly did Buffett feel this way that Berkshire eventually accumulated just under 9 percent.": 1984 Chairman's Letter.

p. 160 " 'I really had no idea what he did,' his son Peter said recently. 'But he read a lot. I knew that.'": Interview on Nightly Business Report, May 1, 2008. http://www.pbs.org/nbr/site/onair/gharib/080501c.

PART II

Introduction

p. 167 "The nation's largest mortgage lender . . .": Gretchen Morgenson, "Inside the Countrywide Lending Spree," *New York Times*, August 26, 2007.

p. 167 "The firm—which had survived the Great Crash of 1929 without firing a single employee—collapsed . . .": "A History of Bear Stearns," *New York Times* timeline, March 17, 2008.

Chapter 22

p. 173 "I find it very easy to predict what will happen . . .": "The Sage of Omaha's Trans-Atlantic Game," The Age.Com/The Daily Telegraph, September 24, 2002.

p. 174 "Financial institutions . . . $350 billion in total, and counting . . .": "Clear Channel Banks May Lose $3 Billion in Buyout," Bloomberg LP, March 26, 2008.

p. 174 "On that day, the Blackstone Group . . . Steve Schwarzman hailed as 'The New King of Wall Street' . . .KKR founder Henry Kravis was making fin-de-siècle-style pronouncements of his own.": Frederic Tomesco, "KKR's Kravis Says No End in Sight for `Golden Era' of Buyouts," May 29, 2007 (Bloomberg); "Steve Schwarzman hailed as 'The New King of Wall Street,'" *Fortune*, March 5, 2007, http://www.fortuneeducation.com/preview_guides/fpg_20070305.htm.

p. 174 "So eager was the public . . .": Andrew Ross Sorkin, ed., *New York Times DealBook*, March 16, 2007.

p. 175 "Blackstone's initial public offering turned out to be the *sixth largest* in U.S. history . . .": Hoover's Inc., January 4, 2008.

p. 175 "Shares soared . . .": *Blackstone Group share price information*, Bloomberg LP.

p. 175 "When newly public Blackstone . . . Hilton Hotels takeover at a 40 percent premium . . .": *New York Times*, July 4, 2007.

p. 175 "By late July, word had begun to filter . . .": "First Data says buyout is on track," Reuters.com, July 20, 2007.

pp. 175-176 "A $25 billion buyout . . .": Bloomberg LP.

p. 176 "More than $300 billion worth of debt . . .": "First Data Bankers Reduce Buyout Loan, Offer Discount," Bloomberg LP, September 14, 2007.

p. 176 "In mid-September, thousands of depositors lined up at the branches of Northern Rock . . .": "Crisis Deepens for Northern Rock," *International Herald Tribune*, September 17, 2007.

p. 176 "Four months later came news that a young trader at Société Générale . . . ": *New York Times*, January 28, 2008.

p. 177 "And the value of the U.S. dollar has indeed dropped 10 percent . . .": Bloomberg LP.

p. 177 "And total profits of U.S. companies declined $53 *billion* . . .": Bureau of Economic Analysis, May 29, 2008 press release.

p. 177 "While Armageddon has, thus far . . .": "Buffett May Profit from Wrigley's 'Moat' in Recession," Bloomberg LP, April 28, 2008.

p. 177 "And the price of Berkshire Hathaway . . .": *Berkshire stock price and Dow Jones Industrial Average*; Bloomberg LP.

p. 178 "Dairy Queen is being sued . . . ": "Dairy Queen Sued by Franchises," *Twin Cities Business Journal*, February 28, 2008.

p. 178 "Speaking of baseball . . .": Alex Rodriguez talks to Buffett, *Wall Street Journal*, September 17, 2007.

p. 178 "Four executives of Berkshire's General Re division . . . once lauded . . .": press release; "Chairman and CEO Ron Ferguson to Retire in June 2002 after 33 Years of Service," *Business Wire*, September 5, 2001; General Re convictions, *Bloomberg News*, Tuesday, February 26, 2008; p. D02.

p. 179 "One other thing has changed . . .": "Jimmy Buffett DNA test results," *Fortune*, May 28, 2007.

Chapter 23

p. 181 "If you're in the luckiest 1 percent . . .": "Buffett, at Clinton Fund-Raiser, Says Congress Favors the Rich," *Bloomberg News*, June 27, 2007.

p. 183 "She does not, however, approach Bill Gates . . .": *secret Yahoo!/Microsoft talks*; "Microsoft Withdraws Yahoo Offer after Attempt to Bridge Gap in Price," *Wall Street Journal*, May 4, 2008.

p. 184 "When I heard *Tubular Bells...*": http://www.peterbuffett.com/about.htm.

p. 184 "I have not legally or emotionally adopted you as a grandchild, nor have the rest of my family adopted you as a niece or a cousin.": *Wall Street Journal*, http://online.wsj.com/public/article_print/SB120371859381786725.html.

p. 185 "In a bittersweet interview with Charlie Rose . . .": *Charlie Rose interview, aired August 26, 2004. It was filmed, he says in the introduction, in May.* http://www.charlierose.com/guests/susan-buffett. *Quotes from Susan Thompson Buffett from Charlie Rose interview; transcribed by the author. Susie Thompson biography from DATA Web site:* http:///www.data.org/about/bod_buffett.html.

p. 185 "I knew when I talked to Dad...": Charlie Rose interview; *transcribed by author.*

p. 186 "Now 53 . . . ": *Howard Buffett biographic material;* BuffettImages.com.

Chapter 24

p. 189 "The 2006 Berkshire holiday card was a photograph of Buffett, Munger, and the rest of the Berkshire board of directors . . ." Kilpatrick, *Of Permanent Value, p. 1748.*

Chapter 25

p. 194 " And neither man will resist frequent wisecracks at the expense of graduate schools . . ."; *Buffett rejected by Harvard Business School;* Lowenstein, *Making of an American Capitalist*, p. 35.

p. 195 "It is 58 years since Buffett was rejected by Harvard . . . 'luckiest thing' . . .": *Fortune*, October 16, 1995.

p. 196 "We were two parallel lines.": *Charlie Rose interview; transcribed by the author.*

Chapter 26

p. 197 "And then I read a book . . .": *Intelligent Investor.*

p. 198 "My cousin has written a book . . .": Bill Buffett, *Foods You Will Enjoy—The Story of Buffett's Store* (Tradepaper, 2008).

p. 198 "The second question of the day . . .": *The 63 questions asked and other shareholder statistics are from the author.*

p. 201 "Mrs. B worked for us . . . ": *Rose Blumkin split,* Lowenstein, *Making of an American Capitalist,* p. 359.

p. 201 "'My God,' he told Carol Loomis of *Fortune* in a 1988 article on his skill at running the Berkshire businesses . . .": Loomis, "The Inside Story."

p. 202 "As Jeff Comment, the CEO of Berkshire's Helzberg Diamonds jewelry retailer, told author Robert P. Miles, author of the excellent book, *Warren Buffett CEO: Secrets from the Berkshire Hathaway Managers. . .* ": *telephone interview with Robert P. Miles.*

p. 202 "Today, however, Internet retailer Blue Nile sells . . .": Bloomberg LP.

Chapter 27

pp. 203-204 "Perhaps they first heard of Buffett five years ago . . ..": *Bono appearance with Buffett,* "Bringing Star Power to AIDS Fight," December 2, 2002, http://www.u2station.com/news/archives/2002/12/bringing_star_p.php.

p. 204 "Or perhaps they watched the breathless televised coverage of his trip to China last year, with a CNBC reporter in tow . . .": *Buffett on CNBC in China;* http://www.cnbc.com/id/21470503.

p. 206 "Sokol has done a spectacular job . . .": *details; Barron's,* May 5, 2008.

Chapter 28

p. 211 "Berkshire was a small business at one time . . .": Berkshire May 10, 1965 earnings report: *New York Times* archives, May 11, 1965. *Berkshire 2008 earnings;* Berkshire press release.

p. 213 "Why, then, should Charlie and I . . .": 1993 Chairman's Letter.

Chapter 29

pp. 217-218 "I do not advocate extreme frugality . . .": *Buffett refers to wedding ring as percent of net worth, New York Times,* June 27, 2006.

p. 218 "I have an e-mail from Chris Wagner . . .": Francesco Guerrera and Justin Baer, "Buffett loses $1.bn on derivatives," May 2, 2008. http://us.ft.com/ftgateway/superpage.ft?news_id=fto050220081902312163.

p. 220 "We have a number of important negatives . . .": Warren Buffett, letter to Buffett Partnership, Ltd., January 22, 1969, *available at various online sources.*

Chapter 30

pp. 224-225 "The pardon shocked the Street and made *Time* magazine's list of '10 Most Notorious Presidential Pardons.'": http://www.time.com/time/2007/presidential_pardons/10.html.

Chapter 31

p. 227 "At least $50 billion . . . they're stuck with over $200 billion . . .": Pierre Paulden and Don Jeffrey, "Clear Channel Banks May Lose $3 Billion in Buyout (Update3), Bloomberg, March 26, 2008.

p. 233 "Yet out of the roughly $12 trillion . . . ": *mutual fund data;* "Trends in Mutual Fund Investing," March 2008, http://www.ici.org.

Chapter 32

p. 236 "In fact, Buffett put *two-thirds* of his net worth in shares of GEICO . . .":
1995 Chairman's Letter.

Chapter 33

p. 241 "Warren Buffett told me . . .:
http://www.guardian.co.uk/world/2005/jun/16/g8.usa.

p. 243 "Buffett's biggest influence . . .": *on church upbringing;* Loomis, "The
Inside Story."

Chapter 34

p. 245 "When it's Berkshire promising...": 1996 Chairman's Letter.

p. 246 "In many areas, including acquisitions . . .": memo from Warren
Buffett to Berkshire managers, August 20, 2000; reprinted in Robert P. Miles,
Warren Buffett CEO.

p. 248 "Third, federal prosecutors reportedly pressured . . .": *Wall Street
Journal,* April 7, 2008.

Chapter 36

p. 262 "It's no wonder . . . only two of See's 200 U.S. stores are east of the
Mississippi River . . ": See's Web site.

p. 263 "Starbucks was not in existence . . .": *Starbucks financial information;*
Starbucks Corporation.

Chapter 38

p. 273 "Buffett's upcoming European tour, in fact, was planned in part by the
CEO of ISCAR . . .": Bloomberg LP, June 25, 2008.

p. 275 "NetJets founder Rich Santulli . . .": He is sometimes referred to as
"Rick."

Coda

p. 283 "Over the next 13 years, Warren Buffett grew Buffett Partnership Ltd.
into a $100 million fund. . . .": Loomis, "The Inside Story."

INDEX

ACKNOWLEDGMENTS

The first question people ask is, "Did you get to talk to Buffett?" The answer is, "I never tried." I wanted the book as clear-eyed as possible, to avoid what Charlie Munger calls "the reciprocation tendency" all human beings possess. I did, however, speak to individuals who have met or reported on Warren Buffett, and I thank them for their insights.

Many people have helped to shape this book. Chris Wagner's urgings to go to Omaha started it all. Readers of my blog, JeffMatthewsIsNotMakingThisUp, provided encouraging feedback as I wrote about that trip. Most crucially, Leah Spiro, my editor, helped me turn that travelogue into a journey to what I hope you'll find is the heart of Berkshire Hathaway.

In reporting on that journey I have tried to capture Buffett and Munger's distinct voices in the text. I thank Whitney Tilson—cofounder of T2 Partners hedge funds, Tilson Mutual Funds, Value Investor Insight, and the Value Investing Congress—for allowing me the use of his comprehensive notes from the May 2007 meeting. I was well prepared in 2008, and except for the reconstructed conversation with Berkshire managers and the reporter, all quotes are as I or Whitney transcribed them—as best we could—with a handful of minor edits for clarity. I want to thank McGraw-Hill's Ruth Mannino, Gaya Vinay, and Lydia Rinaldi for getting this book out into the world.

Warts and all, this pilgrimage was my experience, and any blame for errors of fact or judgment should accrue to me alone.

My father, who died before this booked commenced, would, I know, be proud—and I thank him for always being proud, however contrary my career path seemed at times. My mother encouraged my interest in stocks, even though she and my father had never owned any. Before I was old enough to vote, she took me to the local Merrill Lynch office so that I could buy a few shares of Dr. Pepper. The idea that you could buy *ownership* in your favorite soft drink astonished me. It still does—and I owe her much for that encouragement.

Many people assisted in shaping my investment career once it got underway, particularly Gus Fliakos, Gerry Smith, John Frick, and John Furth. I thank David Rocker, without whom I wouldn't have started my own hedge fund, for his example; Doug Kass, Dan Loeb, Art Spinner and the Brahman boys, Mitch, Peter, and Bob, for their friendship over the years; and Steve Mandel for his lunches, which allow "the two-and-twenty crowd" to get together and do what this business is all about: talk stocks. Marc Cohodes is simply one of the all time good guys, period.

Professionally, I owe the most to those who invested not only their money but their trust in me. Lyell and Nancy Williams did so 18 years ago on a handshake and a term sheet scribbled on a napkin. Bob and Moira Eick invested "the first dollar" when we opened for business three years later.

Those who either helped us get off the ground, or stay there, or both, are Heather and Steve Aveson, Barry Bailey, Jim Balakian, Ed Bell, Elaine Bundock, Tom Bundock, John and Barbara Burgess, Lise Buyer, Jamie and Charlie Campbell, Murray Chassin, Genni Combes, André Couture, Tom DiBartholomeo, Susan and Al Dragone Jr., Chris Dragone, Gus and Jill DuPont, Jack Eizikovitz, Joe Evans, Nicole and John Hill, Mike Homer, Dan McNichol, Gar Miller, Steve Miller, Keith Newman, Frank O'Keefe, Helen and Rock Routhier, Roy and Edith Simpson, Tom and Kathy Smith, George Tall, Will Tienken, Jeff Tunkel, Tom and Ann Weiss, Peter Wright, and Vic Zimmermann. Nick Ohnell has been my consigliere since day one.

(*For the record, our firm is closed to new investors and this book should not be, in any way, construed as an effort to market our services.*)

Kurt Vonnegut, Jr. once said that if you want to be a writer, you shouldn't get married. It's the worst advice I've ever heard. This book would not have existed without my wife, Nancy. And it wouldn't have been worthwhile without our daughters, Sarah and Claire.

Jeff Matthews
Fairfield, CT